HEALTHY AGEING

The Science and
the Myths

Ken Watson PhD

Healthy Ageing
The Science and the Myths

First published in Australia by Kenneth Watson 2020

Copyright © Kenneth Watson 2020
All Rights Reserved

 A catalogue record for this book is available from the National Library of Australia

ISBN: 978-0-6489493-0-5 (pbk)
ISBN: 978-0-6489493-1-2 (ebk)

Typesetting and design by Publicious Book Publishing
Published in collaboration with Publicious Book Publishing
www.publicious.com.au

No part of this book may be reproduced in any form, by photocopying or by any electronic or mechanical means, including information storage or retrieval systems, without permission in writing from both the copyright owner and the publisher of this book.

For the quintessential healthy agers (Maurice, Lena, Elizabeth, Nora and all their soulmates) of the Falkirk and Linlithgow walking group. It is no coincidence that the Scottish town of Falkirk was voted Britain's Best Walking Neighbourhood 2019.

Contents

Chapter 1
Healthy Ageing: Application of the *Pub Test*   1

Chapter 2
Genes and Healthy Ageing: A Beginner's Guide to DNA   21

Chapter 3
Nutrition: 101: What Are the Facts on Fats and Sugars?   67

Chapter 4
Diets and Dietary Supplements: The Truth,
the Whole Truth and Nothing but the Science   112

Chapter 5
Alcohol and Coffee: Drinking to Your Healthy Ageing   164

Chapter 6
Physical Activity: Keep Calm and Walk the Dog   188

Chapter 7
The Gut Microbiota: It's a Small World After All   217

Chapter 8
If We All Lived to a Healthy 100:
Where Would We All Park?   276

About the Author   311

Chapter 1
Healthy Ageing

Application of the Pub Test

The purpose of this book is to summarize the latest scientific findings on healthy ageing in a readable form that is understandable to the general public. Many publications on healthy ageing are too simplistic, non-scientific (therefore not subject to critical analysis), highly biased and largely motivated by commercial interests. Others are written in technical language, such as in academic books and in peer-reviewed scientific journals, that are not easily comprehended by the general public.

Simple explanations and points of view are actually good if based on a non-biased assessment of data. Data by itself may be non-biased: it is the human interpretation of the data that is frequently biased. Unfortunately, much of the available information on health and ageing is highly biased and often confusing, in many cases deliberately so as in food labelling.

The information provided in this book is based on prime quality publications in high-impact peer-reviewed scientific journals. In these publications there is a considerable amount of technical language, vast amounts of data and with that comes lots of statistical analyses. The fact that much data crunching is required for the statistical analysis immediately alerts one to the observation that perhaps data on health and ageing is not that clear-cut. On the other hand, one can equally argue that application of precise statistical analysis to the data is a good thing and suggests a rigorous assessment of the scientific data.

The Reader is encouraged to consult any publications cited in this book which are of personal interest. Many scientific publications are freely available to the general public. For example, try searching PubMedCentral which is an archive of scientific journal articles (www.ncbi.nim.nih.gov/pmc/articles) and lets you know if free access or download is available; other publications may require a fee (expensive) for a single item while others may be available through a higher education facility.

In any case, the *Abstract* or *Summary* of many scientific publications is generally freely available. Although scientific publications are written for a specialized audience, you are encouraged to read the *Abstract/Summary* of articles of interest to you, and the *Introduction* and *Conclusion* are generally also worthy of a read although these can be quite daunting for readers with non-scientific backgrounds. The most difficult and technically challenging sections are the *Methods*, the *Results* and, of course, the inevitable statistics.

Here, I express my bias with respect to statistics in that I do not get very excited if a researcher concludes that their data demonstrates 'a statistically significant 10% decrease in mortality' as a result of, say, a certain diet or lifestyle. In my opinion, a 10% decrease or increase is within experimental error, especially when one is considering health and ageing in humans given the fact that every human is unique with respect to genetics, diet and lifestyle. The 10% figure should be used as a guide as to the trend towards a decrease or increase in mortality or health benefit. Moreover, statistical corrections for confounders affecting health and ageing such as smoking, education, exercise, alcohol, occupation, weight and marital status are so highly personal that statistical corrections for these confounders may not be, well, statistically meaningful. Statistically significant does not automatically translate to 'clinically significant' when it comes to health and ageing. Nevertheless, for a balanced view, many of the publications on health and ageing do apply a statistical correction for some of these confounders.

One definition of a statistician is a person who has their feet in a bucket of ice-water and their head in an oven but claims on average that everything is fine.

One has to be aware that a study published in a peer-reviewed scientific journal, that is an article that has been appropriately refereed by acknowledged experts in the field, signifies that the research is of a certain standard but may be subject to modification should further research provide contradictory or supportive data. This is the nature of scientific research.

The world is rapidly changing. By that we mean not only the environment (e.g. think climate change) but also in the very short term the ageing human population. In many nations the ageing population is currently, and most certainly will be, in the next ten to twenty years, providing real challenges. The data are impressive. For example, in Western European nations, 15% to 20% of the population are over 65 and in Japan it is already 27% (World Bank, type 'population over 65'). Thus, it is not surprising that there is widespread interest in the demographics of ageing by governments, businesses and individuals given the social and financial impacts on society.

There is a paradox, at least in developed nations. Health care consumes a very high proportion of private and public funds and is very much focused on treatment (e.g. general practitioners, hospitals) as opposed to prevention. The latter is surely the preferred option as prevention is better than cure (certainly much cheaper). Not smoking is the classic example. In relation to healthy ageing, there is no doubt prevention or at least slowing down the ageing process is the way to go. Once you have aged, there is simply no cure; it's much better to age well and healthily.

What Do We Mean by Healthy Ageing?

In 2015, the Gerontological Society of America solicited articles specifically focused on the concept of successful ageing. In the Editorial of the special issue of the journal of the Gerontology Society (Pruchno, Editorial, 2015) it was quoted that in an article by Depp and Jete (2006), a review of twenty-eight published studies on successful ageing, resulted in twenty-nine definitions of successful ageing. It is most unlikely that any definition of successful ageing will be universally acceptable, at least in the academic arena. There are simply too many egos at stake.

To some extent, individuals who have reached their one hundredth birthday, the centenarians, may be deemed to have aged successfully. Individuals in good health and relatively free of chronic disease who are in their eighties and nineties, the octogenarians and nonagenarians respectively, may also be regarded as having aged successfully.

In much the same way as people judge other people on first observation as, say, charismatic, attractive, unattractive, trustworthy etc, a successfully aged individual may be judged by body language as in e.g. how they talk and walk. The latter, as in walking gait and speed, is actually a reasonable assessment about the physical condition of an elderly individual and their progress towards health ageing (Studenski *et al.*, 2011; Boulifard *et al.*, 2019; Rasmussen *et al.*, 2019). Of course, one is very well aware that judging a person by appearance is deceptive, as in judging a book by the outside cover; the inside or contents of the book is what really matters.

Facial recognition software is increasingly used for identification and security purposes and is claimed to be extremely accurate. Interestingly, when it comes to ageing, there have been numerous studies in which participants are asked to guess the age of individuals merely by looking at their photographs, with individuals looking older and others looking younger than their actual age.

There are various apps, such as developed by Google and Apple, available for your computer or smartphone which scan photographs of individuals and come up with an estimated age. There is also an app available which provides a projection of a younger or older you. A word of caution: choose your photographs carefully. A photograph of myself scanned at an estimated age of 87 and another, taken one month later, scanned at an estimated age of 52, although my chronological age is 78 and my personal age is 60.

Personal age may be defined as selecting an age at which you are most comfortable with and sticking to it. In reality, we were all born at a certain time on a precise day on a precise month in a precise year. This is your chronological age (CA). It is recognized in documents such as in your birth certificate, passport, driver's license, tax file number, social security number etc and is required or at least requested by the myriad of government, internet and social media sites. There is simply no way of denying one's CA.

Chapter 1: Healthy Ageing: Application of the Pub Test

On the positive or, in some cases, negative side, your CA may bear little relationship to age when we consider the concept of healthy ageing. If you have a positive outlook to life in general, you may consider yourself as younger than your CA; if you have a negative outlook you may consider yourself older than your CA.

What does the scientific methodology have to say about assigning your age? Surely, you say, there must be good scientific evidence that can accurately assign an age to individuals in relation to healthy ageing. After all, we have smartphones which are many more times powerful than the computers which successfully guided men to the Moon and back (1969), we have autonomous or driverless cars, we have radio telescopes which can 'see' almost to the beginning of time, we have the complete genetic code of the human DNA (genome) including the Neanderthals (and the chimpanzee, wooly mammoth and thousands of bacteria, fungi and viruses), and we have free Wi-Fi (well, in some places).

Thus, is there a scientific biomarker of ageing (BMA) that acts as a milestone as to one's continual progress from birth to death, following a pathway towards healthy ageing? Biomarkers of ageing are not to be confused with biomarkers of disease. The latter is conceptually easier to envisage as in e.g. high blood glucose level/low insulin is indicative of type 2 diabetes, or a number of very specific markers of very specific diseases including some cancers. At this point in time, there is no single BMA but rather there are a number of biomarkers, which are indicative of healthy ageing. Biomarkers are further discussed in Chapter 2: Genes and Healthy Ageing.

A routine blood sample, say 20-30 ml, taken for an annual medical check-up, and sent to a pathology laboratory for common clinical tests can provide informative measures of an individual's health status. The application of such analyses to predict an individual's biological age (BA) as compared to CA has been reported in the scientific literature (Chapter 2: Genes and Healthy Ageing). A predictive BA is much more informative than CA with respect to overall health status and thus a measurable milestone towards healthy ageing. Moreover, the BA measurements should also include physiological, neurological and physical measurements. Physiological tests may include body mass index (BMI = weight kg/ height m^2), full blood count, liver function tests, lipid profile (HDL- and LDL- cholesterol, triglycerides) and C-reactive protein (as a measure of inflammation). Neurological tests may include cognitive function and physical measurements may include motor function (e.g. walking speed, balance, unipedal stance) and grip strength.

In a study of n = 954 individuals from the Dunedin Longitudinal Study (Belsky *et al.*, 2015), researchers were able to assign individuals as ageing well (BA less that CA), ageing as per CA and ageing more rapidly (BA more than CA). The assessments were on the basis of a twelve-year follow-up of eighteen biomarkers of physiological status (initial age of participants was 37-38, all born in the same year in the same city, Dunedin, New Zealand). Importantly, measurements of neurological and physical parameters were consistent with the physiological tests in the assignment of BA. In another study of older cohorts (n = 9,389, mean age of 48, 50% female), comparing BA with CA in an eighteen-year follow-up it was concluded that BA, as measured by twenty-one biomarkers of physiological status, was a significantly more accurate predictor of mortality that CA (Levine, 2013).

We can conclude that the scientific consensus is that BA is a more accurate and thus useful measure of healthy ageing than CA.

A yearly check-up with your local physician is thus highly recommended as a key element in maintaining a healthy age profile. Your BA profile would also allow the identification of any lifestyle changes to be addressed should there be issues with parameters outside the expected norm. Early attention to these issues would certainly assist in the progress towards healthy ageing. Prevention or, at least, slowing down the rate of ageing is always better than cure; there is simply no cure for ageing. There is much publicity and hype regarding reversal or rejuvenation of human ageing, but it is just that, hype.

There is no substantive scientific evidence that supports the concept that we currently have the knowledge and capability of reversing human ageing. For example, cosmetic surgery and the hugely popular Botox treatments may have positive psychological effects as well as projecting a positive image of youthfulness and hence perception of CA. Nevertheless, BA is not likely to be greatly influenced and hence neither is one's rate of ageing.

Does your DNA age? The simple answer is yes. As to the how, what and why, that is the mechanism of DNA ageing, a scientific researcher would say we need more data and, importantly, more funds to do more research on more individuals over a very long time frame. The scientific consensus is thus very much non-consensual.

However, there is agreement that DNA is subject to constant challenges as a result of everyday living associated with natural metabolic processes of eating and drinking. These metabolic processes generate chemical reactions some of which result in the formation of highly reactive molecules termed free radicals. Free radicals also result from the essential process of breathing oxygen (try not breathing for, say, five minutes to test the concept of essential; kids, don't try this at home without adult supervision). The formation of highly reactive molecules via oxygen-related processes is, not surprisingly, called oxidative stress. Oxidative stress and free radicals are capable of damaging not only DNA but also proteins, lipids and carbohydrates. The concepts of oxidative stress and free radicals form the cornerstone of the free radical theory of ageing, first postulated by Denham Harman (Harman,1956).

It is now universally recognized that DNA is also subject to lifestyle and environmental stressors, which impinge on DNA structure and function. These stressors include financial and social stressors, exercise, smoking and alcohol. These stressors have profound effects on DNA and greatly influence healthy ageing. Parts of your DNA that you inherited from your parents are thus not fixed throughout your life but are dynamic and modulate as a function of your lifestyle and environment.

Research in the past few decades has demonstrated significant DNA modifications with age. The two most studied DNA modifications associated with ageing, are the telomeric age and the epigenetic age, both of which have been proposed as biomarkers of ageing. Importantly, the telomeric age and epigenetic age modulate not only with age but also are subject to alteration by lifestyle and environment. The telomeric age and epigenetic age in relation to healthy ageing is discussed in Chapter 2: Genes and Healthy Ageing.

There are a number of inconvenient questions to be raised in the context of healthy ageing. These questions are at the core of our understanding or lack of understanding of issues which are the elephant in the room in that these issues are to be conveniently avoided as they do not fit the established way of thinking and indeed, in most cases, also the general public's view of healthy ageing. However, to have any appreciation or understanding of healthy ageing we must address these issues in a non-biased way.

1. Telomeric DNA (DNA sequences at the end of chromosomes) has been proposed as a key marker of ageing with maintenance of telomere DNA length as a key biomarker of healthy ageing. How is it then that there is clear scientific evidence that cells that maintain long telomeres have a high probability of attaining the cancerous state and that healthy centenarians have relatively short telomeres? (Chapter 2 Genes and Healthy Ageing: A Beginner's Guide to DNA).

2. The Dietary Guidelines for Americans, based on the very best available scientific data, have been issued every five years since 1980, the latest is the 2015-2020 edition. How is it then that overweight and obesity in the developed and increasingly also in the developing nations have rapidly increased in the past thirty years ? (Chapter 3 Nutrition 101: What Are the Facts on Fats and Sugars?).

3. Fats, especially saturated fats, have been implicated as a, if not the, major culprit in the obesity epidemic. How is it then that there is no, and has never been, substantive scientific data that actually provides evidence that consumption of foods (e.g. dairy) containing saturated fats leads to weight gain? (Chapter 3 Nutrition 101: What Are the Facts on Fats and Sugars?).

4. After decades of scientific research, supported by many millions of dollars of funding, by some of the world's most distinguished scientists in some of the world's most distinguished universities, the consensus has now been reached that highly processed packaged foods may not

be that good for one's health. How is it then that your grandmother, with limited financial support, came to that exact same conclusion many, many years ago? (Chapter 3 Nutrition 101: What Are the Facts on Fats and Sugars?).

5. The Mediterranean diet has been universally praised as the diet for successful health and healthy ageing. How is it then that individuals living in countries (e.g. Greece, Italy, Spain) that traditionally follow a Mediterranean diet do not live any longer or, importantly, do not have a longer healthy lifespan than individuals who live in countries (e.g. U.K., Canada, Australia) that do not follow the Mediterranean diet? (Chapter 4 Diets and Dietary Supplements: The Truth, the Whole Truth and Nothing but the Science).

6. It has been well documented, ever since the original observations in 1935, in the most highly ranked scientific journals that food restriction (termed calorie restriction) leads to a substantially longer life in the flagship animal model for ageing research, the rodent. How is it then that calorie restriction is most unlikely to be a key aspect of healthy ageing in humans? (Chapter 4 Diets and Dietary Supplements: The Truth, the Whole Truth and Nothing but the Science).

7. It is conservatively estimated that 50% of the adult population, especially women, in the USA and Europe takes dietary supplements such as herbal and vitamin supplements in the belief that they would enhance one's health and thus lead to healthy ageing. How is it then that there is little or no scientific evidence that these supplements have any beneficial health effects? (Chapter 4 Diets and Dietary Supplements: The Truth, the Whole Truth and Nothing but the Science).

8. It has been estimated that, at any given time, 30% to 40% of the population in the developed world is on some kind of weight-loss diet. How is it then that all the evidence clearly shows that in the long-term (> one year) weight-loss diets simply do not work for the great majority of individuals? (Chapter 4 Diets and Dietary Supplements: The Truth, the Whole Truth and Nothing but the Science).

9. It is well established that excess consumption of alcohol or coffee has negative effects on health. How is it then that data in prestigious scientific journals have consistently reported health benefits of moderate alcohol or coffee consumption? (Chapter 5: Alcohol and Coffee: Drinking to Your Healthy Ageing).

10. It has been frequently reported in leading scientific and health related publications that exercise adds years to one's life, with estimates that regular exercise can add around two years to one's life. How is it then that if you exercise one hour every day for fifty years this equates to almost exactly two years? (Chapter 6 Physical Activity: Keep Calm and Walk the Dog).

11. In the past decade or so, a major recognition has been the demonstration that our microbiota (microbes that inhabit on and in our bodies) plays an absolutely essential role and has profound effects on our health and thus healthy ageing. How is it then that the general public has no concept and little knowledge that microbes are essential for life and our well-being? (Chapter 7 Your Gut Microbiota: It's a Small World After All).

Each of these questions will be addressed in the indicated Chapters in this book. Maximum benefit will be obtained on these and other topics on healthy ageing when one approaches these issues from a non-biased and informed viewpoint.

Bias is the tendency, either conscientiously or unconscientiously, to look at and absorb information that supports your biases (i.e. preconceived conclusions) and ignores, again conscientiously or unconscientiously, those that are against your biases. Discussions or arguments, and there are many disagreements as to the nature of healthy ageing, that are one-sided are perceived to be superior to those that present other sides of the argument.

We see what we are looking for and search for confirming evidence or selective findings for our biased views, termed confirmation bias or personal truths. In other words, we may place a very high weighting on one piece of evidence supportive of a biased view and ignore or apply a very low weighting on evidence that does not agree with one's biased view. Of course, one should have confidence in one's judgmental ability to make a conclusion or decision. On the other hand, overconfidence may lead to overlooking important alternative aspects of one's conclusions. It is relatively easy to find fault with other peoples' beliefs but extremely difficult to find fault with one's own beliefs.

It is most important to recognize that we are all inherently biased. Your biases are part of your personality that has been moulded by your life experiences and interactions with family, friends and colleagues, and even influenced by your environment. Consider the weather. On a wet, cold, dark winter day, you are biased towards a certain conclusion or belief. Now consider the same conclusion or belief on a warm, sunny summer day in a pleasant and relaxed atmosphere such as having a coffee at your favourite cafe. Or try the same belief after a stressful day at work. In fact, reading this book and selected Chapters, in different environments (ideally reading the same Chapter say a month or two later but in a different environment) will very likely influence your judgement and hence biases.

A recent publication in the journal Scientific Reports (Seresinhe *et al.*, 2019) concluded that individuals are more likely to have positive thoughts in scenic environments, and not only in natural environments but also in built-up areas.

Anecdotal evidence (translation: some years ago, I read an article in a reputable newspaper and recall some of the details) suggests that in a real democracy (and including only individuals who actually bother to vote), 80% of voters have political views (biased) that are not influenced by advertising, television debates or opinion polls and 20% are undecided or don't care. It is that 20% that greatly influences which political party actually forms government. The point here is another example of inherent biases. Changing one's vote for another political party really challenges our most cherished biases.

One final test of your biases is to apply the following experiment. Select an issue (e.g. from one of the book Chapters) that you have a very strong opinion on, let's say you strongly believe that substance A or lifestyle B has a positive effect on the attainment of healthy ageing. Now imagine or, better still, actually explain to family members and close friends why you believe that substance A or lifestyle B does provide real benefits for healthy ageing. Given that these individuals are very likely to share your values (read biases) and indeed lifestyle, the exercise is much more effective and challenging when you attempt to explain the benefits to individuals who are not within your circle of family or friends.

Finally, as ultimate tests of your biases, try explaining your conclusions to a journalist and then to a scientist. Apply this exercise to your consensus viewpoint to all the Chapters. You have now addressed your biases and achieved the maximum benefit from reading this book.

The information in this book is derived from articles published in peer-reviewed scientific journals of the highest standard. Some Readers may find these references challenging with articles on observational and clinical trials providing extensive details of the methodology (including statistics), duration of the studies and number of participants with ages, sex, lifestyle, clinical parameters etc. These details are absolutely necessary. They provide authenticity to the conclusion of the authors and act as a standard on which to compare other studies, confirmatory or otherwise, on the specific topic. These standards are the basis on which the informed Reader may compare their own conclusions and information sources with respect to the topics covered in the Chapters of this book.

Although I have exhaustively scanned the scientific literature (up to January 2020) for relevant information, one may have inadvertently omitted or failed to quote references that the Reader may deem to be important. I take full responsibility for these omissions and invite the interested Reader to forward details of these omissions via email to kfhwatsonia@gmail.com. There is limited input from the more popular literature such as magazines and newspapers, nevertheless, these have to some extent influenced the subject matter of each Chapter given the public interest in specific topics related to healthy ageing.

The scientific community is very conservative and there is the tendency on some issues to provide equivocal messages to the general public, particularly pertaining to healthy ageing. Scientific publications on ageing frequently conclude that further studies, particularly longer term (and hence more funding), are required to clarify the results and conclusions. This has led to considerable confusion in areas such as nutrition and has allowed commercial exploitation of products (e.g. superfoods, dietary supplements, anti-ageing pills) that have never been subject to scientific studies and peer-reviewed publication. On the other hand, the general public, the ageing general public, demands immediate answers and are open to claims of eternal youth, the ultimate 'fountain of youth,' by way of promotion of certain beliefs, lifestyles and anti-ageing health therapies by commercial entities.

The constrained expectations of the scientific community can be contrasted with the ebullient expectations of the general public in the following example.

Some years ago, I attended a scientific meeting on ageing at which around 120 of the top international scientists presented the very latest research on ageing, a few involving humans albeit mostly research involving model systems from yeast to fruit flies, worms and rodents (all these models are still the predominant model systems for human ageing research). In addition, there were around twenty or so commercial companies exhibiting the latest in scientific instrumentation, chemicals and enzymes associated with laboratory research on ageing. The overall conclusion from the conference was that much further research was required to clarify the detailed mechanisms of ageing in humans and in model systems.

A few days later, and frankly out of curiosity, I attended the annual meeting of the American Academy of Anti-Aging Medicine in Las Vegas.

Nothing had prepared me (as a typical university scientist of many years) for the 10,000 plus highly enthusiastic attendees and the hundreds (yes, hundreds) of commercial companies selling their anti-ageing innovations (particularly dietary supplements). Audience participation (e.g. standing, hugging your neighbour, saying a few words in unison) was the norm at the very entertaining conference presentations. I thoroughly enjoyed the experience. It was very clear that the general public was there to adopt anti-ageing therapies irrespective of any peer-reviewed scientific data. The moral of this story is that the general public and commercial enterprises are well ahead of the science.

As is the case of all individuals, the peer-reviewed published scientific literature, including the highest ranked journals, are also biased in that studies which report positive outcomes (e.g. success in obtaining an improved outcome for a medical intervention) receive favourable reviews and hence are accepted for publication. On the other hand, studies which report a negative (e.g. negative outcome of a medical intervention) or neutral (no positive or negative outcome) receive unfavorable reviews and hence are not published.

This is often the case for new or improved pharmaceutical drugs which have been developed for a specific medical condition (e.g. cardiovascular disease) in which positive trials are reviewed favorably for publication but neutral or negative outcomes (e.g. side effects) are not accepted for publication or, more commonly, not even submitted for publication. Such is the reality of peer-reviewed scientific publications.

Nevertheless, peer-reviewed scientific publications are certainly to be trusted far above any commercial self-promotion of a particular therapy (e.g. an in-house publication such as a glossy brochure) or any anecdotal evidence, generally in the form of an opinion (on what evidence?) provided by a friend, work colleague or family relation.

In this book, and in the appropriate Chapters, we subject the claims for healthy ageing to the *Pub Test* in which we ask a simple question and we *provide a simple Yes or No answer*, based on the best available scientific evidence.

The Pub Test

The origin of the *Pub Test* is debatable: from the Australian perspective it is when, say a group of friends, meet at a pub or bar for a social occasion and after a few drinks the conversation leads to animated discussions in which general agreement is reached with resolution on all the world's problems.

The *Pub Test* works best after a few drinks. It has its origins in politics, in that when a politician is asked a simple question requiring a simple yes or no, invariably there is much talk but essentially the simple question is never answered. The essence of the *Pub Test* is basically this: has the politician really addressed the simple question, that is, has it passed the *Pub Test*? The *Pub Test* can be seen as a gauge of public opinion: is the answer believable and trustworthy as far as the general public is concerned?

In this book, we apply the *Pub Test* to the most important questions relating to healthy ageing. We leave you, the informed Reader, to pass your own judgement on the answers to the Pub Tests. Your health is much too important an issue to be left unanswered by political and scientific rhetoric or, importantly, left to be answered by commercial, for-profit enterprises.

Belsky, DW, Caspi, A, Houts, R, et al. 2015. Quantification of biological aging in young adults. *Proceedings of the National Academy of Sciences* 113:4104-4110. doi:10.1073/pnas.1506264112.

Boulifard, DA, Avers, E. Verghese, J. 2019. Home-based gait speed assessment: normative data and racial/ethnic correlates among older adults. *Journal of the American Medical Director's Association* 20:1224-1229. doi:10.1016/j.jamda.2019.06.002.

Depp, CA. and Jeste, DV. 2006. Definitions and predictors of successful aging: a comprehensive review of larger quantitative studies. *American Journal of Geriatric Psychiatry* 14:6-20. doi:10.1097/01.JPG0000192501.03069.bc.

Harman, D. 1956. Aging: a theory based on free radical and radiation chemistry. *Journal of Gerontology* 11: 298-300. doi:10.1093/geronj/11.3.298.

Levine, ME. 2013. Modeling the rate of senescence: can estimated biological age predict mortality more accurately than chronological age? *The Journals of Gerontology: Series* A 68:667-674. doi:10.1093/gerona/gls233.

Pruchno, R. Editorial. 2015. Successful aging: Contentious past, productive future. *The Gerontologist* 55:1-4. doi:10.1093/geront/gnv002.

Rasmussen, LJH, Caspi, A, Ambler, A, et al. 2019. Association of neurocognitive and physical function with gait speed in midlife. *JAMA Network Open* 2:e1913123. doi:10.1001/jamanetworkopen.2019.13123.

Seresinhe, CI, Preis, T, MacKerron, G, *et al.* 2019. Happiness is greater in more scenic locations. *Scientific Reports* 9:4498. doi:10.1038/s41598-019-40854-6.

Studenski, S, Perera, S. Patel, K. 2011. Gait speed and survival in older adults. *JAMA* 305:50-58. doi:10.1001/jama.2010.1923.

Chapter 2
Genes and Healthy Ageing

A Beginner's Guide to DNA

Longevity or a long lifespan is a family thing. There is no doubt that, in the past, humans have observed that their life expectancy at birth was somehow associated with the lifespan of their parents and other immediate family members. However, it is only relatively recently that data from studies on identical and non-identical twins have concluded that between 25% to 30% of lifespan can be attributed to familial DNA (inherited genes), while studies on data obtained from the general population have indicated a smaller heritable percentage (Hjelmborg *et al.*, 2006; Ruby *et al.*, 2018, and references therein). These studies have been extremely valuable in the cases where one twin was raised in a different family environment and thus one could differentiate to some extent the genetic components (nature) of ageing from the environmental aspects (nurture).

A long-term study of twins (n = 20,502) from the Nordic countries (Denmark, Finland and Sweden) has concluded that genetic influence on longevity is modest up to age 60 but at more advanced ages the genetic influence appears to be significantly stronger (Hjelmborg *et al.*, 2006). Moreover, heritability or genetics of lifespan may be substantially less than 20% if one accounts for sociocultural effects and take into consideration genetically unrelated family clusters but sharing similar lifestyles and environments such as ethnic, economic, education, occupation and diet (Ruby *et al.*, 2018).

Does this mean that approximately 80% of lifespan is attributed to factors other than genetics? Well, yes and no.

There are also inherited factors associated with healthy ageing, loosely defined as attaining a good age (> 80 years), physically and cognitively competent and relatively free of chronic disease. Healthy ageing would mean maintenance with age of physical attributes such as good walking speed and strong handgrip and absence or low values of clinical parameters associated with symptoms of cardiovascular disease, low bone density and high blood pressure. The relative heritable contribution to healthy ageing of each of these health parameters is extremely variable and essentially an individual or within family characteristic. Moreover, although heritable to a variable extent, many of these health parameters can also be modulated by lifestyle and the environment.

The key question then is, what are the genetic factors or genes that influence healthy ageing?

A Beginner's Guide to DNA

There are constant advances in DNA technology that allow more and more detailed analyses of genes and proteins which modulate ageing and healthy ageing. It is true to say that as we accumulate more and more data on this subject, we reach the conclusion that ageing is highly complex and that in fact we know less and less.

A draft DNA sequence of human DNA (the Human Genome) was first published in 2001 (Lander *et al.*, 2001; Venter *et al.*, 2001) and cost around $3 billion. An essentially complete human DNA sequence was completed in 2003 (International Human Genome Sequencing Consortium, 2004). By 2010, the DNA sequences of many hundreds of individuals were available and by 2016, many thousands were completed. Current technology allows an individual's complete DNA to be routinely sequenced at a commercial cost of less than $1000.

The relatively routine process of analyzing specific sections of human DNA can be judged by the popularity of tracing one's ancestry through DNA analysis. Note that this type of analysis does not involve sequencing the complete or almost complete DNA of an individual but only specific sections (inherited from the father, the mother or from both parents) known to be associated with specific world geographic areas. To date, many millions (> 30 million) of individuals have had their DNA analyzed for ancestry purposes.

The human DNA consists of approximately 3.2 billion letters, designated as a series of four bases or more precisely nucleotides: A (adenine), T (thymine), G (guanine) and C (cytosine). The precise order of these nucleotides defines the genetic code.

How large is the human DNA ? If you were to type out a typical human genome as a random series of A's, T's, G's and C's (e.g. AGATTTCCCGCCTAA....) on your computer and using 12 fonts Times New Roman with 1.5 line spacing, the entire human DNA would require > l million sheets of A4 paper. There is thus clearly a need for high-powered computers to analyze human DNA.

Detailed analyses have shown that about 1% of human DNA (termed coding sequences) codes for specific genes (approximately 23,000 genes). A gene may be defined as a specific sequence of A's, T's, G's and C's which codes for a specific protein.

The often-quoted comment that all humans are 99.5% genetically related refers to the fact that the DNA sequences of the 1% of human DNA that codes for protein are almost identical in all humans. You may also wish to contemplate that a comparison of selected genes found in common in humans, chimpanzees and gorillas has shown that in 70% of the genes, the chimpanzee sequences are more similar to humans than to those in the gorilla (Scally *et al.*, 2012). However, in the remaining 30%, the gorilla DNA base sequences are more closely related with either the human or the chimpanzee than these two share with each other.

If only 1% of the human DNA codes for protein does that mean that 99% of human DNA does not have a function? Well, no. Previously, most of this 99% DNA was designated as junk DNA, however, we now know that much (80-90%) of this DNA, termed non-coding sequences, plays key roles in gene regulation in that genes can be fully or partially switched on (and thus translated into functional proteins) or fully or partially switched off (not translated into functional proteins).

Although humans share 99.5% of their DNA with respect to the 1% coding sequences, when one examines the entire DNA (the coding and non-coding sequences) of individuals there are substantial differences from one individual to another. Even identical twins may be differentiated on the basis of their DNA, although a simple hand fingerprint may distinguish one twin from another.

Identifying individuals on the basis of their DNA is based on examining differences in short tandem repeats of between four to ten bases in the A's, T's, G's and C's which are repeated many hundreds of times. In practice, to provide a highly statistically significant DNA profile (also termed DNA fingerprint) of an individual, multiple loci for short tandem repeats (STRs) are examined: for example, 17-STRs in the UK or 20-STRs in the USA are analyzed. STRs are used extensively in forensics, most notably in criminal investigations to implicate or exonerate individuals potentially associated with a crime investigation.

DNA profiling is also used in parental disputes in respect to determination of paternity issues. Consider the classic example of a woman taking a man to court in a case involving the dispute of paternity of her child. The man consents to a DNA profile. The laboratory results return a positive: the DNA (20-STRs) of the child corresponds to the man as the father, a clear case of paternity identification. However, it turns out that the DNA blood sample provided by the man was in fact that of his best friend. The moral of that story is to consent to a DNA profile if innocent but if guilty, perhaps not.

A particular class of non-coding sequence, termed single nucleotide polymorphisms (SNPs, pronounced as snips) are DNA variations in which a single nucleotide, say A, is replaced by another nucleotide, say T. SNPs are the most common genetic variations among individuals. These SNPs may occur within a coding gene, in between genes or at some distance from a gene and may influence the function of a particular gene (e.g. switch on/off, activity increase/decrease). There are more than 10 million SNPs in the human genome. This pool of SNPs accounts for much of the genetic variation of the human population and the heritable risk of common diseases. A significant number of these SNPs are located in the vicinity of genes associated with health and age-related diseases, including cardiovascular disease, Alzheimer's and cancers. Studies on SNPs have therefore provided new information as to the influence of DNA on human longevity and healthy ageing.

The approach to research on the coding and non-coding DNA sequences, particularly the SNPs, influencing human ageing and healthy ageing basically falls into three main areas.

Longevity Genes

Studies on longevity associated genes initially involved examining genes in humans that were originally identified as influencing ageing in model organisms, including yeast (*Saccharomyces cerevisiae*), the fruit fly (*Drosophila melanogaster*), the nematode worm (*Caenorhabditis elegans*) and the perennial favourite of experimental scientists, the rodent (the mouse, *Mus musculus* and the brown rat, *Rattus norvergicus*).

The normal lifespans of these model organisms range from a few days or weeks to a maximum of three to four years for the rodent. The relatively short lifespan of these model organisms is an advantage in that one can follow biological changes from birth to death. Moreover, scientists can observe these changes under strict, albeit artificial, highly controlled laboratory conditions such as variations in nutrition, physical activity, social interactions and the all-important genetics of their chosen model organism. On the other hand, extrapolation of study outcomes on model organisms to humans is problematic given the free-living nature of humans and the substantial differences in genetics, physiology, biochemistry and psychology. Oh, and not to mention that humans can live to > 120 years, and thus following biological ageing in humans from birth to death is experimentally demanding to say the least. Nevertheless, experiments on model organisms have been and continue to be an important resource for studies on human ageing.

Despite extensive research, to date, only a few specific genes (e.g. APOE and FOXO3A) and their regulatory sequences (SNPs) have been consistently associated with longevity and age-related diseases in humans (Brooks-Wilson, 2013; Broer et al., 2015).

The apolipoprotein E (APOE) gene, for example, is associated with cardiovascular disease and carrying one copy of the APOE-ε4 gene allele in one's DNA increases the risk of late-onset Alzheimer's and carrying two copies greatly increases the risk. It should be noted that carrying the APOE-ε4 allele does not mean that one will definitely progress to Alzheimer's, but there is clearly an increase risk. Some individuals with two copies of the APOE-ε4 allele do not progress to Alzheimer's and conversely, some individuals with no copies of the APOE-ε4 allele progress to Alzheimer's. In this respect the APOE gene may be regarded as more a frailty rather than a longevity marker. In terms of longevity, having one copy of a genetic variant (APOE-ε4) of the APOE gene is associated with a decrease in maternal (minus 1.24 years) and paternal (minus 0.79 years) lifespans. In the rare instances of carriers of two copies of the APOE-ε4 allele they are predicted to have between 3.3 and 3.7 years shorter lifespan (Joshi et al., 2016).

The Foxhead box 3A (FOXO3A) gene regulates a wide range of biological functions including DNA repair, oxidative stress, insulin regulation and glucose metabolism (Morris et al., 2015). The gene is known to influence traits associated with type 2 diabetes and cardiovascular disease. These influences may be positive or negative depending on individual circumstances and concentration of specific SNPs which occur close to the location of the gene.

A study involving n = 6,247 individuals over a seventeen-year study period reported that carriers of a certain FOXO3A allele (the G allele) had a 10% decrease in all-cause mortality, with an approximately 26% decrease in risk of cardiovascular disease (Wilcox et al., 2016).

A study of oldest-old Danes (n = 1,088, aged 92-93, 7 years of follow-up) found no association between age-related phenotypes (including cognitive performance, daily activities, hand-grip strength and self-rated health) and over 100 genes and gene variants selected on the basis of their previously reported association with longevity (Sorensen et al., 2016).

Studies to date on the quest for specific longevity genes have all indicated that candidate genes only show modest contributions to human lifespan. The biology of human ageing is highly complex, involving genetics and a myriad of interactions involving individual lifestyles and the environment. It is likely that individual genes make only small but significant contributions to longevity and that many, perhaps hundreds, of genetic variants all contribute in modest ways to complex traits as in human ageing.

Genome-Wide Association Studies

The second approach is to examine the entire DNA sequence, termed whole genome sequencing, of family pedigrees consisting of relatively healthy long-lived parents (> 80 years) and their middle-aged children (45-60 years) as the experimental and compare with a suitable control cohort. In these studies, emphasis is placed on genetic variations in the SNPs of individuals. A related approach, termed genome-wide association studies (GWAS), is based on scanning DNA for variations in SNPs associated with age-related physical characteristics (e.g. walking speed, hand-grip strength) and age-related disease traits.

It is most important here to understand the difference between lifespan and healthy ageing. You may live until, say, aged 90 (lifespan) but with the last ten years or so be in poor health, as opposed to living to aged 90 with the last ten years in relatively good health as in healthy ageing. Thus, screening DNA for SNPs associated with susceptibility or resistance to age-associated disease and age-related physical and physiological (as in e.g. cognitive decline) characteristics provides key information as to healthy ageing.

The GWAS approach has its emphasis on the phenotype of the individual as compared with studies on the search for longevity genes. The phenotype is the physical characteristics of the individual and, although primarily influenced by the genotype, can also be influenced by lifestyle and the environment. The genotype, on the other hand, is one's complete heritable DNA. To complicate matters further, it is now known that selective parts of one's heritable DNA can also be altered by lifestyle and the environment (see later section on Telomeres and Epigenetics).

In one recent study (n = 1,384, mean age of 84.2, 61% female) using whole-genome sequencing, of relatively healthy individuals (defined in the study as the Wellderly phenotype), a number of genetic variants were identified as contributing to healthy ageing (Erikson *et al.*, 2016). A significant decrease in genetic risk for Alzheimer's and coronary artery disease was identified in the Wellderly cohort as compared with an ethnicity-matched control cohort. It is important to note that the Wellderly cohort differed from the control group in a number of ways. In particular, > 80% had completed a tertiary education certificate in contrast to < 20% of the control group and 67% reported exercise as part of their lifestyle compared with 44% of the control group. It is not inconceivable that education level and exercise had positive effects on the healthy profiles of the Wellderly cohort. For example, a high education level had been reported to decrease risk of cognitive decline (e.g. Marioni *et al.*, 2015) and exercise is consistently reported to improve cardiovascular health and cognitive performance (see Chapter 6: Physical Activity).

In a large study of n = 75,244 individuals of British descent, evidence was provided for a genetic basis of longevity and healthy ageing (Pilling *et al.*, 2016). In these studies, one cohort (n = 8,655) consisted of middle-aged individuals (mean age of 63.5) whose parents were identified as long-lived with mean ages at death of the father and mother of 82 and 87 respectively. Two other larger control cohorts (each n > 20,000 individuals) consisted of middle-aged individuals (mean age of 62.5) whose parents were identified as medium-lived (father and mother's mean ages at death of 77 and 82 respectively) and short-lived (father and mother's mean ages at death of 64 and 72 respectively).

In the siblings of long-lived parents, a number of genetic variants (alleles), previously associated with common risk traits and diseases, were identified as protective (i.e. lower risk) with respect to health-related phenotypes particularly cardiovascular risk with a weaker association for lower risk of Alzheimer's. On the other hand, in this study, the FOXO gene was not apparently associated with longevity. The authors concluded that there was an overlap between living to a very long age (longevity) and genetic variants associated with lower risk factors for age-related diseases, notably cardiovascular disease.

Centenarians

The third approach is to analyze the DNA and SNPs of exceptionally long-lived individuals, the centenarians (individuals who have lived to 100 years or more) and nonagenarians (individuals aged 90 and above), and compare the DNA and SNPs of their siblings and with an appropriate control cohort of non-long-lived families. It has been only relatively recently that researchers have turned their attention to these long-lived individuals as prime examples of successful ageing.

The number of centenarians world-wide in 1990 was estimated to be around 100,000 with a current (2015) estimate of around 500,000 (Robine and Cubaynes, 2017), a fivefold increase in twenty-five years. In the same period, by comparison, the world population had increased from around 5.285 billion to around 7.250 billion, about a 1.5 fold increase (US Census Bureau).

The importance here is the authentication of chronological age given that claims of individuals living to 120-150 years, for example in rural regions of the Caucasus, had long proved to be fraudulent. For example, it was common practice, particularly for males, to claim to be the village elder with inherent privileges of high social standing. However, these regions kept limited local records of birth certificates providing documentation of age. The fact that such documents related to their father's birth or marriage with exactly the same names as their sons appeared to have been conveniently overlooked. Simply stating or observing that an individual had been living in a particular town or village for a very long time does not constitute definitive proof that the individual was a long-lived individual or for that matter a centenarian.

It is now recognized that centenarians, a significant number of whom are in relatively good health and free from common age-related diseases, represent a unique resource as models for successful ageing. An early observation was the recognition of hot spots or clusters, the so-called Blue Zones, of centenarians in specific geographic locations (Buettner, 2012). These regions include the islands of Okinawa (Japan) and Sardinia (Italy), specific regions of Costa Rica and Greece, communities around Loma Linda (California, USA) and the New England and Utah regions of the USA.

Previous studies on centenarians (n = 348, birth cohort of 1890) and their siblings (n = 1,142) in the Okinawa Centenarians Study had pointed out genetic components associated with longevity and healthy ageing. In these studies, although acknowledging the possible influence of lifestyle and environmental factors, plausible arguments were presented for a strong genetic component for successful ageing (Wilcox et al., 2006). The authors emphasized that the long-lived individuals and their siblings represented a relatively homogeneous genetic cohort given the low migration status within the island of Okinawa, particularly the rural population. Furthermore, the availability of well-documented records of births dating back to the mid-nineteenth century, added to the authenticity of the data.

A study of long-lived individuals and their families in Utah (USA) with well documented birth and death records and relatively low migration (at the time of the studies) had concluded that heritable genetic components were contributory factors in longevity and healthy ageing at the same time acknowledging that lifestyle and environmental factors were also significant (O'Brien et al., 2007). The Utah study (individuals n = 666,921) concluded that:

'A family history of disease increases one's risk of dying from the same cause, whereas a family history of longevity is protective (lower risk of cardiovascular disease), except in the case of cancer.'

Similarly, in a study of n = 40,000 individuals, all born in 1905 in Denmark, a country with relatively low migration and with excellent public health records as well as documented births and deaths going back to the late nineteenth century, it was found that centenarians and nonagenarians had significantly fewer days in hospitalization as compared with non-long-lived individuals at a similar age (Engberg et al., 2009). The analyses were conducted from 1977, at which time the participants were all aged 71-72, and completed in 2006, a Herculean twenty-nine-year follow-up study.

In a very recent related study of long-lived individuals (n = 1,588 nonagenarians, mean age of 93.1) all born in 1905 in Denmark, a genetic variant (allele rs2149954, located on chromosome 5) was associated with decreased risk of coronary artery disease and increased physical function as compared to an elderly control cohort (n = 677, mean age of 78.7) (Nygaard et al., 2017).

Interestingly, in a more genetically diverse population, characterized by migration of individuals of European origin, studies on families from the New England Centenarian Study had provided evidence that healthy ageing was associated with heritable genetic components. In these studies (3 to 4 years of follow-up) healthy ageing was estimated by onset of age-related diseases which were delayed in siblings (n = 370) of centenarians by comparison with individuals (n = 140) from less long-lived families (Adams et al., 2008).

In a 2016 study of Italian subjects, researchers compared the health status of siblings (n = 247, mean age of 70) having a centenarian parent with that of siblings (n = 107, mean age of 71) having a parent classified as non-long-lived (Bucci et al., 2016). The researchers compiled a comprehensive medical history of the participants and these included clinical parameters (e.g. lipid profiles, hypertension, BMI and medications), physical measurements (e.g. hand-grip strength and walking speed) and cognitive performance. The siblings of a centenarian parent presented a significantly healthier profile than the siblings of non-long-lived parents. The absolute scientific proof of these observations would be to record the ages of death of the two cohorts. However, the complete data would not be available for at least another twenty to thirty years, thus, highlighting that studies on human ageing are long-term, the conclusions of which, by default, can only be probabilities or extrapolations based on highly sophisticated statistical analyses.

Studies on centenarians and their siblings have greatly advanced our understanding of ageing with particular emphasis on heritability and maintenance of health well into the nineties and beyond. However, a genetic basis in the sense of specific genes responsible for heritability of longevity has, to date, not been conclusively established. Nevertheless, in a study of long-lived individuals and appropriate controls, a signature of 281 genetic variants in SNPs of 130 genes has been associated with exceptional longevity providing a tool for differentiating centenarians from non-centenarians, particularly if the former were over 105 years old (Sebastiani *et al.*, 2013).

The search for genes associated with longevity has also been extended to examining the DNA of supercentenarians, that is individuals who have lived to 110 years or more. A study of the DNA of seventeen supercentenarians, all female Caucasians, has been published (Gierman *et al.*, 2014). The authors examined the DNAs in considerable detail for rare protein coding genes and SNPs but were unable to identify any single gene or variants associated with the exceptional longevity of the individuals.

Overall, scientific studies on long-lived individuals, including centenarians and their siblings, have confirmed the strong heritability of longevity and, just as importantly, that of delayed onset of age-related diseases. However, despite these extensive studies, no single gene or variation of a gene (allele) or clusters of genes have been implicated as keys to healthy ageing. Claims to the contrary simply do not pass the *Pub Test*.

Pub Test 2.1:

Question:

In deep and meaningful discussions, and after having a few drinks, in a pub or bar with friends, can analysis of your DNA at age 25, 50 or 70, accurately provide information that you will live to be a centenarian in relatively good health?

Answer:

No

Although it is common knowledge that a family history of longevity (and good health) suggests the likelihood of long-lived offspring, other lifestyle factors are significantly more important than the genetics. On the other hand, analysis of your DNA can be informative in respect of specific genetically inherited disorders and diseases.

However, before we abandon the DNA test as a measure for healthy ageing, we have to look at two aspects of DNA which have recently been touted as holding the keys to longevity: telomeres and epigenetics.

What Are Telomeres?

Telomeres are repetitive segments (tandem repeats of the sequence TTAGGGn where n can be from several hundred to several thousand) of DNA at the ends of our chromosomes. These repetitive segments are non-coding in the sense that these sequences do not translate into proteins. They form a kind of protective cap at the end of chromosomes and prevent instability and damage to our DNA.

A key feature of telomeres is that they shorten each time a cell divides and thus as we age telomeres get progressively shorter. The rate of telomere attrition or shortening is most rapid in the first few years after birth and then less rapidly up to middle age (40-55 years) after which it has been noted to increase as one ages. It is noteworthy that not only telomere length varies considerably from one individual to the next but also the age-related rate of shortening. Cells may reach a stage at which they become senescent (stop dividing or dividing very slowly). Importantly, stem cells which can potentially differentiate into many different cell types such as immune, skin, nail and hair cells, are capable of indefinite renewal provided they are healthy.

Telomere length is maintained by the enzyme telomerase. However, the latter activity is low in most cell types (somatic cells) and cell division is limited when telomeres reach a certain critical length. On the other hand, too much telomerase may lead to a cancerous state, characterized by indefinite cell proliferation. Cancerous and malignant cells overexpress telomerase and thus maintain telomere length and have high replicative activity i.e. rapid growth.

Telomere length can act as an indicator or biomarker of age, given that telomeres shorten with age, thus the older the individual the shorter the telomeres. However, telomere length is quite dynamic in that an individual's inherited DNA, lifestyle and environment all influence telomere length. Nevertheless, it is now recognized that telomeres have high heritability with reports suggesting around 40% to 60%. Some studies have shown that heritability to offspring is greater from fathers than mothers, others have shown the reverse and yet others have shown little or no bias as to parent. On the other hand, it is frequently observed that females, from birth onwards, have longer telomeres than males (Lapham et al., 2015).

In the past decade, there has been a massive increase in publications on telomeres and their potential role in health and disease. The obsession with the length of one's telomeres is understandable given that telomeres progressively shorten with age and, as previously mentioned, may reach a critical stage at which cells are unable to divide, become senescent and die or turn cancerous. Thus, it is postulated that maintaining long telomeres should be the goal for healthy ageing.

Claims that telomeres hold the key to the fountain of youth and ageing healthily requires very careful reading of the published literature. A thorough understanding of the assumptions is required, the science and the statistics behind the publications, many of which appear in the highest ranked scientific journals, before a critical appraisal of the data and non-biased conclusions can be made.

The first issue to consider is how exactly is telomere length determined.

The most common procedure is estimating the leucocyte telomere length (commonly abbreviated as LTL). In essence, this involves taking a blood sample, separating out the leucocytes (white blood cells), amplifying the DNA by real time quantitative polymerase chain reaction (RT-QPCR) and determining the relative telomere length as a ratio of the telomere repeat copy number (T) to that of a reference single-copy gene copy number (S) to give the T/S ratio. The absolute LTL can then be estimated by graphing the T/S ratio against the known telomere length of the reference DNA gene, e.g. if the T/S is 1 the LTL is the same as the telomere length of the reference gene, say, 5,260 base pairs (bp). Similarly, if the T/S ratio is less than one or more than one, then the LTL would be < 5,260 bp or > 5,260 bp respectively. Another common and more direct procedure for determining LTL is by the Southern blot method (Lai *et al.*, 2018).

Although LTL is by far the most common procedure, telomere lengths may also be determined, albeit much less frequently, in saliva, skin cells and skeletal muscle cells.

Apart from attrition due to ageing, telomere length is also known to be modified by lifestyle and environmental factors (see later). In order to minimize these issues and to focus on genetic factors, researchers have recently examined DNA gene variants (alleles or SNPs), previously established to be associated with telomere maintenance, to indirectly infer telomere lengths. These methodologies, using the genetic loci technique, have provided new insights into potential associations between telomere lengths and cancer.

It has been known for some time that 80-90% of human cancers characteristically have relatively short telomeres. Cells which have aged, ceased replicating and become senescent or dormant as their telomeres have reached a critical short length may progress to become cancerous. The latter state may lead to mutation with progression to rapid growth and malignant cancer (activation of telomerase) or benign cancer (inactivation or low telomerase). Targeting telomerase as a potential treatment for human cancers is currently an area of intense research.

Paradoxically, very recent studies using the genetic loci method for estimating telomere length had provided evidence that long telomeres were a risk factor for some specific cancers. In an impressive study on non-Hodgkin lymphoma cases (n = 10,102) and appropriate controls (n = 9,562), the authors concluded that longer telomeres increased the risk of the four common non-Hodgkin lymphoma by 1.49 times and chronic lymphocytic leukaemia by 2.60 times (Machiela et al., 2016). In a very large study of individuals of Danish ancestry (n = 95,568) using three genetic markers (SNPs) associated with telomere length, longer telomeres were associated with a 1.19 and 1.14 increased risk of melanoma and lung cancer respectively (Rode et al., 2016)

A comprehensive review of telomere length and cancer risk concluded that longer telomeres were associated with increased odds of disease for nine of twenty-two primary cancers examined (Haycock et al., 2017).

Despite these reported associations between increased risk of specific cancers and longer telomeres, many issues have to be addressed, both clinical and methodological. Perhaps the most critical issue is in the timing of samples taken for analysis of LTL. Samples taken pre-diagnosis, post-diagnosis or even after commencement of treatment will almost certainly differ in LTL. Longitudinal samples, perhaps taken over several years, to follow the progression of cancer will be crucial. A single sample taken at a single time point will hardly be adequate in the case of most cancers.

Another issue is that comparison of data across publications is difficult if different methodologies have been used for LTL measurements. Ideally, not only the same methodology but also the same laboratory should be used for the analyses.

It should be appreciated that scientific research at this level is technically challenging and extremely costly. There are very few granting bodies that would be willing to fund this type of costly research for many years. Applications for research funding much beyond three to five years, the typical time frame for scientific grant applications, are very unlikely to be funded.

Overall, the relationship between risk of cancer and telomere length is highly complex, to say the least. Publications on the topic rely on very large numbers, appropriate age-matched controls and complex statistical analysis. Determination of a single individual's LTL will not be informative as to risk of cancer. Even for values beyond the norm for short or long telomeres, these are more likely indicative of other issues related to genetic, lifestyle and environmental factors. At this stage, conventional diagnosis for cancer is the best option.

Telomeres

In terms of heritability and successful ageing, the key observation is that offspring of long-lived parents retain relatively long telomeres as compared with offspring of non-long-lived parents (Honig *et al.*, 2015).

This observation is also related to the observations that long-lived individuals (and their offspring) appear to have a genetic predisposition or health advantage in that such individuals show a delay in the onset of aged-related disorders such as cardiovascular disease, Alzheimer's and cancer.

Just on the subject of Alzheimer's, an aged-related disorder, there are conflicting reports as to any relationship between LTL and cognitive decline.

In a two-year follow-up study of n = 449 individuals (mean age of 85), including n = 205 controls (cognitively normal), LTL was not predictive of dementia or mild cognitive impairment (Zekry *et al.*, 2010).

In a larger study (Harris *et al.*, 2016), the Lothian Birth Cohorts of 1936 (n = 1,091, 6 years of follow-up, measurements at aged 70, 73 and 76) and Lothian Birth Cohorts of 1921 (n = 550, 13 years of follow-up, measurements at ages 79, 87, 90 and 92) the authors concluded that telomere length shortening, although decreasing with age, was independent of decreased cognitive and physical abilities (e.g. walking speed, grip strength, lung capacity).

In a study of non-demented community dwelling individuals (n = 2,734, mean age of 74, 7 years of follow-up), longer telomere LTL was associated with better cognitive function. However, absolute LTL values could not be assigned with level of cognitive performance (Yaffe *et al.*, 2011). In a very recent review of thirteen published studies (termed meta-analysis referring to a general conclusion from statistical analyses of results from multiple studies of published research) it was concluded that the studies were generally consistent with shorter telomeres in patients with Alzheimer's (Forero *et al.*, 2017).

There is increasing evidence that shorter LTL is indicative of increased risk of cardiovascular disease (CVD). Several recent studies have addressed this topic.

In a meta-analysis encompassing 24 independent studies (n = 43,725 individuals including n = 8,400 with cardiovascular disease), half of which were prospective in design (before diagnosis) and half retrospective (after diagnosis), there was a

1.34 increase in relative risk of CVD with shorter telomere length after allowing for what the authors termed as publication bias (Haycock et al., 2014).

In a very large study of ischaemic heart disease (a subset of CVD) in an ethnically homogeneous population of Danish origin (n = 62,966), the authors (Madrid et al., 2016) calculated a hazards ratio of 1.21 (similar to relative risk) between individuals with the shortest and longest telomere lengths, with appropriate adjustments for confounders (e.g. age, smoking, exercise and clinical parameters of CVD including lipid profiles).

A study of LTL in an ethnically diverse U.S. population (n = 7,252, mean age of 45.7) demonstrated an association of telomere length to seventeen established clinical markers of CVD (Rehkopf et al., 2016). The authors concluded that LTL was a potential biomarker for risk of CVD, the shorter the LTL the greater the risk.

A very recent meta-analysis of several very large genetic associated studies (GWAS) examined the potential association between telomere length and risk factors for CVD (Zhan et al., 2017). The study combined data from a study (n = 37,684) which utilized telomere length as a genetic measurement, a case-controlled CVD study (cases, n = 22,233 ; controls, n = 64,762) as well as several other very large studies on risk factors for CVD. In brief, the authors concluded that short telomere length was potentially linked to fasting insulin levels, the latter a known biomarker for CVD.

In the case of centenarians, several studies have reported that offspring of centenarians retain relatively long telomeres as compared with offspring of non-long-lived parents (Tedone et al., 2014).

In an earlier study on Ashkenazi centenarians (Atzmon et al., 2010), it was reported that centenarians and their offspring maintained longer telomeres and better health parameters than an appropriate age-matched control group. Also in an early publication (Terry et al., 2008), it was reported that healthy centenarians (n = 19), defined as living relatively independently and with relative absence of age-related disorders (e.g. hypertension, heart disease, dementia, cancer) had significantly longer telomeres (mean length of 5,771 bp) than relatively unhealthy centenarians (n = 19, mean telomere length of 3,657 bp).

A more recent study (Aoki et al., 2017) on longevity in Japanese centenarians (n = 23) found a correlation between longer telomeres and performance status (essentially walking ability), but only after excluding two individuals with diagnosed cancer. On the other hand, a large study on Japanese centenarians (n = 684) and their offspring concluded that LTL was not indicative of successful ageing, although heritability of LTL was demonstrated (Arai et al., 2015). The authors concluded that inflammation, as determined by levels of proteins (e.g. C-reactive protein, interleukin-6, tumour necrosis factor-α) associated with the inflammatory response, was a better predictor of cognitive function and all-cause mortality than telomere length.

This leads to the question as whether centenarians and supercentenarians (individuals aged at least 110 years) have exceptionally long telomeres. Well, no. Telomeres in centenarians and supercentenarians are reported to be quite short, not surprisingly given that telomeres shorten with age, averaging 4,000 bp (4 kb) or less and depending on the method used to measure TL (Arai et al., 2015; Tedone et al., 2018).

The key question is the one that asks what is the optimum or indeed the 'best' TL for an individual to have with respect to healthy ageing? Frankly, there is simply no obvious answer, given the wide variations in TL from one individual to another not only at birth but also in the individual differences in the rate of decrease in TL as one ages. In addition, one has to consider the added complication that the rate of TL attrition is greatly influenced by a myriad of environmental and lifestyle factors.

It is beyond the scope of this book to consider the details of TL and modulation by lifestyle and environmental factors, and the interested reader is referred to the literature quoted in this Chapter for more details as well as a recent book on the topic of telomeres and health (Blackburn and Epel, 2017). It is sufficient to note that TL has been reported, in a very limited number of studies, to be influenced by: stress (increased stress, shorter TL, Darrow *et al.*, 2016; Whisman and Richardson, 2017), social and educational status (mixed results, Robertson *et al.*, 2013), exercise (variable results, depending on duration and type of exercise, Arsenis *et al.*, 2017) and diet (variable results, depending on duration and generally based on food questionnaire recall by participants, Milte *et al.*, 2018; Rafie *et al.*, 2017). As with all such reports, one must carefully and critically read the publications, which is no easy task even with a sound scientific background.

A recent article in *Ageing Research Reviews*, an umbrella review of systematic reviews of observational studies on telomere length and health outcomes, concluded that the level of evidence was high only for the association of short telomeres with higher risk (1.95 relative increase) of gastric cancer in the general population (Smith *et al.*, 2019).

One thing that is clear from the scientific literature is that longer telomeres and slower telomere attrition as one ages are seen as having a positive health outcome, with the caveat that some specific cancers have been associated with longer telomeres. Nevertheless, despite extensive studies, there is no clear indication as to the optimum TL (at what age and at what rate of attrition as one ages?) that would lead to healthy ageing. If longer telomeres are positive for healthy ageing then, conversely, shorter telomeres are negative for healthy ageing. What is the published evidence for this conclusion?

In a large study of n = > 12,000 individuals (aged from 20 to > 100) of European ancestry, a critical telomere length, termed the 'telomere brink', was defined as a LTL threshold (as determined by the Southern blot method) below which the probability of survival ('imminent death') was extremely low. The critical LTL was defined as 5 kb or less (Steenstrup *et al.*, 2017). The data confirmed previous findings that females had longer telomeres than males with an estimate of 150 bp longer, adjusted for age. Furthermore, if one assumes a typical LTL attrition rate of 30 bp per year, the 150 bp difference would equate to five years of longer life for females. Interestingly, current data for life expectancy at birth for individuals of Western European descent indicate that female life expectancy is approximately four to five years longer than males (Table 1, p.154).

Should you therefore rush out to have a laboratory measure your LTL, preferably by one with high technical expertise in the measurement of LTL? Well, firstly consider that the telomeric brink of 5 kb LTL specifically refers to the above-mentioned study which used the Southern blot methodology, many thousands of individuals and sophisticated statistical analysis. Telomere measurements may only be useful over large populations in statistical studies but not at all helpful for individuals. One would have to consider the age of the individual, ethnic background, lifestyle and environmental variables and certainly take into consideration conventional health parameters of the individual.

Consider again that the 5 kb LTL may only apply to that specific study (and the specific laboratory that measured the LTL) given that some publications report LTL values significantly less than 5 kb in individuals who are very much alive and well such as centenarians and their offspring.

LTL is unlikely to be a helpful marker with respect to an individual's current health status as compared with conventional markers such as lipid profile (cholesterol HDL/LDL, triglycerides), BMI, blood pressure and inflammatory indicators.

A recent study of n = 351 individuals, aged 49 to 51, found no association between LTL and conventional health biomarkers (Appleby *et al.*, 2017). In a three-country (USA, Taiwan, Costa Rica) study of middle-aged individuals (n = > 4,500, aged 54-61) with a five-year follow-up, LTL did not predict survival or all-cause mortality (Glel, 2016). Indeed, age itself was a much better predictor of mortality. Apart from age, the strongest predictors of mortality were mobility, cognitive function and conventional clinical and lifestyle parameters of health, including exercise and BMI.

In summary, although telomeres have attracted considerable attention with respect to health and ageing, there are conflicting findings. Some of these conflicting findings can be related to study design with respect to e.g. age and number of participants, short-term studies, baseline health of participants (TL at birth being a key factor but generally unavailable), a single one-time measurement of TL (with long-term longitudinal studies the desirable objective) and modulation of TL by a myriad of lifestyle and environmental parameters. Having said that, two consistent observations are that telomeres shorten as we age (albeit with wide individual attrition rates) and females have longer telomeres than males (Gardner *et al.*, 2014; Lapham *et al.*, 2015).

There are also reported ethnic differences, with African-Americans having longer telomeres at birth and into adulthood than Hispanics which in turn have longer telomeres than Whites (Hunt et al., 2008; Needham et al., 2013; Lynch et al., 2016). If longer telomeres are better for ageing, then this pattern does not reflect data for the United States which show that life expectancy is actually highest for Hispanics (especially for females) followed by Whites than African-Americans (CDC 2015). Several reports have addressed this paradox by assessing that the rate of telomere attrition is higher for African-Americans than Whites, given the higher social and economic stressors (leading to telomere shortening) of the former ethnic group but the issue is far from clear (Rewak et al., 2014; Chae et al., 2016). In a study of a large multi-ethnic US population (n = 11,934, mean age of 68), with estimation of saliva TL using genetic markers (seven SNPs associated with telomere maintenance), it was reported that African-Americans have genetic markers which favour longer telomeres from birth (Hamad et al., 2016).

Pub Test 2.2

Question:

Will the determination of your DNA telomere length in your leucocytes provide a good measure of your projected longevity?

Answer:

No

A single determination of telomere length in an individual at, say, aged 50 is not that useful. On the other hand, if one also has the telomere lengths at birth, early teens and early adulthood, then perhaps an indication of how the individual was ageing could be provided. Nobody currently aged 50 years or more will have had their telomeres measured at birth, early teens and early adulthood (the latter certainly not accurately). Furthermore, for any meaningful measure one would also have to have a control cohort of individuals (ideally hundreds) matched for a myriad of lifestyle and environmental factors, only possible in large observational studies.

Epigenetics

The science of epigenetics is complex, and thus in this section some aspects have been simplified, not too much but sufficient to provide an understanding of the topic for individuals with a limited background in DNA science.

Epigenetics refers to chemical modifications in DNA and associated proteins resulting in alterations in the way genes are switched either on or off. Recall that a gene is a DNA sequence (CGATGCAT…..etc) that translates into a functional protein. The most common and best studied of these chemical modifications occurs by the addition of a methyl group (CH_3-, where C designates carbon and H designates hydrogen, in this case three hydrogens) characteristically at a cytosine (C) linked via a phosphate (p) to guanine (G): abbreviated as CpG. Approximately 1% to 1.5% of human DNA consists of CpG sites of which 70-80% are methylated, conventionally designated as DNAm (DNA methylation). Many of these methylated CpG sites are located close to genes and have a marked influence on gene regulation with respect to which and when genes are switched either on or off (or indeed more active or less active) to be or not to be translated into functional proteins. In this respect, DNAm does not result in changes in the DNA sequence, that is the genetic code of an individual, but does influence gene expression and thus protein synthesis.

It is known that DNAm is heritable, approximately 40% to 50%, and that DNA methylation and DNA demethylation is subject to modification as one ages and, importantly, by lifestyle and environmental factors. It is known that DNA methylation increases (hypermethylation) from birth to about middle-age (30-50), after which there is a relatively rapid decrease (hypomethylation) (Tsang *et al.*, 2016). It is also known that, as one ages, concurrent with global DNA hypomethylation, there also occurs specific or local DNA hypermethylation, the significance of which is not entirely clear. Nevertheless, DNAm has been proposed as a key factor in determining which genes are switched on or off (or more active or less active) at any one time.

As with LTL, a number of techniques have been developed to quantify DNAm in individuals using various tissues, most commonly blood but also saliva and brain, liver and kidney tissues. In consulting scientific publications, one has to take into account these different methodologies in any comparison between studies (Chatterjee *et al.*, 2017).

Humans have approximately 23,000 genes which potentially can be translated into many more thousands of proteins given that genes can be translated to synthesize more than one protein or modifications thereof. The key point here is that genes are highly regulated and this is dependent on the tissue (e.g. brain, liver, kidney, muscle), the age of the tissue (and by implication the age of the individual), the lifestyle of the individual (e.g. smoking, exercise, diet) and a myriad of other behavioural and environmental factors.

Early studies on DNAm indicated modifications with individual lifestyles and a recent study of n = 4,173 individuals (females, mean age of 64) showed modest (around 10% or less) but statistically significant correlations of epigenetic age with lifestyle parameters of diet, exercise, moderate alcohol consumption and socio-economic status (Quach et al., 2017). Overall, a diet rich in fruit, vegetables and fish, moderate physical activity, moderate alcohol intake and a sound education correlated with a lower epigenetic age or clock than chronological age.

As a potential biomarker for ageing, DNA methylation age abbreviated as DNAm age (also termed epigenetic age) has been claimed to be a better marker than chronological age in determining healthy ageing and mortality. The two most widely used measures of DNAm age are based on the Horvath (2013) and Hannum et al. (2013) procedures, both of which are correlated with chronological age. The difference between DNAm age and chronological age is an estimate of age acceleration, a parameter that is individually variable and generally three to five years higher or lower than chronological age, at least when measured in older adults.

In a study of female centenarians (n = 21), their female offspring (n = 21) and the female offspring (n = 21) of non-long-lived parents, all of Italian descent, it was concluded that DNAm age profiles matched the improved health status (age-related diseases such as cardiovascular disease, hypertension, cancer and respiratory disease) of the centenarians and their offspring as compared to the offspring of non-long-lived parents (Gentilini et al., 2013).

In another study of centenarians also of Italian descent (n = 82, mean age of 105.6), their offspring (n = 63, mean age of 71.8) and a control group (n = 47, mean age of 69.8), it was determined that the centenarians and their offspring had a lower (approximately 5.1 years) DNAm age or epigenetic age with respect to chronological age than the control group (Horvath *et al.*, 2015). Moreover, the same group also exhibited a slower epigenetic ageing than the control cohort These observations would appear to confirm the concept that longevity is a heritable trait and that DNAm age or epigenetic age is a better marker for healthy ageing than chronological age.

In a large meta-analysis (n = 13,089, individuals aged from early sixties to late seventies) epigenetic age acceleration (difference between DNAm age and chronological age) was statistically significantly better at prediction of all-cause mortality than chronological age and health-related risk factors (e.g. smoking, exercise, BMI, chronic diseases) (Chen *et al.*, 2016). This study was particularly significant as it included a wide range of ethnic groups consisting of Caucasians, Hispanics and African-Americans. In another study (n = approximately 6,000) of individuals of different ethnic groups, it was determined that males had a higher epigenetic age acceleration than females (Horvath *et al.*, 2016). On the other hand, there were mixed results with respect to age acceleration in Hispanics and African-Americans.

In a study of four different cohorts (n = 4,678, aged from late sixties to late seventies) an epigenetic age difference of five years (higher as compared to chronological age) was estimated to be associated with a 16% increased risk of all-cause mortality (Marioni *et al.*, 2015). A recent review concluded that individuals with symptoms of age-related diseases (e.g. cardiovascular disease, musculoskeletal frailty) tend to be epigenetically older than healthy individuals (Gensous *et al.*, 2017).

One may have noted from the scientific literature that there are very few studies on DNAm and epigenetic age in relation to younger individuals; most studies have been confined to individuals from middle-age to the elderly, including centenarians. Understandably, as one considers healthy ageing and age-related diseases, both aspects of which involve elderly individuals. Moreover, as in the case of LTL, there is clearly a need for longitudinal studies, that is measurements taken over time, ideally, but essentially impractical, from birth to death. The scientific data is thus restricted to complex statistical analysis involving many thousands of middle-aged to elderly individuals.

The potential of using DNAm age or epigenetic age as a predictor of health and development was illustrated by a recent longitudinal study of adolescents from birth to 17 years (Simpkin et al., 2017). In this study (n = 1,018) epigenetic age acceleration was estimated at birth, at age 7 and at age 17, with physical development (e.g. BMI, fat and lean body mass) also measured at each time point. Although mixed results were found, this was a pioneering study on the use of epigenetic age in relation to predictions of individual health and development in a young population.

Pub Test 2.3:

Question:

Will analysis of your DNA methylation age or epigenetic age accurately state that you, say at age 25, 50 or 70, will have a healthy lifespan to your eighties and beyond?

Answer:

No

DNA methylation age or epigenetic age may provide an estimate for rate of ageing, but any meaningful interpretation will also require comparative data from many other individuals (hundreds) of similar sex, age, ethnicity and lifestyle. Furthermore, do you have your DNA methylation age at birth and at appropriate chronological points and what about the data for the control cohort as a comparison?

Biomarkers of Ageing

In the context of this book, we should be discussing biomarkers of healthy ageing rather than the conventional concept of biomarkers of ageing. It is clearly important to discriminate between healthy and unhealthy ageing.

The simplest parameter is one's chronological age (CA), that is our birthdate. However, CA is an inadequate marker of ageing: we all age differently, depending on our DNA, lifestyle and environmental factors. A family history of longevity or healthy longevity, as documented by long-lived parents, grandparents and other family members, is indicative that, barring unforeseen accidents, children will also attain a healthy lifespan.

Relatively recent research examining the relationship between human DNA and ageing has provided a wealth of data on the association of telomeres and DNAm (methylation of DNA, specifically at the CpG dinucleotides) with age and age acceleration/deceleration. In particular, the latter has provided the concept of an epigenetic clock (the difference between CA and epigenetic age based on the degree of DNAm) as a measure of age acceleration (epigenetic clock > CA, unhealthy ageing) and age deceleration (epigenetic clock < CA, healthy ageing).

As previously discussed, the epigenetic clock has been reported to be correlated with conventional clinical measures of health and age-related diseases. It should be noted, however, that there are also conflicting reports as to the merits of the epigenetic clock as compared with conventional clinical parameters.

Several clinical or physiological measures of ageing have recently been proposed, and some of these have been reported to be highly predictive of morbidity (health) and mortality (death).

These include the so-called frailty index based on thirty-four clinical health measures (termed FI34) which include parameters for heart and lung function, incidence of stroke, type 2 diabetes, BMI, hypertension, lipid profile and physical and mental function. In a study of older individuals (n = 262, mean age of 86, 62.9% female), the frailty index was reported to be superior to DNA methylation age as a predictor for biological age (Kim et al., 2017). On the other hand, in a cohort (n = 1,820, average age of 62.5) of individuals of German origin, a frailty index (based on thirty-four deficits associated with e.g. cardiovascular issues, lipid profile, diabetes and cancer, together with ratings for daily physical activities) was reported to be associated with the epigenetic clock but not telomere length (Breitling et al., 2016).

In another study (n = 4,704, ages 30-110), biomarker signatures of ageing consisting of nineteen blood biomarkers (associated with e.g. inflammation, renal function, diabetes, lipid disorders) were correlated with longitudinal changes in predictive risk of morbidity (e.g. CVD, diabetes, cancer) and mortality (Sebastiani et al., 2017).

In one of the very few publications on ageing in young individuals, the Dunedin Study Birth Cohort study on individuals of New Zealand origin (n = 954, all aged 38 and born in Dunedin), eighteen biomarkers (e.g. BMI, blood pressure, lipid profile, lung function) were measured to assess individual risk factors and establish a biological age profile in relation to the rate of ageing (Belsky et al., 2015, 2017). The key points of this study were that all individuals were the same chronological age (38 years old, all born in 1972-73) and biomarkers were measured at three time points, at ages 26, 32 and 38. Importantly, the researchers were able to demonstrate that individuals varied in their biological age estimates, some ageing more and others less rapidly than their CA. The implications of this study were that even at an early age, mid-to-late thirties, and before obvious symptoms of age-related diseases, it was possible to predict individual healthy and unhealthy rates of ageing.

All of these studies emphasize the use of multiple biomarkers of ageing, essentially conventional or established clinical parameters of health, as opposed to a single biomarker such as LTL or DNAm age (epigenetic age). It is very likely that the latter two molecular biomarkers of ageing provide quite different ageing parameters both from each other as well as from that provided by conventional clinical markers. What is absolutely clear is that CA offers limited information regarding healthy or unhealthy ageing.

Pub Test 2.4:

Question:

Do established clinical markers of health provide a good indication of your healthy ageing?

Answer:

Yes

Clinical markers may well indicate potential issues such as in high blood pressure, high BMI, high cholesterol, heart, liver and kidney problems, anaemia and type 2 diabetes. Next time, also check out your score on physical activity.

Most importantly, as you enter midlife (say, 50-60 years) and beyond it is highly recommended that a regular appointment (annually if > 50, or less often if < 50 and in good health) be arranged with your doctor for assessment of clinical markers of health, markers of which would be dependent on the individual and appropriate medical assessment. These should include as a minimum, a full blood count, liver function test, lipid profile, and cardiovascular health and lung function, in addition to BMI and blood pressure. Of course, selection of appropriate clinical tests is very much dependent on the individual and their health profiles. It would be most unlikely that your doctor would recommend determination of your DNAm age (epigenetic age) or your LTL as measures of your health/unhealthy ageing profile.

Adams, ER, Nolan, VG, Andersen SL, *et al*. 2008. Centenarian offspring: start healthier and stay healthier. *Journal of the American Geriatrics Society* 56: 2089-2092. doi:10.1111/j.1532-5415.2008.01949.x.

Aoki, Y, Aoki, M, Yamada, K. 2017. Leucocyte telomere length and serum levels of high-molecular-weight adiponectin and dehydroepiandrosterone-sulfate could reflect distinct aspects of longevity in Japanese centenarians. *Gerontology & Geriatric Medicine* 3:1-6. doi: 10.1177/2333721417696672.

Appleby, S, Pearson, JE, Aitchison, A, *et al*. 2017. Mean telomere length is not associated with current health status in a 50-year population sample. *American Journal of Human Biology* 29:e22907. doi:1002/ajhb.22906.

Arai, Y, Martin-Ruiz, CM, Tkayama, M, *et al*. 2015. Inflammation, but not telomere length, predicts successful ageing at extreme old age: a longitudinal study of semi-supercentenarians. *EBiomedicine* 2:1549-1558. doi:10.1016/j.ebiom.2015.07.029.

Arsenis, NC, You, T, Ogawa, EF, *et al.* 2017. Physical activity and telomere length: impact of aging and potential mechanisms of action. *Oncotarget* 8:45008-45019. doi:10.18632/oncotarget.16726.

Atzmon, G, Cho, M, Cawthon, RM, *et al.* 2010. Genetic variation in human telomerase is associated with telomere length in Ashkenazi centenarians. *Proceedings of the National Academy of Sciences* 107:1710-1717. doi:10.1073/pnas.0906191106.

Belsky, DW, Caspi, A, Houts, R, *et al.* 2015. Quantification of biological aging in young adults. *Proceedings of the National Academy of Sciences* 112:E4104-4110. doi:10.1073/pnas.1506264112.

Belsky, DW, Moffitt, TE, Cohen, AA, *et al.* 2017. Eleven telomere, epigenetic clock, and biomarker-composite quantifications of biological aging: do they measure the same thing? *American Journal of Epidemiology* 187:1220-1230. doi:10.1093/aje/kwx346.

Blackburn, EH, Epel, ES. 2017. The Telomere Effect. Orion Spring: Orion Publishing Group, London.

Brietling, LP, Saum, K-U, Perna, L, *et al.* 2016. Frailty is associated with the epigenetic clock but not with telomere length in a German cohort. *Clinical Epigenetics* 8:21-29. doi:10.1186/s13148-016-0186-5.

Brooks-Wilson, AR. 2013. Genetics of aging and longevity. *Human Genetics* 132:1323-1338. doi:10.1007/s00439-013-1342-z.

Broer, L, Buchman, AS, Deelen, J, et al. 2015. GWAS of longevity in CHARGE consortium confirms *APOE* and *FOXO3* candidacy. *The Journals of Gerontology: Series A* 70:110-118. doi:10.1093/gerona/glu166.

Buettner, D. 2012. The Blue Zones. National Geographic Society: Washington, D.C.USA.

Bucci, L, Ostan, R, Cevenini, E, et al. 2016. Centenarians' offspring as a model of healthy aging: a reappraisal of the data on Italian subjects and a comprehensive overview. *Aging* 8:510-519. doi:10.18632/aging.100912.

Chae, DH, Epel, ES, Nuru-Jeter, AM, et al. 2016. Discrimination, mental health, and leucocyte telomere length among African American men. *Psychoneuroendocrinology* 63:10-16. doi:10.1016/j.psyneuen.2015.09.001.

Chatteriee, CA, Rodger, EJ, Morison, IM, et al. 2017. Tools and strategies for analysis of genome-wide and gene-specific DNA methylation patterns. *Methods in Molecular Biology* 1537:249-277. doi:10.1007/978-1-4939-6685-1-15.

Chen, BH, Marioni, RE, Colicino, E. et al. 2016. DNA methylation-based measures of biological age: meta-analysis predicting time to death. *Aging* 8:1844-1858. doi:10.18632/aging.101020.

Darrow, SM, Verhoeven, JE, Revesz, D, et al. 2016. The association between psychiatric disorders and telomere length: a meta-analysis involving 14,827 persons. *Psychosomatic Medicine* 78:776-787. doi:10.1097/PSY.0000000000000356.

Engberg, H, Oksuzyan, A, Jeune, B, et al. 2009. Centenarians - a useful model for healthy aging? A 29-year follow-up of hospitalizations among 40,000 Danes born in 1905. *Aging Cell* 8:270-278. doi:10.1111/j.1474-9726.2009.00474.x.

Erikson, GA, Bodian, DL, Rueda, M, *et al.* 2016. Whole-genome sequencing of a healthy aging cohort. *Cell* 165:1002-10011. doi:10.1016/j.cell.2016.03.022.

Gardner, M, Bann, D, Wiley, L, *et al.* 2014. Gender and telomere length: systematic review and meta-analysis. *Experimental Gerontology* 51:15-27. doi:10.1015/j.exger.2013.12.004.

Gensous, N, Bacalini, MG, Pirazzini, C, *et al.* 2017. The epigenetic landscape of age-related diseases: the geroscience perspective. *Biogerontology* 18:549-559. doi:10.1007/s10522-017-9695-7.

Gentilini, D, Mari, D, Castaldi, D, *et al.* 2013. Role of epigenetics in human aging and longevity: genome-wide DNA methylation profile in centenarians and centenarians' offspring. *Age* 35:1961-1973. doi:10.1007/s11357-012-9463-1.

Glel, DA, Goldman, N, Risques, RA, *et al.* 2016. Predicting survival from telomere length versus conventional predictors: a multinational population-based cohort study. *PLoS ONE* 11:e0152486. doi:10.1371/journal.pone.0152486.

Gierman, HJ, Fortney, K, Roach, JC, *et al.* 2014. Whole-genome sequencing of the world's oldest people. *PLoS ONE* 9:e112430. doi:10.1371/journal.pone.0112430.

Hamad, R, Tuljapurkar, S. Rehkopf. DH. 2016. Racial and socio-economic variation in genetic markers of telomere length: a cross-sectional study of U.S. older adults. *EBiomedicine* 11:296-301. doi:10.1016/j.ebiom.2016.08.015.

Hannum, G, Guinney, J, Zhao, L, et al. 2013. Genome-wide methylation profiles reveal quantitative views of human aging rates. *Molecular Cell* 49: 359-361. doi:10.1016/j.molcel.2012.10.016.

Harris, SE, Marioni, R, Martin-Ruiz, C, et al. 2016. Longitudinal telomere length shortening and cognitive and physical decline in later life: the Lothian Birth Cohorts 1936 and 1921. *Mechanisms of Ageing and Development* 154:43-48. doi:10.1016/j.mad.2016.02.004.

Haycock, PC, Heydon, EE, Kaptoge, S, et al. 2014. Leucocyte telomere length and risk of cardiovascular disease: systematic review and meta-analysis. *British Medical Journal* 349:g4227. doi:10.1136/bmj.g4227.

Haycock, PC, Burgess, S, Nounu, A, et al. 2017. Association between telomere length and risk of cancer and non-neoplastic diseases. A Mendelian randomization study. *JAMA Oncology* 3:636-651. doi:10.1001/jamaoncol.2016.5945.

Hjelmborg, JvB, Iachine, I, Skytthe, A, et al. 2006. Genetic influence on human lifespan and longevity. *Human Genetics* 119:312-321. doi:10.1007/s00439-006-0144-y.

Honig, LS, Kang, MS, Cheng, R, et al. 2015. Heritability of telomere length in a study of long-lived families. *Neurobiology of Aging* 36:2785-2790. doi:10.1016/j.neurobiolaging.2015.06.017.

Horvath, S. 2013. DNA methylation age of human tissues and cell types. *Genome Biology* 14: R115. doi:10.1186/gb-2013-14-10-r115.

Horvath, S, Pirazzini, C, Bacalini, MG, et al. 2015. Decreased epigenetic age of PBMCs from Italian semi-supercentenarians and their offspring. *Aging* 7:1159-1170. doi:10.18632/aging.100861.

Horvath, S, Gurven, M, Levine, ME, *et al*. 2016. An epigenetic clock analysis of race/ethnicity, sex, and coronary heart disease. *Genome Biology* 17:171-193. doi:10.1186/s13059-016-1030-0.

Hunt, SC, Chen, W, Gardner, JP, *et al*. 2008. Leucocyte telomeres are longer in African Americans than in whites: the National Heart, Lung, and Blood Institute Family Heart Study and the Bogalusa Heart Study. *Aging Cell* 7:451-458. doi:10.1111/j.1474-9726.2008.00397.x.

International Human Genome Sequencing Consortium. 2004. Finishing the euchromatic sequence of the human genome. *Nature* 431: 931-945. doi:10.1038/nature.03001.

Joshi, PJ, Fischer, K, Schraut, KE, *et al*. 2016. Variants near *CHRNA3/5* and *APOE* have age- and sex-related effects on human lifespan. *Nature Communications* 7:11174. doi:10.1038/ncomms11174.

Kim, S, Myers, L, Wyckoff, J, *et al*. 2017. The frailty index outperforms DNA methylation age and its derivatives as an indicator of biological age. *GeroScience* 39:83-92. doi:10.1007/s11357-017-9960-3.

Lai, T-P, Wright, WE, Shay, JW. 2018. Comparison of telomere length measurement methods. *Philosophical Transactions of the Royal Society B* 373:20160451. doi:10.1098/rstb.2016.0451.

Lander, ES, Linton, LM, Birren, B, *et al*. 2001. Initial sequencing and analysis of the human genome. *Nature* 409: 860-921. doi:10.1038/35057062.

Lapham, K, Kvale, MN, Lin, J, *et al*. 2015. Automated assay of telomere length measurement and informatics for 100,000 subjects in the genetic Epidemiology Research on Adult Health and Aging (GERA) Cohort. *Genetics* 200:1061-1072. doi:10.1534/genetics.115.178624.

Lynch, SM, Peek, MK, Mitra, N, *et al.* 2016. Race, ethnicity, psychosocial factors, and telomere length in a multicentre setting. *PLoS ONE* 11:e0146723. doi:10.1371/journal.pone.0146723.

Marioni, RE, Shah, S, McRae, AF, *et al.* 2015. DNA methylation age of blood predicts all-cause mortality in later life. *Genome Biology* 16:25-37. doi:10.1186/s13059-015-0584-6.

Machiela, MJ, Lan, Q, Slager, SL, *et al.* 2016. Genetically predicted longer telomere length is associated with increased risk of B-cell lymphoma subtypes. *Human Molecular Genetics* 25:1663-1676. doi:10.1093/hmg/ddw027.

Milte, CM, Russell, AO, Ball, K, *et al.* 2018. Diet quality and telomere length in older Australian men and women. *European Journal of Nutrition* 57:363-372. doi:10.1007/s00394-016-1326-6.

Morris, BJ, Willcox, DC, Donlon, TA, *et al.* 2015. *FOXO3*: A major gene for human longevity - a mini-review. *Gerontology* 61:515-525. doi:10.1159/000375235.

Needham, BL, Adler, N, Gregorich, S, *et al.* 2013. Socioeconomic status, health behaviour, and leucocyte telomere length in the National Health and Nutrition Examination Survey, 1999-2002. *Social Science and Medicine* 85: 1-8. doi:10.106/j.socscimed.2013.02.023.

Nygaard, M, Thinggaard, M, Christensen, K, *et al.* 2017. Investigation of the 5q33.3 longevity locus and age-related phenotypes. *Aging* 7:247-253. doi:10.18632/aging.101156.

O'Brien, E, Kerber, R, Smith, K, et al. 2007. Familial mortality in the Utah population database: characterizing a human aging phenotype. *The Journals of Gerontology* 62A;803-812. doi:10.1093/gerona/62.8.803.

Pilling, LC, Atkins, JL, Bowman, K, et al. 2016. Human longevity is influenced by many genetic variants: evidence from 75,000 UK Biobank participants. *Aging* 8:547-560. doi:10.18632/aging.100930.

Quach, A, Levine, ME, Tanaka, T, et al. 2017. Epigenetic clock analysis of diet, exercise, education, and lifestyle factors. *Aging* 9:429-446. doi:10.18632/aging.101168.

Rafie, N, Hamedani, G, Barak, F, et al. 2017. Dietary patterns, food groups and telomere length: a systematic review of current studies. *European Journal of Clinical Nutrition* 71:151-158. doi:10.1038/ejcn.2016.149.

Rehkopf, DH, Needham, RL, Lin, J, et al. 2016. Leucocyte telomere length in relation to 17 biomarkers of cardiovascular disease risk: a cross-sectional study of US adults. *PLoS Medicine* 13:e1002188. doi:10.1371/journal.pmed.1002188.

Rewak, M, Buka, S, Prescott, J, et al. 2014. Race-related health disparities and biological aging: does rate of telomere shortening differ across blacks and whites? *Biological Psychology* 99: 92-99. doi:10.1016/j.biopsycho.2014.03.007.

Robertson, T, Batty, GD, Der, G, et al. 2013. Is socioeconomic status associated with biological age as measured by telomere length? *Epidemiologic Reviews* 35:98-111. doi:10.1093/epirev/mxs001.

Robine, J-M, Cubaynes, S. 2017. Worldwide demography of centenarians. *Mechanisms of Ageing and Development* 165:59-67. doi:10.1016/j.mad.2017.03.004.

Rode, L, Nordestgaard, BG, Bojesen, SE. 2016. Long telomeres and cancer risk among 95,568 individuals from the general population. *International Journal of Epidemiology* 45:1634-1643. doi:10.1093/ije/dyw179.

Ruby, JG, Wright, KM, Rand, KA, *et al*. 2018. Estimates of the heritability of human longevity are substantially inflated due to assortative mating. *Genetics* 210:1109-1124. doi:10.1534/genetics.118.301613.

Scally, A, Dutheil, JY, Hillier, LW, *et al*. 2012. Insights into hominid evolution from the gorilla genome sequence. *Nature* 483:169-175. doi:10.1038/nature 10842.

Sebastiani, P, Bael, H, Sun, FX, *et al*. 2013. Meta-analysis of genetic variants associated with human exceptional longevity. *Aging* 5: 653-661. doi:10.18632/aging.100594.

Sebastiani, P, Thyagarajan, B, Sun, FX, *et al*. 2017. Biomarkers of aging. *Aging Cell* 18: 329-338. doi:10.1111/acel.12557.

Simpkin, AJ, Howe, LD, Tilling, K, *et al*. 2017. The epigenetic clock and physical development during childhood and adolescence: longitudinal analysis from a UK birth cohort. *International Journal of Epidemiology* 46:549-558. doi:10.1093/ije/dyw307.

Sorensen, M, Nygaard, M, Debrabant, B, *et al*. 2016. No association between variation in longevity candidate genes and aging-related phenotypes in oldest-old Danes. *Experimental Gerontology* 78:57-61. doi:10.1016/j.exger.2016.03.001.

Smith, L, Luchini, C, Demurtas, J, et al. 2019. Telomere length and health outcomes: an umbrella review of systematic reviews and meta-analyses of observational studies. *Ageing Research Reviews* 51:1-10. doi:10.1016/j.arr.2019.02.003.

Steenstrup, T, Kark, JD, Verhulst, S, et al. 2017. Telomeres and the natural lifespan limit in humans. *Aging* 9:1130-1142. doi:10.18632/aging.101216.

Tedone, E, Arosio, B, Gussago, C, et al. 2014. Leucocyte telomere length and prevalence of age-related diseases in semisupercentenarians, centenarians and centenarians' offspring. *Experimental Gerontology* 58:90-95. doi:10.1016/j.exger.2014.06.018.

Tedone, E, Huang, E, O'Hara, R, et al. 2018. Telomere length and telomerase activity in T cells are biomarkers of high-performing centenarians. *Aging Cell* 18:e12859. doi:10.1111/acel.12859.

Terry, DF, Nolan, VG, Andersen, SL, et al. 2008. Association of longer telomeres with better health in centenarians. *The Journals of Gerontology: Series A* 63:809-812. doi:10.1093/gerona/63.8.809.

Tsang, S-Y, Ahmad, T, Mat, FWK, et al. 2016. Variation of global DNA methylation levels with age and in autistic children. *Human Genomics* 10:31-37. doi:10.1186/s40246-016-0086-y.

Venter, JC, Adams, MD, Myers, EW, et al. 2001. The sequence of the human genome. *Science* 291: 1304-1351. doi:10.1126/science.1058040.

Whisman, MA, Richardson, ED. 2017. Depressive symptoms and salivary telomere length in a probability sample of middle-aged and older adults. *Psychosomatic Medicine* 79:234-242. doi:10.1097/PSY.0000000000000383.

Wilcox, BJ, Wilcox, DC, He, Q, *et al.* 2006. Siblings of Okinawan centenarians share lifelong mortality advantages. *The Journals of Gerontology: Series A* 61:345-354. doi:10.1093/gerona/61.4.345.

Wilcox, BJ, Tranah, GJ, Chen, R, *et al.* 2016. The FoxO3 gene and cause-specific mortality. *Aging Cell* 15:617-624. doi:10.1111/acel.12452.

Yaffe, K, Lindquist, K, Kluse, M, *et al.* 2011. Telomere length and cognitive function in community-dwelling elders: findings from the Health ABC Study. *Neurobiology of Aging* 32:2055-2060. doi:10.1016/j.neurobiolaging.2009.12.006.

Zerky, D, Herrmann, FR, Irminger-Finger, I, *et al.* 2010. Telomere length is not predictive of dementia or MCI conversion in the oldest old. *Neurobiology of Aging* 31:719-720. doi:10.1016/neurobiolaging.2008.05.016.

Zhan, Y, Karlsson, IK, Karlsson, R, *et al.* 2017. Exploring the causal pathway from telomere length to coronary heart disease. *Circulation Research* 121:214-219. doi:10.1161/CIRCRESAHA.116.310517.

Chapter 3
Nutrition: 101

What Are the Facts on Fats and Sugars?

This Chapter will most definitely test your biases as it provides information on a subject, namely nutrition, that has been imprinted into our lifestyles over the last fifty years.

One of the three basic essentials for human life is food (the other two are water and oxygen; surprisingly, the mobile or cell phone is not a basic essential for life). A healthy diet should add real value to your life and should stand the test of time. So, what constitutes a healthy diet and thus a long and healthy lifespan? A simple question with no simple answer it seems.

In this Chapter, we explore the biases and the scientific myths that have surrounded the issue of what constitutes a healthy diet. It is necessary before reading further that you critically address your biases regarding food; in particular ask yourself where did you get the information on the foods that are good or bad for your health? (family, friends, internet-online, advert, book, magazine).

Try this question:

Where is the scientific information that dietary fats make you fat?

Try another question:

What is the best healthy diet? For example, type in the words 'best healthy diets 2020' in an internet search engine.

Now, make an informed decision as to a healthy diet for a healthy lifespan. The fact that there are so many different diets, all claiming to be the 'best healthy diet' should immediately say to you that there is little consensus about what a healthy diet is. At this point you may turn to the scientific community for guidance, but you may be sadly disappointed. Why?

It's not because of lack of trying by the scientific community. There are many scientific journals exclusively devoted to nutrition and thousands of publications every year on the topic of nutrition and its effect on health, morbidity (disease) and mortality (death).

The most significant and influential publication on nutrition is 'The Dietary Guidelines for Americans' first published in 1980 and updated every five years, with the latest being the 2015-2020 version (https://health.gov/dietaryguidelines/2015/guidelines). The guidelines, jointly produced by the US Department of Agriculture and the Department of Health and Human Services, are based on the very latest research on human nutrition and the best scientific evidence.

The general public in the USA and elsewhere have been following these Guidelines for many years (Cohen *et al.*, 2015) and so, how is it that obesity in the adult population in the USA and Europe in 2016 has essentially doubled since 1990, with a steady increase of about 5% every five years? And what about type 2 diabetes?

Concurrent with dietary guidelines for the general population, governments in the developed world (e.g. Australia, Western Europe, North America) have required the food industry to provide detailed nutritional information on all packaged food items in supermarkets to include not only the ingredients (and sometimes, if you carefully read the label, even the country of origin) but also the calorie content, recommended dietary intake (RDI, sometimes also designated as recommended dietary allowance RDA) and the percentages of protein, fat and carbohydrate. Frequently, these food labels include a standard serving size plus all these quantities expressed as per 100 gm. The food industry considers itself very responsible in providing these details, but the general public is thoroughly confused and has no idea what all these calories, percentages, RDIs and servings/100 gm mean. Perhaps that is the required outcome?

The most contentious current topics on nutrition are:

- the calorie content of foods and drinks
- the concept of good and bad fats
- the sugar content of foods and drinks
- the ubiquitous highly processed foods in supermarkets

The often-quoted equation of calories in = calories out, meaning that food calories intake should not greatly exceed the calories expended by the individual (otherwise, weight gain), is far too simplistic and at best misleading. The sugar content of foods is obscured by the term 'added sugar' which is singled out as the problem when the general public has little concept about what that exactly means; in fact, the major problems are soft drinks or soda (sugar-sweetened beverages [SSBs] as termed by the scientific community) and highly processed foods.

The issue of fats has been the cornerstone of expert scientific advice on nutrition for the last fifty years; that fats make you fat when, in fact, there has been and is little scientific evidence for that statement. Publications over the last decade in the most highly ranked scientific journals have been critical of that statement. Recent reviews of the scientific literature have shown that a diet consisting of fats, including saturated fats, may be more beneficial with respect to clinical parameters of health than a low-fat diet. The only consensus on nutritional advice appears to be that fruit and vegetables are healthy and highly processed foods are unhealthy, a fact that your grandmother could have told you.

Now that we have raised these issues and confronted some of the accepted dogma on what constitutes a healthy diet, one is required to provide the information that challenges the last fifty years of nutritional advice.

A Calorie Is Not Equal to a Food Calorie

We are all familiar with the concept of calories with respect to our nutritional needs. We are constantly reminded to 'watch your calories' if we are dieting or not, exercising or sedentary and checking the calories on every food item we consume etc. The recommended calorie intake per day (e.g. in the UK, USA and Australia) is around 2,500 calories (10,500 kJ) for men and 2,000 calories (8,400 kJ) for women. This figure is very much dependent on age, lifestyle and body mass index (BMI = weight kg/height m^2).

Nutritional scientists use the term kilocalorie (Calorie, with a capital C = 1,000 calories) for the energy value of foods. A calorie is a unit of heat energy defined as the amount of heat required to raise the temperature of one gram of water one degree Celsius °C at one atmosphere pressure. The term Calorie refers to the heat required to raise the temperature of one kilogram of water one degree Celsius °C. This is the common term used in the food industry and the term 'calories' is actually kilocalories where the kilo part is omitted.

To further complicate the matter, the scientific community redefines the energy value of foods in terms of the International System of Units (metric units), and thus we have the kilo Joule (kJ) in which 4.184 kJ = 1 Cal (Calorie = 1,000 calories). However, throughout the book and for consistency with current food labelling, the small letter c for calories refers to the capitalized Calorie.

Food labels refer to the energy value of foods as kJ or calories. The conventional food energy content is as follows:

> 1 gram of protein = 17 kJ or 4 calories
> 1 gram of fat = 37 kJ or 8.8 calories
> 1 gram of carbohydrate = 17 kJ or 4 calories

The key issue here is to recognize that the calories assigned to one gram (gm) of protein, fat or carbohydrate refers to the *values as measured in the laboratory*. However, we rarely consume food in the form of pure protein, pure fat or pure carbohydrate.

Consider the following scenarios: swallow one level teaspoon of egg white (say 4 gm, approximately 80% pure protein) or one level teaspoon of olive oil (say 4 gm, approximately 98% fat) or one level teaspoon of white sugar (say 4 gm, 99.9% carbohydrate as sucrose). Assuming the approximations that the egg white, olive oil and sugar represent pure protein, pure fat and pure carbohydrate respectively then the calorie values will be 16, 35.2 and 16 respectively. However, your digestive system from the mouth down through to your gut expends energy in the digestive process, the value of which is essentially impossible to calculate, and what about the role of your gut microbes? (see Chapter 7: The Gut Microbiota).

In terms of health, the egg white also contains some fat, carbohydrate and trace amounts of B vitamins. Olive oil also contains small amounts of polyphenols, chlorophylls, carotenoids and trace amounts of the fat-soluble vitamins E and K. Sugar is essentially pure sucrose. Remember that the consensus is that the olive oil is healthy (a monounsaturated good fat, as part of a Mediterranean diet) with a whopping 35.2 calories at twice the calories when compared with 16 for the egg white (protein) and 16 for the sugar (carbohydrate). The consensus is that the latter (sugar) would be the unhealthiest although at one half the calories of the fat.

For a reality check, now consider the calories of a relatively simple breakfast of bacon (two rashes cooked with a teaspoon of olive oil), eggs (two eggs, scrambled, cooked with a teaspoon of olive oil), one slice of sourdough bread (toasted, spread on a teaspoon of butter) and washed down with one generous cup of freshly brewed coffee (one teaspoon sugar plus some full-cream milk). One can calculate a calorie count for this simple breakfast by consulting any reference booklet with listed calories for these food items. For information, this simple breakfast would theoretically amount to approximately 680 calories or 2,856 kJ. This calorie count is, at best, a very rough estimate as there is no way to accurately account for the following:

- The method of cooking the food which will significantly modify the chemical structure and composition of the food.
- The fact that one will have to chew (masticate) the food to further assist the digestive process.
- The passage of the food through the digestive system (small intestine, large intestine) during which time energy (calories) is required and numerous enzymes will act on the chemical bonds in the food matrix to break down the proteins, fats and carbohydrates.
- Selective constituents (e.g. amino acids from the proteins, fatty acids from the triglycerides, simple sugars from the carbohydrates) from the digestive process will be transported to appropriate parts of the body (e.g. liver) where specific enzymes will further metabolize them (e.g. for energy production) and indeed also synthesize these products of digestion into new products (e.g. proteins, fats and carbohydrates).
- The role of the gut microbes in the utilization of the digested food products.

The calories the body obtains from protein, fat and carbohydrate are clearly dependent on the method of food preparation, the Interactions of the different foods and the food matrix from which they originate. The more complex the food matrix, the more energy is required to extract the nutrients from the food and subsequently utilize the nutrients and/or synthesize new protein, carbohydrate and fat as required.

A simple example further illustrates this important concept. Consider 120 calories from consuming 30 gm of sugar (pure sucrose, approximately 6 generous teaspoons, 4 calories per gm of carbohydrate) or 120 calories from consuming one large banana (contains 25% carbohydrate [e.g. fructose], minerals [e.g. potassium, phosphorus], vitamins [e.g. vitamins B, C and folate]) or 120 calories from consuming 20 gm of peanuts (contains 73% fat, 15% protein, 12% carbohydrate, fibre, vitamins E and B and numerous minerals [potassium, manganese, magnesium, phosphorus, calcium, zinc, iron]).

In the case of the sugar, your digestive system will break it down as sucrose into glucose and fructose (sucrose = glucose + fructose) using the enzyme sucrase, after which the glucose will rapidly enter your bloodstream (leading to a spike in your insulin levels) to be transported to appropriate parts of your body and utilized as a source of energy or converted to more complex carbohydrates. The fructose, on the other hand, is not that readily metabolized and ends up largely in the liver, where at high concentrations it is converted to triglycerides which can lead to abdominal fat.

On the other hand, for the equivalent number of calories (120) in the banana, the presence of fibre, protein, carbohydrate, minerals and vitamins help mitigate the negative effects of the fructose (the primary sugar in fruit) as compared with pure sugar. Similarly, the 120 calories from the peanuts are metabolized quite differently from the 120 calories from the pure sugar.

At this point, you might also consider the effects of consuming the 120 calories from sugar, fruit or peanuts on healthy ageing. The bottom line is that calories from different foods are clearly different and one has to take into consideration the food matrix, the food composition and the digestive/metabolic process.

Pub Test 3.1

Question:

Is a calorie the same as a food calorie?

Answer:

No

A calorie is most definitely not a food calorie.

The calorie unit is the energy released from pure fat, pure carbohydrate or pure protein as measured under strictly defined laboratory conditions. However, food is rarely consumed as pure protein, fat or carbohydrate. The nature of the food matrix (e.g. the chemical structure of the food including the digestible and non-digestible components such as the fibre content), the chemical composition of the food (e.g. vitamins, minerals) and the digestion process (including method of food preparation) are all key issues with respect to estimation of calorie intake. The concept that 'a calorie in = a calorie out' is totally misleading.

Are Fats Bad for Healthy Ageing ?

As previously mentioned, the most influential guide on dietary matters in the Western world is the Dietary Guidelines for Americans and, for the last forty years or so, the guidelines have perpetuated the central dogma that fats are bad for health. These guidelines have been progressively updated to state that fats, especially saturated fats, are unhealthy leading the food industry to understandably develop a massive range of foods labelled 'no fat', 'low-fat', 'lite' etc. This has created a whole new range of food products.

One outcome of the low-fat dietary intake advice was the replacement of calories from fats by calories from carbohydrates, especially highly processed or refined carbohydrates, as in many of the low-fat food items. However, numerous studies have shown that a low-fat / high-carbohydrate diet, at best, has no better health outcomes (e.g. clinical parameters of cardiovascular disease, relative risk for mortality) than a 'normal' fat and carbohydrate diet and indeed, in most cases, has significantly worse outcomes.

It was then proposed that the issue was that the carbohydrate component of the diet consisted largely of refined carbohydrates (e.g. white bread, pasta, pizza, white rice) and that replacement with wholegrain or unrefined carbohydrate (e.g. wholegrain bread) would be a healthier option. In other words, adopt a healthier diet and avoid highly processed foods. The most recent research has indeed demonstrated that a diet containing minimally processed foods (e.g. fruit, vegetables, whole grains) and low in highly processed foods (e.g. most packaged foods) is a healthy option.

At about the same time as the low fat/high carbohydrate diet was recommended and adopted by the general public, it was considered that foods containing monounsaturated (e.g. oleic acid, designated C18:1) and polyunsaturated fats (e.g. linoleic acid, designated C18:2; fish oils, designated as C20:5, C22:6) have positive health outcomes.

The scientific establishment thus introduced the concept of good fats (unsaturated fatty acids) and bad fats (saturated fatty acids). However, this clearly confused the general public as it was seen as a mixed message for a healthy diet. The most recent refinement of the concept of bad fats is to target a specific saturated fatty acid, namely palmitic acid (designated as C16:0), as a major culprit (Zong *et al.*, 2016). This fatty acid is the main saturated fatty acid in dairy foods and is also found in variable amounts in almost all foods high in fats, such as nuts, seeds and vegetable oils. The concept of a single very specific nutrient affecting health status has been very successful in historical studies related to nutrient deficiencies as seen in early research on specific single vitamin and trace element requirements for human health.

However, we rarely, if ever, consume fats and certainly not palmitic acid as a single nutrient. Fats are essentially always consumed in highly complex food matrices as in e.g. fish, meat and dairy. It is extremely doubtful that a single nutrient such as saturated palmitic acid (C16:0) in a highly complex dairy food matrix (e.g. milk, yoghurt, cheese) containing a wide range of fatty acids, numerous minerals, fat-soluble vitamins (e.g. A, D, E, K) and water-soluble vitamins (e.g. B, C), would have a major specific detrimental health issue.

In summary, the dietary advice has gone from 'fats are bad', to recommending a 'low-fat/high-carbohydrate diet', to 'good fats and bad fats', to recommending a 'low-fat/less-refined-carbohydrate diet' (avoid highly processed carbohydrates) and finally to suggesting to 'avoid palmitic acid' (C16:0, saturated fatty acid). So, what about a diet with simply 'normal' high-fat foods (e.g. dairy, nuts, seeds) combined with minimally processed carbohydrates (e.g. whole grains), plus of course vitamins, minerals, fibre and protein?

However, the message that the public is still receiving is that fats, particularly saturated fats, are to be avoided when in fact there is simply little evidence that fats are a health hazard. Indeed, the evidence appears to be to the contrary. A recent review (BioMed Central, open-access publication) in the *Nutrition Journal* provides a balanced account of the current (at least at the date of publication, 2017) approach to dietary fats (Liu *et al.*, 2017).

What Are *Trans*- and *Cis*-Fats?

Unsaturated fatty acids generally occur in nature in the *cis*-configuration as opposed to the *trans*-configuration (the interested Reader can check out these different configurations on the internet). Some vegetable oils contain *trans*-fats as a by-product resulting from chemical modification (a process termed partial hydrogenation) of a portion of the unsaturated fats in the vegetable oils. The *trans*-fats when incorporated into processed foods (e.g. pies, pastries, cakes, muffins, shortening) confer stability on the product and hence extend the shelf-life.

There is scientific consensus that the consumption of foods high in *trans*-fats should be minimized as this type of fat has a negative impact on health, an observation that has been known for several decades (e.g. Willett *et al.*, 1993). Recognition of this consensus can be gauged by the gradual phasing out of *trans*-fats in foods in many developed countries, with Denmark (2003) setting the example.

Confirmation of the negative health outcomes associated with intake of *trans*-fats continues to receive scientific consensus with a recent systematic review and meta-analysis of observational studies concluding increased relative risk of all-cause mortality (34% increase) and cardiovascular disease (28% increase) between cohorts with high and low intakes of industrially produced (chemical hydrogenation of vegetable fats) *trans*-fats (de Souza *et al.*, 2015). On the other hand, in the same study, saturated fat intake (comparing cohorts with highest to lowest intake) was not associated with all-cause mortality and coronary heart disease.

It should be noted that *trans*-fats occur in dairy products (1% to 6% of the total fat) and meat, as a natural product of bacterial fermentation in ruminants (e.g. cattle, sheep). However, these naturally occurring *trans*-fats, as compared with the *trans*-fats from chemical modification of vegetable oils, have been reported to have no adverse effects on risk factors associated with cardiovascular disease, at least at the levels of normal consumption (Gayet-Boyd *et al.*, 2014; de Souza *et al.*, 2015, and references therein).

Pub Test 3.2:

Question:

Are *trans*-fats from chemical modification of vegetable oils bad for health?

Answer:

Yes

There is good scientific evidence that *trans*-fats increase the 'bad' cholesterol (LDL-cholesterol) and decrease the 'good' cholesterol (HDL-cholesterol). One should always read the label on packaged foods to check the content of *trans*-fats. The advice is to minimize intake as it is difficult to totally eliminate *trans*-fats from the modern diet given that many foods, particularly baked and fried foods, still contain significant amounts.

Let us now examine the most recent scientific evidence about the dietary advice that fats, particularly saturated fats, are bad for health.

Randomized Controlled Trials

It would be appropriate to take a step back and review how data on nutrition and health are collected. In the case of randomized controlled trials (RCTs) or clinical trials, participants are randomly assigned to two groups: a control cohort in which participants are assigned a regular or normal diet with say 10% to 15% food energy (calories) from saturated fats and an experimental cohort on a diet in which, say, 1% to 5% of the food energy from saturated fats is replaced by unsaturated fats, in the form of vegetable oils (e.g. soybean, corn, olive oil) or more realistically real food high in unsaturated fats (e.g. nuts, seeds, fish).

In general, the trials will run for at least four weeks or, in the well-funded trials, several years. In the latter case, compliance by the participants becomes a major issue. Size really does matter in that hundreds and ideally thousands of participants are required in order to obtain results that are statistically valid.

The control and experimental groups should consist of approximately the same numbers and be matched for e.g. age, gender, ethnic and cultural background, socio-economic status, smoking, alcohol consumption and physical activity. Outcomes may be measured by e.g. analysis of blood samples (e.g. HDL-, LDL-, VLDL-cholesterol) taken at baseline, at several time points in long-term studies and at the end of the experimental period. Parameters to be measured will dependent on e.g. the design of the trial, age and health status of the participants, and being short- or long-term. Hard end-points such as mortality and cardiovascular health (morbidity and mortality) require very long-term (years) studies and are prohibitively costly.

The main issues with RCTs are the relatively small number of participants, the short-term nature of the studies and compliance with the diet under test.

Observational Studies

Long-term nutritional studies that include large numbers (thousands) of participants are conducted as observational studies in which participants are required to fill-in frequent food questionnaires (FFQs). These are generally self-assessed FFQs and thus subject to error. These include:

- Remembering exactly what you have eaten today, last week, last month and what about last year?
- Individuals frequently underestimate food intake as well as underestimate alcohol consumption
- Food and drink consumption vary substantially depending on the day of the week, the weekend, when on vacation and where and with whom one consumes the food and drink
- A significant percentage of individuals may be on a specific diet
- Lifestyle, especially exercise, has a profound effect on food metabolism
- Estimation of calorie intake should take into consideration the cooking methodology, the food matrix (e.g. unprocessed, highly processed) and the combination of food and drink consumed

Another issue with long-term observational studies with large numbers of participants is that data from FFQs are generally only collected at baseline and thus, over the long term, individuals may have changed their dietary habits. Ideally FFQs should be collected at frequent time-points and not just at baseline.

As in the case of RCTs, data should also take into account participant variables, termed confounders, such as age, sex, ethnic and cultural background and socio-economic status.

Strengths of FFQs and observational studies include large numbers of participants and the long-term nutritional outcomes in contrast to RCTs (relatively small numbers and short-term).

Are Saturated Fats Bad for Healthy Ageing?

An appropriate starting point is the initial recommendations that dietary fats are a health issue as outlined in the Dietary Guidelines released in the late 1970s/early 1980s. The latest edition of the Dietary Guidelines for Americans 2015-2020 (https://health.gov/dietaryguidelines/2015/guidelines) continues to advocate a low-fat diet, with recommendations to restrict saturated fat intake to less than 10% of the daily calories, albeit the latest recommendations do not place an upper limit on total calories from fat, previously limited to 30% of total calorie intake. Furthermore, the guidelines recommend that, where possible, saturated fat be replaced by unsaturated fat (monounsaturated and polyunsaturated). In addition, although dairy was listed as an important food item, low-fat dairy continued to be advocated.

Public release of the guidelines led to considerable debate, both in the public arena and within the scientific community. A peer-reviewed critique (Teicholz, 2015) of the guidelines in the *British Medical Journal* (BMJ), a pre-eminent medical journal, highly critical of the recommendations evoked a sharp response from the Advisory Committee for the Guidelines which requested a retraction of the publication. However, after an external review, the BMJ found no grounds to retract the article (www.bmj.com/company/wp-content/uploads/2016/12/the-bmj-US-dietary-correction.pdf).

Two further publications in the *British Medical Journal* added to the controversy about the dietary fat guidelines. One article concluded that there was no sound scientific evidence to support the original guidelines on dietary fat (Harcombe et al., 2017a). The other article was a systematic review and meta-analysis of prospective cohort studies (up to mid-2016) in which the authors concluded there was no statistically significant increase in risk of coronary heart disease mortality associated with total fat or saturated fat intake (Harcombe et al., 2017b).

In the last decade, numerous systematic reviews published in high-ranking scientific journals, have provided conflicting conclusions for an association of saturated and total fat intake with health outcomes. However, the most recent reviews of the scientific literature have concluded that fats, particularly dairy fats, have positive health outcomes.

It is important to provide a balanced view on dietary fats given the 2015-2020 Dietary Guidelines. In this respect, the American Heart Association has provided support for a low saturated fat diet in an article published in *Circulation*, a high-impact peer-reviewed journal, in a review (up to mid-2016) of the scientific literature (Sacks et al., 2017).

The article advocates a low saturated fat diet on the basis that there is sufficient evidence that saturated fats have a negative health impact on heart disease, linking saturated fats to levels of both good and bad cholesterols. In the case of the latter, there are conflicting reports as to exactly which LDL-cholesterol, if at all, is affected: is it the large LDL, the small LDL (also termed VLDL, very low-density lipoprotein) or in fact both? In the case of the good cholesterol (HDL-cholesterol), saturated fats have been variously reported as having a neutral response or actually increasing levels of HDL-cholesterol. The review article also cited four core trials on food intake in which saturated fats were replaced by polyunsaturated fats (primarily from vegetable oils), outcomes from which indicated lowered incidence of a cardiovascular event or mortality from coronary heart disease. However, it should be noted that all four trials included a significant number of individuals with pre-diagnosed heart conditions.

A review (Cochrane review, completed in mid-2014) on saturated fatty acid and risk of cardiovascular disease concluded that there was: 'a small but potentially important reduction in cardiovascular risk on reduction of saturated fat intake' and that replacement of food energy from saturated fatty acid with polyunsaturated fatty acid (inconclusive for monounsaturated fatty acid) was beneficial (Hooper et al., 2015a).

A second review (Cochrane review, completed at the end of 2014) covering randomized controlled trials (RCTs) with measurements extending to at least six months, on total fat intake and body weight provided somewhat ambiguous conclusions (Hooper et al., 2015b). Compared with a control group (on a normal or moderate fat intake), participants on a relatively low-fat diet 'showed a consistent, stable but small effect of low-fat intake on body fatness: slightly lower weight (mean weight reduction of 1.5 kg), BMI and waist circumference.' On the other hand, it was also concluded that 'this effect of reducing total fat was not consistently reflected in cohort studies assessing the relationship between total fat intake and later measures of body fatness or change in body fatness in studies on children, young people or adults.'

In another review of RCTs (data to mid-2014 and trials lasting at least twelve months), it was concluded that clinical trials involving a high-fat/low-carbohydrate diet led to statistically significantly greater weight loss than low-fat intervention trials (Tobias et al., 2015).

In a large prospective study of individuals (n = 136,384, aged 35-70, median 9.1 years of follow-up) from twenty-one countries in five continents, total fat and types of fat (saturated, unsaturated) were associated with lower (17% to 24% decrease risk) of all-cause mortality including cardiovascular mortality and stroke (Dehghan et al., 2018). Reduced risk, comparing highest with lowest intake, of all-cause mortality was decreased by 14% for saturated fat and approximately 20% for mono- and polyunsaturated fat intake.

It should be noted that fat intake of the participants (~ 75% obtained less than 10% of energy from saturated fats) was lower than generally observed in previous studies involving participants from USA and Europe (~ 50% obtained less than 10% of energy from saturated fats). Furthermore, the study was notable in that the participants were classified as urban-rural from low- to middle-income countries and did not include individuals from USA or Europe (with the exception of Sweden).

In another large prospective cohort study of individuals (non-European and non-North American origin) from Iran comparing high with low dairy food intake, there was a 19% decreased risk of all-cause mortality and 28% decreased mortality associated with cardiovascular disease (Farvid et al., 2017). This was a relatively long-term study (11 years of follow-up) involving a large number of individuals (n = 42,403, male and female). This study confirmed earlier observations that saturated fat intake was associated with lower risk of coronary heart disease and stroke (Alexander et al., 2016).

An earlier review (Mozaffarian et al., 2010) concluded that replacement of saturated fats by monounsaturated and polyunsaturated fats in the diet would have health benefits related to coronary heart disease. This view was further endorsed in an update on a large prospective observational study (n = 115,782, 63% female) of health professionals (Zong et al., 2016). This study was based on food frequency questionnaires (e.g. food recall over the past year) and an impressive follow-up of twenty-one to twenty-eight years. Replacing 1% of energy (calories) intake from saturated fatty acids reduced the risk of coronary heart disease by 5% when replaced by monounsaturated fat and by 8% with polyunsaturated fat. Replacing 1% energy (calories) from palmitic acid (a saturated fat) reduced the risk of coronary heart disease by 8% and 12% when replaced by monounsaturated or polyunsaturated fat respectively. One should not get too excited by these very modest decreases in risk, confounders due to individual variations in lifestyle (e.g. physical activity, socio-economic status) may easily account for these differences.

A key point to note is that in studies on dietary food intake in which saturated fat is partially replaced by unsaturated fat, the food matrix of the unsaturated fat is crucial. For example, if from fish, nuts, seeds and vegetables then the protein, vitamins, minerals and fibre components of these will greatly influence the health outcomes and not just the fat. In other words, substituting saturated fats with unsaturated fats in the diet also introduced a healthier overall diet and not just replacement of saturated fats.

Earlier reports of negative health outcomes from a diet high in fats, particularly saturated fats, failed to recognize that individuals on a high-fat diet also consumed significantly large amounts of fried and processed foods high in sugar and salt, and possibly also *trans*-fats.

And remember, as previously discussed, a calorie is most definitely not a food calorie.

The high calorie content of fats (as determined in the laboratory as a single pure entity) simply does not take into account the cooking procedure, the digestive process and the food matrix (e.g. dairy, nuts, seeds, fish, meat) in which the fats are contained. This food matrix also comes with the bonus of proteins, minerals and vitamins, many of which (e.g. vitamins A, D, E and K) are fat-soluble and thus the fat is essential to assist proper digestion of these essential nutrients.

Pub Test 3.3:

Question:

Are saturated fats bad for health?

Answer:

No

However, if your diet also includes high amounts of saturated fats and refined carbohydrates from highly processed foods (e.g. pastries, pies, cakes, cookies, packaged foods) and sugar (particularly soft drinks or soda), you will have a problem.

Are Dairy Products a Health Hazard?

Although the 2015-2020 Dietary Guidelines for Americans lists dairy as part of a healthy diet, the continued advocacy for low-fat dairy is debatable given that there is no clear and certainly no strong clinical evidence that normal dairy has detrimental health effects (apart from individuals allergic to milk products as in lactose intolerance).

Recent publications have continued to confirm that a normal dairy intake (e.g. milk, cheese, yoghurt) in healthy individuals is either neutral or indeed protective against all-cause mortality and cardiovascular disease (Drouin-Chartier et al., 2016; Guo et al., 2017).

An umbrella or overview of the published scientific literature (as at April 2018), in the American Society for Nutrition journal, *Advances in Nutrition*, concluded that dairy product consumption (milk, cheese, yoghurt, butter) consistently showed no association with risk of all-cause mortality (Cavero-Redondo et al., 2019). This comprehensive review covered studies from data obtained from > 3.6 million individuals (> 680,000 mortality in follow-up). Furthermore, in a comparison of studies involving a high-dairy or low-dairy diet, there was no increased risk of all-cause mortality with a high-dairy diet.

Another very recent study in the *American Journal of Clinical Nutrition*, a high-ranked journal, examined the effect of low- versus high-dairy intake on blood pressure in overweight adults (Rietsema et al., 2019). This was a randomized controlled trial (n = 52, mean age of 58.6, 56% female, mean BMI of 28,) in which one set of participants were put on a low-dairy diet for six weeks, followed by a four week wash-out (on a normal diet) and then a high- dairy diet for six weeks. Conversely, another set of participants (matched for age, BMI and sex) were on high-dairy, wash-out and low-dairy. Thus, in this cross-over experiment, participants acted as their own controls.

A high-dairy diet resulted in reduction in both systolic (mean decrease of - 4.6 mm) and diastolic (mean decrease of - 3 mm) blood pressure.

One should not get too excited by this result given the low number of participants and the short-term experimental diets. These data need to be confirmed in long-term studies with many more participants from diverse ethnic backgrounds, different age groups and with different health issues (e.g. healthy, type 2 diabetes, overweight).

Nevertheless, this publication additionally confirms that consumption of dairy, even at high amounts, is not associated with adverse health outcomes.

This conclusion may be hard to accept by a large proportion of the general public, given the contrary has been essentially ingrained into our psyche regarding dairy products and health. Here is a simple test to examine your ingrained biases:

Where is the evidence that consumption of dairy products is detrimental to human health?

Information from a family member, friend, associate or your grandmother (on this topic at least) is invalid (highly biased) as is information from commercial enterprises selling low-fat dairy products (highly biased and conflict of interest).

What is valid is a scientific study on long-term dairy product consumption involving a well-designed clinical trial (e.g. randomized clinical trial) with several hundred participants. Alternatively, observational studies based on food frequency questionnaires allow large numbers of participants to be recruited with data available over a long-term (years). The interested Reader may have noted that much of this information is already available and the consensus conclusion is that dairy consumption does not have adverse health outcomes (with exceptions such as individuals with lactose intolerance).

It is ironic to note that the opposite of low-fat dairy (purposely created by the food industry as a marketing tool) is natural or regular dairy or should that now be termed high-fat dairy? Interestingly, the replacement of regular dairy milk by a plethora of 'healthier' milk alternatives (e.g. soymilk, rice milk, almond milk) is puzzling.

Vague health claims based on e.g. low-calorie, low-fat, good protein, antioxidants etc are simply that, vague, with no clear experimental evidence. Consequently, one is unable to conduct any review or meta-analysis as there are simply very few publications (essentially none involving well-designed long-term clinical studies with large numbers of individuals) in high-ranked peer-reviewed scientific journals on the health benefits of commercially available milk alternatives as compared with regular dairy milk.

Nevertheless, if one continues to enjoy consumption of milk alternatives then by all means do so. Many of them are very palatable and I personally enjoy soy milk. Just keep in mind that, at this stage, there is simply no evidence that milk alternatives are healthier (or indeed less healthy) than regular milk.

Here are some intriguing pieces of trivia. The Dutch (and Finns, Danes and Swedes) have a very high consumption of dairy fats in their diets, mostly in the form of milk and cheese. The Dutch are designated as one of the tallest nations with average male and female heights at 1.82 and 1.69 metres respectively. Moreover, the Dutch (and Finns, Danes and Swedes) are ranked highly for lifespan and healthy ageing at 84 years and 72 years respectively for females and 79 years and 70 years respectively for males (World Health Organisation 2016). And what about butter and the French? The French also rank very high in lifespan and healthy ageing, at 86 and 75 years respectively for females and 80 and 72 years respectively for males (see Table 1 p. 154).

Where again is that evidence that dairy is a health hazard for healthy ageing?

Pub Test 3.4:

Question:

Is regular dairy bad for you?

Answer:

No

There is no scientific evidence which shows that regular dairy fat is a health hazard (unless you have an allergy to dairy), in fact the evidence is neutral or in most studies positive for health.

A regular dairy diet with unrefined carbohydrates (e.g. whole grains, fruit, vegetables) and a minimum of processed/packaged foods would be alarmingly healthy. A low-fat dairy diet may in fact be negative for health as the dairy fat is required to assist in digestion and metabolism of minerals and fat-soluble vitamins from the dairy. Moreover, a low-fat diet generally means a high-carbohydrate diet, in which case absolutely avoid processed foods rich in highly refined carbohydrates.

Fats Are Absolutely Essential for Healthy Ageing

The key issue here is that fats are essential for health. The average adult female is 20% to 35% fat, the average adult male is 18% to 25% fat (depending on age, lifestyle and BMI) and our brain is absolutely dependent on fat, both unsaturated and saturated fatty acids (approximately 60% wet weight of the human brain is lipid consisting of complexes of cholesterol, myelin, phospholipids and fatty acids). And, just like humans, fats come in all shapes and sizes within our bodies and in the food we consume.

The proper functioning, and hence health, of our cell membranes (e.g. membranes surrounding the nucleus, mitochondria, neurons) is critically dependent on the maintenance of an optimum fluidity: a Goldilocks state, not too solid, not too fluid but just right. Saturated and unsaturated fats contribute in making cell membranes more solid and more fluid respectively, thus maintaining the 'just right' degree of membrane fluidity in the optimum combination (Nicolson, 2014).

Our core body temperature is around 37^0C, and any deviation of a few degrees either up or down can lead to serious complications (e.g. death). Our cell membranes have to function optimally at 37^0C and it is the combination of saturated and unsaturated fats that is the major determinant of the optimal membrane fluidity (note: proteins, cholesterol and other complex lipids and carbohydrates also influence membrane fluidity).

For example, the saturated fatty acid, palmitic acid (16:0, melting point 63.1^0C) is a solid at 37^0C. By comparison, both the monounsaturated fatty acid, oleic acid (18:1, melting point 13.4^0C) and the polyunsaturated fatty acid linoleic acid (18:2, melting point -5^0C) are liquids at 37^0C, thus an optimum combination of fats is required for cell membranes to properly function at 37^0C.

Pub Test 3.5:

Question:

Are fats bad for health?

Answer:

No

In fact, fats are essential for health. For example, fats are an integral part of the brain and a proper balance of saturated and unsaturated fats is essential to maintain our cell membranes (e.g. in the nucleus, mitochondria) at equilibrium for optimum functioning at 37^0C.

Are Sugars Bad for Healthy Ageing?

There is compelling evidence that sugar is a health hazard. An increasing number of countries (e.g. Chile, Mexico, France, Germany, a few states in the USA) have introduced or are in the process (Australia, U.K.) of introducing a tax on sugar. It is premature to make judgment on the outcomes of the sugar tax although there are some early signs of a decrease in consumption of soft drinks, the latter termed sugar-sweetened beverages (SSBs). There is criticism that the level of tax is too low (e.g. 5% to 10%) and that it is too little, too late to have much effect on the world-wide obesity epidemic. Interestingly, there are signs that obesity may be declining in some parts of the developed world but worryingly increasing in some parts of Asia, the Middle East, Pacific Islands and Polynesia.

As in the case with fats and health, there is a massive literature on sugar and health. Articles in health magazines frequently have a commercial slant and articles in popular magazines are generally too simplistic. Newspaper articles are sometimes more informative but there is a tendency for exaggeration given the requirement to attract reader attention and hence sales: basically 'don't let the facts spoil a good story.' In reality, we have to turn to the peer-reviewed scientific literature for the truth, or can we?

In keeping with the theme of quoting the most recent scientific publications only references in the last few years are reviewed herein.

Sugars May Not Be a Health Hazard: Where is the Evidence?

A systematic review, published in 2017 in the *American Journal of Clinical Nutrition*, a top-ranked clinical nutrition journal, of randomized controlled trials (RCTs) in which glucose, sucrose or both were replaced by fructose (energy-equivalent calories) concluded that fructose substitution in food may be of benefit to individuals with type 2 diabetes (Evans *et al.,* 2017). The review included eleven RCTs involving a total of 277 individuals. The duration of the trials was extremely short term, only two to four weeks with one trial at six weeks and one trial at ten weeks. Thus, both the very limited number of individuals and the short time frame of all eleven studies raised serious scientific criticisms about the validity of these studies.

An earlier study, published in 2013 in the *Journal of Nutrition* (Slujs *et al.,* 2013), suggested that digestible carbohydrates (including sucrose) were not associated with risk of diabetes. This was a very large study in eight European countries involving a representative cohort (n = 16,835) and incident type 2 diabetes cases (n = 12,403) with a median follow-up of twelve years. Interestingly, in the UK cohort, there was a reported 34% and 54% decreased risk of diabetes in respect of food intake of digestible carbohydrates and sucrose respectively. However, these studies may have been compromised in that it was stated in the methodology section of the publication that most of the UK-Oxford cohort consisted of vegetarians and health-conscious volunteers. Presumably their diets would have been high in fruit and vegetables, as sources of digestible carbohydrates and sugar, and low in highly processed foods, both known factors of a healthy diet profile. The observed decrease risk in diabetes (and less risk of overweight) in this cohort may thus be related to their healthy diet profile and healthy lifestyle.

The 2013 publication was extensively quoted (seven out of fifteen cohort studies reviewed) in a recent literature review (Tsilas et al., 2017) that concluded that:

'Current evidence does not allow us to conclude that fructose containing sugars independent of food form are associated with increased risk of type 2 diabetes.'

Importantly, the authors proposed that high intake of SSBs may be generally indicative of individuals with unhealthy lifestyle choices, such as less physical activity, high alcohol intake and smoking.

The scientific basis of public guidelines on sugar intake by government and scientific organizations was recently reviewed in the *Annals of Internal Medicine*, a highly prestigious medical journal (Erickson et al., 2017). In this review the authors stated that there was a conflict of interest in that funding was provided by the food and agriculture industry.

'However, given the funding source our study team has a financial conflict of interest and readers should consider our results carefully'

Nevertheless, it was concluded that:

'Guidelines on dietary sugar do not meet criteria for trustworthy recommendations and are based on low-quality evidence'

This conclusion could not be more different from the consensus of much of the scientific studies of the past decade on sugar and health and highlighted the role of the food industry in influencing government bodies with respect to dietary recommendations for the general public (Nestle, 2007, 2015; Teicholz, 2015; Kearns, 2016).

It is recognized that the food industry has provided cheap and, if one shops carefully, relatively healthy food for the general public. On the other hand, the competitive nature of the food industry and the business requirement for profit have led to the production of highly processed foods with long shelf-life (with the assistance of preservatives and antioxidants), and artificially flavoured and coloured, calorie-dense and nutrient-poor food. Sugar sweetened beverages, including sports and energy drinks and fruit juices, have been especially targeted as a source of 'empty calories' and as a factor in the world-wide obesity epidemic.

In a balanced view, one should consider that individuals who consume large amounts of SSBs may frequently also consume large amounts of highly processed foods (see Steele *et al.*, 2017 for types of processed foods) and adopt unhealthy lifestyles e.g. physical inactivity, smoking, drinking in excess.

Sugars Are a Health Hazard: Where is the Evidence?

There is substantial anecdotal evidence that increased sugar consumption (a fact; simply read the food nutrition label on soft drinks, low-fat foods and processed foods) which has occurred since the end of sugar rationing (a result of the Second World War), is associated with the world-wide increase in overweight individuals (a fact; simply just look around your neighbourhood).

The history of sugar and its introduction into almost every aspect of the human food market, especially in processed foods, is beyond the scope of the present discussion. The interested Reader can find entertaining and informative aspects of these issues in several scientific articles (Kearns *et al.*, 2016; Nestle, 2016), selected books (Nestle, 2015; Gameau, 2015; Taubes, 2017) and even a popular video (Gameau, 2015). One is encouraged to research these references and others to obtain an overview of the sugar-health debate and thus come to an informed decision (non-biased).

Obesity levels are currently at record highs and there appears to be a strong association between sugar and the prevalence of overweight and obesity world-wide. Note that there is an association not absolutely a causal effect and therein lies the conundrum.

To start with, what is sugar? The most common form of table sugar is the carbohydrate sucrose (a disaccharide) that consists of equal amounts (50%) of one molecule of glucose (a monosaccharide) and one molecule of fructose (a monosaccharide). Commercial sucrose is mainly extracted from sugar cane (e.g. North and South America, Australia) or from sugar beet (e.g. Europe). Natural foods are also rich in sugars. Fruit is rich in fructose. Honey has a mixture of fructose (~40%), glucose (~30%) and sucrose (~3%). Maple syrup has ~60% sucrose. Sweet potato (~5% sucrose-glucose-fructose) releases the additional sugar disaccharide maltose (consists of glucose-glucose units) on baking. Fruit, vegetables and grains contain complex carbohydrates, including fibre, as well as variable amounts of sucrose, glucose and fructose. The complex carbohydrates are broken down on cooking and on digestion yielding simple sugars, particularly glucose and fructose. Lactose, the main sugar in milk, is a disaccharide consisting of one molecule of glucose and one molecule of galactose. High-fructose corn syrup (e.g. HFCS-55, 55% fructose, 45% glucose) is the sweetener commonly added to soft drinks (soda).

Now that we have covered food-sugar-chemistry in one paragraph, no mean feat, we turn to the question: which foods provide us with our daily sugar fix?

Foods that have essentially no or minimal sugars include meat, fish, eggs and non-starchy vegetables (e.g. cauliflower, lettuce, broccoli). On the other hand, starchy vegetables (e.g. sweet potato, carrot, peas, corn) contain variable amounts of sugar (maltose, sucrose, glucose, fructose), which also depends on how they are cooked.

Lactose is the sugar in dairy products and includes milk with around 4% to 5%, natural yoghurt at < 5% and with low amounts in cheese (e.g. cheddar < 0.5%) and butter (< 0.2%). Fruit contains relatively high amounts of sugar (sucrose, glucose, fructose) and the sweeter the fruit the higher the sugar (particularly fructose which is much sweeter, approximately 1.7 times, than sucrose). Dried fruit (e.g. raisins, prunes) have high amounts of sugar.

It is most important to note that the sugar in real, natural foods comes with the additional bonus package of fats, proteins, fibre, minerals, vitamins and antioxidants. The sugar in these foods is metabolized differently from sugar in soft drinks (soda) and processed foods, as it is metabolized significantly slower and leads to controlled release of sugars (e.g. glucose, fructose) into the bloodstream, tissues and organs (e.g. liver). Moreover, the additional nutrients as listed above further assist in ameliorating the metabolic effects of the sugars. The scientific consensus is that sugar from natural foods, in particular fruit, vegetables and dairy, are not a major health issue. So, what are the sources of sugar that constitute a health hazard?

The 2015-2020 Dietary Guidelines emphasized the need to decrease the amount of added sugar in the diet without explicitly stating, at least in the Executive Summary document, what added sugar is. The general public will be as confused as I have been in deciding what added sugar is, e.g. are soft drinks classified as having added sugar? A search of the scientific literature would partially clarify this issue: it is the sugar in soft drinks, energy drinks, flavoured milk and yoghurt and processed foods (essentially anything in a package with more than two or three ingredients and not recognized by your granny as real food).

The sugar in soft drinks (including in fruit juices and energy drinks) comes in liquid form and thus is easily digested leading to a rapid rise in blood glucose and thus insulin levels. This is liquid calories or sometimes termed 'empty calories' as it comes with very little or no nutrients.

Food manufacturers frequently add minerals (e.g. potassium, sodium, magnesium), vitamins (especially C and B-type, both water-soluble vitamins) and even caffeine to their products (e.g. energy drinks) in attempts to make their drinks appear healthier with 'added minerals, vitamins and energy.' In the same way, food manufacturers add minerals and vitamins to highly processed breakfast cereals, many of which contain high quantities of added sugar.

It should be recognized that most processed foods are generally manufactured in a way that removes most of the food fibre and much of the natural ingredients such as vitamins, minerals and fats (e.g. ready-made meals, cereals, sauces, canned soups, snacks, in fact most food items in a packet, can or bottle). The addition of sugar, salt, antioxidants and preservatives adds to a long shelf-life which allows the manufacturer to store and transport goods as required and is also convenient for the consumer. Processed foods are relatively cost-effective, again to the benefit of both the manufacturer and consumer. The trade-off is that most processed foods are relatively easily digested and calorie-dense as compared with unprocessed, fresh or natural foods. Importantly, they have that 'added sugar' problem (and salt).

A comprehensive survey of the US population on the intake of added sugars was recently published in the *British Medical Journal*, a highly ranked medical journal (Steele *et al.*, 2017). The survey (n = 9,317) was based on at least one twenty-four-hour dietary recall (food frequency questionnaire) and classified food groups into essentially three categories:

1. *unprocessed or minimally processed* (e.g. fruit, vegetables, meat, eggs, dairy)
2. *processed* (e.g. cheese, ham, salted meats)
3. *ultraprocessed* (e.g. bread, cakes, pies, snacks, soft drinks, cereals, desserts)

The authors concluded that in a typical US diet, ultraprocessed foods contributed approximately 58% of total calories/day (based on a 2,070 calories/day diet). Significantly, on a daily average, ultraprocessed foods contributed approximately 90% of the added sugars. An earlier study (Yang *et al.*, 2014) of two very large cohorts of US adults (n = 31,147 and n = 11,733) concluded that, on average, approximately 15% of total calories/day were obtained from added sugars, with 37% of the added sugars originating from SSBs. These authors further extrapolated (mean

14.6 years of follow-up) that individuals consuming ≥ seven SSBs/week (360 ml servings) had a 27% increase in risk of cardiovascular disease as compared to individuals consuming ≤ one SSBs/week. In this study, in which participants provided at least one twenty-four-hour dietary recall, adjustments were made for confounders including educational attainment, physical activity and smoking.

In 2016, the American Heart Association (AHA) produced a scientific statement on added sugars and risk of cardiovascular disease in children (Vos et al., 2016). The recommendations were based on a review of the scientific literature up to November 2015. In summary, the AHA recommended that (excluding sugar naturally occurring in e.g. fruit, vegetables, dairy), children consume ≤ 25 gm of added sugar/day, equal to approximately six teaspoons of sugar, to reduce risk of developing CVD. To put this figure in perspective, a Mars bar (53 gm) has 31 gm of sugar and 198 calories, six squares of milk chocolate has 22 gm of sugar and 200 calories and a serving (375 ml) of soft drink has 34 gm of sugar and 160 calories. Complications occur when one factors in 'added sugar' from highly processed foods which would almost certainly be consumed as part of a normal Western diet.

A large observational study (Huang et al., 2017), published in the *American Journal of Clinical Nutrition*, a high impact journal on clinical nutrition, on the incidence of diabetes mellitus (DM) in postmenopausal women (n = 64,850, average 8.4 years of follow-up) examined the association of DM with intake of SSBs and artificially sweetened beverages (ASBs).

Consumption of ≥ two servings of ASBs a day (serving size 355 ml) as compared with never or < three servings a month was associated with a 21% increased risk of DM. Consumption of

≥ two servings of SSBs a day as compared with < one serving a week was associated with a 43% increased risk. It should be emphasized that these observations demonstrate associations and not causality among SSBs, ASBs and DM. For example, individuals consuming ASBs may already constitute a cohort attempting to control weight (e.g. by changing from SSBs to ASBs) and with a predisposition for overweight and thus a pre-diabetic risk.

A Swedish study (Lofvenborg *et al.*, 2016), published in the *European Journal of Endocrinology*, examined sweetened beverages with respect to risk of type 2 diabetes and latent autoimmune diabetes (LADA, with characteristics of both type 1 and type 2 diabetes). In this study (n = 1,371 controls, n = 1,136 type 2, n = 357 LADA), the authors concluded that consumption of each 200 ml serving of SSBs or ASBs conferred a 12% to 18% increased risk of LADA and a higher risk (20%) for type 2 diabetes.

There is compelling evidence from long-term (> one year) observational studies primarily based on FFQ and medical data on large numbers of participants (thousands) have indicated an association between consumption of sugars (particularly from SSBs and processed foods) and increased risk of obesity, type 2 diabetes and CVD (Malik, 2017). However, short-term (< one year) randomized controlled trials (RCTs, generally with less than several hundred participants) have provided only modest support for this association. This has led some researchers to challenge the consensus that sugars, especially added sugars and fructose, are causative agents for health issues related to obesity, type 2 diabetes and CVD.

A long-term study of two distinct cohorts, one the Nurses' Health Study (n = 80,647, 34 years of follow-up, female) and the other the Health Professional's Follow-up Study (n = 37,716, 28 years follow-up, male), on soft-drink consumption and risk of mortality (n = 36,436 deaths) was recently published in *Circulation*, a high-impact medical journal (Malik *et al.*, 2019).

Comparing individuals who consumed on average ≥ two SSBs/day (standard drink reference at about 350 ml) with individuals who consumed < one drink/month, there was a 21% increased risk of all-cause mortality and 31% for cardiovascular mortality. There was a modest increased risk of cancer (16%) in the high consumption cohort. In the case of ASBs, there was a 10% and 15% increased risk of all-cause and cardiovascular mortality respectively but only in the Nurses' Health Study. There was no statistically significant increased risk of cancer for either cohort associated with ASB consumption.

ASBs have been successfully marketed as an alternative to SSBs on the basis of low calories and absence of sugar. A very recent study (n = 81,714, female, aged 50-79, mean follow-up of 11.9 years) published in *Stroke*, a premier publication of the AHA, examined the association of consumption of ASBs with stroke, coronary heart disease and all-cause mortality (Mossavar-Rahmani *et al.*, 2019).

In comparing individuals who consumed ≥ two ASB drinks/day (reference 12 fl.oz. or 355 ml) with infrequent consumers (never or < one drink/week) there was a 25%, 29% and 16% increased risk of stroke, coronary heart disease and all-cause mortality respectively. Data were adjusted for a number of confounders, including socio-economic factors, smoking, alcohol, physical activity and prior health risk variables.

However, the characteristics of the study cohort (85% white, 7% black and 3% Hispanic) required careful consideration. The authors noted that most participants (64%) were infrequent consumers (never or < one drink/week) and only 5% consumed ≥ two drinks/day. The high risk of stroke, particularly ischaemic stroke (1.19 increased risk for whites, as compared with 3.93 for blacks, a substantial difference) was only statistically significant in individuals with BMI > 30. On the other hand, the increased risk of all-cause mortality was only in those with BMI < 30. Increased risk of coronary heart disease was also notably different, with 1.31 for whites and 1.60 for blacks.

A recent long-term (average 16.4 years of follow-up, n = 41,693 deaths) nation-wide study of ten European countries, published in *JAMA Internal Medicine* (Mullee et al., 2019), examined associations between soft drink consumption and mortality. This very large study (n = 451,743, 71.1% female, mean age of 50.8) compared individuals who consumed ≥ two glasses soft drinks/day (glass = 250 ml) with those who consumed < one glass/ month. The authors further divided soft drinks into either SSBs or ASBs.

Comparing participants with high to low consumption, and after adjustments for lifestyle factors, including smoking, physical activity, diet and socio-economic status, there was a 17%, 8% and 26% increased risk of all-cause mortality for total, SSB and ASB soft drink consumption respectively. The authors also reported increased risk for digestive diseases for SSBs and increased risk for circulatory diseases for ASBs. On the positive side, soft drink consumption was not associated with various cancers.

Studies on ASBs have raised various issues about the reasons why individuals consume ASBs. Those who do may have underlying health issues such as being overweight or at risk of type 2 diabetes. Consuming ASBs may also confer a false sense of security (low calories, no sugar) and thus may encourage individuals to indulge in inappropriate eating habits such as intake of high-calorie and sugar-dense foods. Also, the question as to which type and how long the individual has been consuming the ASB of choice needs to be addressed.

One must acknowledge the complexities of obtaining objective diet information in that most observational studies rely on self-reporting (diet recall) by participants and then generally only at baseline or the start of the study. In long-term studies, over many years, individual diets (and lifestyle) are likely to change. However, many of the authoritative studies have included acceptable sensitivity analysis such as regular assessment of diet and lifestyle for a cross-section of cohorts.

Pub Test 3.6:

Question:

Is sugar a health hazard?

Answer:

Yes

The added (hidden) sugar in highly processed foods and the liquid calories in sugar-sweetened beverages provide sugar calories in easily digestible forms which the body readily absorbs, leading to a rapid spike in blood glucose and insulin. There is consensus that sugar in foods such as fruit, vegetables and dairy is much less harmful in that the food matrix acts as a buffer and results in the slow, controlled release of sugar into the bloodstream and organs. Moreover, the nutrients (fibre, carbohydrates, fats, proteins, minerals, vitamins, antioxidants) in the food matrix are an added bonus.

Alexander, DD, Bylsma, LC, Vargas, AJ, et al. 2016. Dairy consumption and CVD: a systematic review and meta-analysis. *British Journal of Nutrition* 115:737-750. doi:10.1017/S0007114515005000.

Cavero-Redondo, I, Alvarez-Bueno, C, Sotos-Prieto, M, et al. 2019. Milk and dairy product consumption and risk of mortality: an overview of systematic reviews and meta-analyses. *Advances in Nutrition* 10:S97-S104. doi:10.1093/advances/nmy128.

Cohen, E, Cragg, M, deFonseka, J, et al. 2015. Statistical review of US macronutrient consumption data, 1965-2011: Americans have been following dietary guidelines, coincident with the rise in obesity. *Nutrition* 31:727-732. doi:10.1016/j.nut.2015.02.007.

Dehghan, M, Mente, M, Rangarajan, S, et al. 2018. Association of dairy intake with cardiovascular disease and mortality in 21 countries from five continents (PURE): a prospective cohort study. *The Lancet* 392:2288-2297. doi:10.1016/S0140-6736(18)31812-9.

Drouin-Chartier, J-P, Cote, JA, Labonte, M-E, et al. 2016. Comprehensive review of the impact of dairy foods and dairy fat on cardiometabolic risk. *Advances in Nutrition* 7:1041-1051. doi:10.3945/an.115.011619.

Erickson, J, Sadeghirad, B, Lytvyn, L, et al. 2017. The scientific basis of guideline recommendations on sugar intake. *Annals of Internal Medicine* 166:257-267. doi:10.7326/M16-2020.

Evans, RA, Frese, M, Romero, J, et al. 2017. Fructose replacement of glucose or sucrose in food or beverages lowers postprandial glucose and insulin without raising triglycerides: a systematic review and meta-analysis. *American Journal of Clinical Nutrition* 106:506-518. doi:10.3945/ajcn.116.145152.

A, et al. 2017. Dairy food intake and all-cause, cardiovascular disease, and cancer mortality: The Golestan Cohort Study. *American Journal of Epidemiology* 185:697-711. doi:10.1093/aje/kww139.

Gameau, D. 2015. That Sugar Book. Pan Macmillan: Sydney.

Gameau, D. 2015. That Sugar Film. Madman Production Company: Melbourne.

Gayet-Boyer, C, Tenenhaus-Aziza, F, Prunet, C, *et al.* 2014. Is there a relationship between the dose of ruminant *trans*-fatty acids and cardiovascular risk markers in healthy subjects: results from a systematic review and meta-regression of randomised clinical trials. *British Journal of Nutrition* 112:1914-1922. doi:10.1017/S0007114514002578.

Guo, J, Astrup, A, Lovegrove, JA, *et al.* 2017. Milk and dairy consumption and risk of cardiovascular diseases and all-cause mortality: dose-response meta-analysis of prospective cohort studies. *European Journal of Epidemiology* 32:269-287. doi:10.1007/s10654-017-0243-1.

Harcombe, Z, Baker, JS, Davies, B. 2017a. Evidence from prospective cohort studies did not support the introduction of dietary fat guidelines in 1977 and 1983: a systematic review. *British Journal of Sports Medicine* 51:1736-1741. doi:10.1136/bjsports-2016-096409.

Harcombe, Z, Baker, JS, Davies, B. 2017b. Evidence from prospective cohort studies does not support current dietary fat guidelines: a systematic review and meta-analysis. *British Journal of Sports Medicine* 51:1742-1748. doi:10.1136/bjsports-2016-096550.

Hooper, L, Martin, N, Abdelhamid, A, et al. 2015a. Reduction in saturated fat intake for cardiovascular disease. *Cochrane Database Systematic Reviews* 10:CDO11737. doi:10.1002/14651858. CD011737.

Hooper, L, Abdelhamid, A, Bunn, D, et al. 2015b. Effects of total fat intake on body weight. *Cochrane Database Systematic Reviews* 8:CD011834. doi:10.1002/14651858.CD011834.

Huang, M, Quddus, A, Stinson, L, et al. 2017. Artificially sweetened beverages, sugar-sweetened beverages, plain water, and incident diabetes mellitus in postmenopausal women: the prospective Women's Health Initiative observational study. *American Journal of Clinical Nutrition* 106:614-622. doi:10.3945/ajcn.116.145391.

Kearns, CE, Schmidt, LA, Glantz, SA. 2016. Sugar industry and coronary heart disease research. A historical analysis of internal industry documents. *JAMA Internal Medicine.* 176:1680-1685. doi:10.1001/jamainternmed.2016.5394.

Liu, AG, Ford, NA, Hu, FB, et al. 2017. A healthy approach to dietary fats: understanding the science and taking action to reduce consumer confusion. *Nutrition Journal* 16:53-68. doi:10.1186/s12937-017-0271-4.

Lofvenborg, JE, Andersson, T, Carlsson, P-O, et al. 2016. Sweetened beverage intake and risk of latent autoimmune diabetes in adults (LADA) and type 2 diabetes. *European Journal of Endocrinology* 175:605-614. doi:10.1530/EJE-16-0376.

Malik, VS. 2017. Sugar sweetened beverages and cardiometabolic health. *Current Opinion in Cardiology* 32:572-579. doi:10.1097/HCO.0000000000000439.

Malik, VS, Li, Y, De Koning, L, *et al.* 2019. Long-term consumption of sugar-sweetened and artificially sweetened beverages and risk of mortality in US adults. *Circulation* 139:2113-2125. doi:10.1161/CIRCULATIONAHA.118.037401.

Mossavar-Rahmani, Y, Kamensky, V, Manson, J, *et al.* 2019. Artificially sweetened beverages and stroke, coronary heart disease and all-cause mortality in the Women's Health Initiative. 2019. *Stroke* 50:555-562. doi:10.1161/STROKEAHA.118.023100.

Mozaffarian, D, Micha, R, Wallace, S. 2010. Effects on coronary heart disease of increasing polyunsaturated fat in place of saturated fat: a systematic review and meta-analysis of randomized controlled trials. *PloS Medicine* 7:e1000252. doi:10.1371/journal.pmed.1000252.

Mullee, A, Romaguera, D, Pearson-Stuttard, J, *et al.* 2019. Association between soft drink consumption and mortality in 10 European countries. *JAMA Internal Medicine* 179:1479-1490. doi:10.1001/jamainternmed.2019.2478.

Nestle, M. 2007. Food Politics. University of California Press: Berkeley & Los Angeles.

Nestle, M. 2015. Soda Politics. Oxford University Press: Oxford.

Nestle, M. 2016. Corporate funding of food and nutrition research: science or marketing? *JAMA Internal Medicine* 176:13-14. doi:10.1001/jamainternmed.2015.6667.

Nicolson, G. 2014. The fluid-mosaic model of membrane structure: still relevant to understanding the structure, function and dynamics of biological membranes after more than 40 years.

Biochimica et Biophysica Acta 1838:1451-1466. doi:10.1016/bbamem.2013.10.019.

Rietsema, S, Eelderink, C, Joustra, ML, et al. 2019. Effect of high compared to low dairy intake on blood pressure in overweight middle-aged adults: results of a randomized crossover intervention trial. *American Journal of Clinical Nutrition* 110:340-348. doi:10.1093/ajcn/nqz116.

Sacks, FM, Lichtenstein, AH, Wu, JHY, et al. 2017. Dietary fats and cardiovascular disease. A presidential advisory from the American Heart Association. *Circulation* 136:e1-e23. doi:10.1161/CIR.0000000000000510.

De Souza, RJ, Mente, A, Maroleanu, A, et al. 2015. Intake of saturated and trans unsaturated fatty acids and risk of all-cause mortality, cardiovascular disease, and type 2 diabetes: systematic review and meta-analysis of observational studies. *British Medical Journal* 351:h3978. doi:10.1136/bmj.h3978.

Sluijs, I, Beulens, JW, van der Schouw, YT, et al. 2013. Dietary glycemic index, glycemic load, and digestible carbohydrate intake are not associated with risk of type 2 diabetes in eight European countries. *The Journal of Nutrition* 143:93-99. doi:10.3945/jn.112.165605.

Steele, EM, Baraldi, LG, Louzada, MLC, et al. 2017. Ultra-processed foods and added sugars in the US diet: evidence from a nationally representative cross-sectional study. *British Medical Journal Open* 6:e009892. doi:10.1136/bmjopen-2015-009892.

Taubes, G. 2017. The Case Against Sugar. Portobello Books: London.

Teicholz, N. 2015. The scientific report guiding the US dietary guidelines: is it scientific? *British Medical Journal* 351:h4962. doi:10.1136/bmj.h4962.

Tobias, DK, Chen, M, Manson, JE, *et al*. 2015. Effect of low-fat vs. other diet interventions on long-term weight change in adults: a systematic review and meta-analysis. *The Lancet Diabetes & Endocrinology* 3: 968-979. doi:10.1016/S2213-8587(15)00367-8.

Tsilas, CS, de Souza, RJ, Mejia, SB, *et al*. 2017. Relation of total sugars, fructose and sucrose with incident type 2 diabetes: a systematic review and meta-analysis of prospective cohort studies. *Canadian Medical Association Journal* 189:E711-720. doi:10.1503/cmaj.160706.

Vos, MB, Kaar, JL, Welsh, JA, *et al*. 2016. Added sugars and cardiovascular disease risk in children. A scientific statement from the American Heart Association. *Circulation* 135: e1017-1034. doi:10.1161/CIR.0000000000000439.

Willett, WC, Stampfer, MJ, Manson, JE, *et al*. 1993. Intake of trans fatty acids and risk of coronary heart disease among women. *The Lancet* 341:581-585. doi:10.1016/0140-6736(93)90350-p.

Yang, Q, Zhang, Z, Gregg, EW, *et al*. 2014. Added sugar intake and cardiovascular diseases mortality among US adults. *JAMA Internal Medicine* 174:516-524. doi:10.1001/jamainternmed.2013.13563.

Zong, G, Li, Y, Wanders, AJ, *et al*. 2016. Intake of individual saturated fatty acids and risk of coronary heart disease in US men and women: two prospective longitudinal cohort studies. *British Medical Journal* 355:i5796. doi:10.1136/bmj.i5796.

Chapter 4
Diets and Dietary Supplements

The Truth, the Whole Truth and Nothing but the Science

What Is a Healthy Diet?

A simple question:

What is the best healthiest diet for healthy ageing?

A simple answer:

A diet consisting of high dietary fibre (e.g. fruit, vegetables, legumes, whole grains) plus natural foods high in protein, minerals and vitamins (e.g. nuts, dairy, fish, poultry, meat), washed down with water and a little alcohol if desired, restrict intake of processed foods and sugar sweetened beverages (SSBs).

However, adopting a healthy diet also requires adopting a healthy lifestyle, particularly maintaining physical activity, not smoking and consuming alcohol in moderation, for healthy ageing.

Eating in moderation is a key factor here, given that, at least in the developed world but also increasingly in the developing world, there is an abundance of food, particularly cheap highly processed calorie-dense foods. Keeping a precise calorie count of your daily food intake is not that helpful, and in any case likely to be inaccurate (Chapter 3: Nutrition 101). One should be conscious of the empty calories from processed foods and beverages. Avoid the daily temptation of buying the large or jumbo-sized drink or food because it makes economic sense since it is cost-effective and costs not much more than the small or medium serving. However, the cost to your waistline and your health is simply not worth it.

Adopt the habit of selecting a smaller plate or bowl for your food choices both inside and outside your home. The psychology of food utensil size is the concept that people consume more when presented with larger size servings or utensils than compared with smaller size versions (Hollands *et al.*, 2015). However, that earlier review may have been compromised on the basis of low to moderate quality of the studies (e.g. small sample size) and possible bias in some of the reviewed studies, as reported in a very recent well-conducted study on plate size and food consumption (Kosite *et al.*, 2019)

Maintaining a healthy body weight, with BMI as a guide, certainly contributes to healthy ageing given that overweight individuals have a definite increase in risk factors for e.g. diabetes, cancer, stroke and heart disease (Lassale *et al.*, 2018; Khan *et al.*, 2018).

There are thousands of books and articles on what constitutes a healthy diet. It is beyond the scope of the present discussion to simply reiterate all that confusing, often contradictory, advice. Simply read the opening paragraphs of this Chapter, digest the information and apply to your current diet.

The advice provided is simple common sense and simply common knowledge, two factors which do not constitute a patentable, profitable or competitive commercial endeavour.

The Mythology of Diets and Weight Loss

There is a difference between a healthy diet and 'going on a diet' to lose weight. The latter subject is addressed in countless books, magazines and newspaper articles, generally all with a commercial outcome in mind. As previously mentioned (Chapter 3: Nutrition 101), the fact that there are so many 'best diets for losing weight' should immediately alert oneself to the very real possibility that diets to lose weight simply do not work, certainly not in the long term.

Almost any diet will result in some weight loss, some faster than others. The weight loss pattern is remarkably predictable, a rapid loss over a short time, generally a few weeks to a few months, then a much slower weight loss followed by a steady state in which weight loss approaches zero. The latter generally corresponds to non-compliance to the recommended diet, after which a return to the original pre-diet weight frequently occurs. Although non-compliance is a major factor, it is known that the human body adjusts to diet-induced weight loss and attempts to reach an equilibrium that corresponds to the long-established weight of the individual before the diet. Hormonal and protein changes which affect appetite may be factors. The microbes or microbiota in our gut (Chapter 7: The Gut Microbiota) also play a key role in the maintenance of body weight.

There is no doubt that weight-loss diets do work for some individuals but for the majority of individuals the 'lost' kilos are rapidly put back on once the discipline of conforming to the prescribed diet is lost. Maintaining a designated diet generally lasts much less than twelve months, even for the most dedicated of individuals. The commercial market for weight-loss diets is totally reliant on this observation.

Two very recent studies illustrate some of the issues relating to diets for weight loss. In a cohort (n = 609, mean age of 40, 57% female) of individuals with high BMI (28 to 40), a comparison was made of two diets, one termed a healthy low-fat diet and the other a healthy low-carbohydrate diet (Gardner et al., 2018). At the end of the twelve-month trial period there was no statistical difference in weight loss for the healthy low-fat (mean loss of 5.3 kg) or low-carbohydrate (mean loss of 6.0 kg) diets.

A second study (Sofi et al., 2018) examined a low-calorie vegetarian diet versus a Mediterranean diet (MD) in a cohort (n = 118, mean age of 51.1, 78% female) of overweight individuals (BMI ≥ 25) with a low to moderate cardiovascular risk profile in a three month cross-over trial, that is, one-half of the cohort went on the low-calorie vegetarian diet for three months and then, after a wash-out period, went on the MD for three months; the other half of the cohort reversed the diet profiles for the two three month periods.

Both diets were effective for weight loss, averaging around 2 kg loss for each three month period. On the other hand, there were measurable differences in lipid profiles with decreases in LDL-cholesterol and triglycerides (both biomarkers for cardiovascular disease) with the low-calorie vegetarian and Mediterranean diets respectively, the significance of which was unknown.

On the topic of an MD, there is much hype in the popular media as to the health benefits of an MD. The scientific literature also contains many hundreds of articles in peer-reviewed journals on the benefits of an MD. So, what is and what are the perceived benefits of an MD?

A typical MD consists of fresh fruit and vegetables, legumes, nuts, fish, poultry, moderate (< two servings/week) of red meat, cheese, yoghurt, minestrone soup and the ubiquitous use of olive oil. Importantly, it is traditional to take meals with family and friends with regular consumption of red wine (1-2 standard drinks/day). In rural communities, physical activity with attention to livestock and crops is also a lifestyle normality as is the consumption of local and seasonal foods e.g. fresh fruit and vegetables often home-grown or from family and neighbours. Basically, it's a combination of a healthy diet and a healthy lifestyle.

A review of eighteen observational studies and thirteen randomized controlled trials (RCTs), essentially a review of published systematic reviews and meta-analysis, concluded that there was moderate scientific evidence from observational studies that adherence to an MD was associated with decreased risk of mortality, diabetes, cardiovascular disease and neurological disorders (Dinu *et al.*, 2018). However, evidence from RCTs was relatively weak for measured health outcomes.

The most recent Cochrane review (data as of September 2018) reviewed thirty RCTs (n = 12,461 total participants, only trials with at least three months of follow-up) on the effectiveness of an MD diet on risk factors for cardiovascular disease and all-cause mortality in healthy individuals and in individuals at high risk of CVD and those with established CVD (Rees *et al.*, 2019).

The authors concluded that there were inconclusive outcomes of an MD in relation to risk factors for CVD in healthy adults and low to moderate quality of publications supporting modest outcomes in individuals at risk of CVD.

Nevertheless, there is one obvious fact (a belief or bias is not the same thing as a fact) that contradicts evidence that an MD is the secret to healthy ageing and is 'the best healthy diet."'

Try this simple question: if the MD is the healthiest or at least one of the healthiest diets, then one will expect that people born and living in countries known to adhere to this type of traditional diet will have the longest life expectancy and, more importantly, the longest healthy life expectancy.

Thus, the people of Spain, Italy and Greece, the three most exemplary of countries with a long-established indigenous population following a traditional MD, indeed have both a long life and a healthy life expectancy (Table 1 p. 154). However, now consider Australia, Canada and Japan, three comparable developed countries, with *totally different diets*. The life expectancies and healthy life expectancies of individuals living in these countries are almost identical to the three Mediterranean countries. For information, Table 1 also includes data for several other developed countries.

There is no doubt that an MD is healthy, at least by comparison to an unhealthy diet (or lifestyle), but one cannot conclude that an MD, as compared with any other diet characteristic of comparable developed countries, leads to any significant increase in healthy life expectancy.

And did someone say what about the keto diet, Paleo diet or intermittent fasting diet? (for the latter, see later section on Fasting and Calorie Restriction).

Pub Test 4.1:

Question:

Is the Mediterranean diet the key to health and, importantly, healthy ageing?

Answer:

No

The Mediterranean diet is certainly a healthy diet for individuals currently on an unhealthy diet (and unhealthy lifestyle). However, people living in comparable developed countries with diets radically different from the Mediterranean diet have just as long life expectancies and, importantly, healthy life expectancies.

After that digression, albeit an important one, we return to the topic of diets and weight loss. A very readable book on how to lose weight and, importantly, maintain that loss is written by two economists (Payne and Barnett, 2018), as opposed to experts on nutritional science or individuals with commercial interests.

The authors utilized their knowledge of economics to provide real-life situations and practical advice about how to reduce the amount of food consumed, lose weight and maintain that loss. One of their prime motivators was a daily weigh-in that they claimed to be a core factor in the success of their weight loss program.

Another simple and obvious advice was to adhere to more home-made meals and less take-away and eating out. Interestingly, a novel suggestion was that instead of spending, say, thirty minutes running on your treadmill spend thirty minutes on preparing a home-made meal.

The concept here is that one should adopt good eating habits first and then do some exercise rather than the other way around. In other words, do not rely on exercise to lose weight or maintain a good weight, it's the food intake that is the primary problem. The authors also state that a degree of self-discipline is required, i.e. no pain, no gain.

One should add that, having read many articles and books on diets, I have come to the conclusion that the general public would find this book a realistic guide to weight loss. (Warning: the book does not have a designated highly disciplined three-month diet plan about precisely when or what foods to eat. Thus, the plan may just be a realistic weight-loss program that actually maintains the weight loss).

Pub Test 4.2

Question:

Do weight-loss diets work

   (a) In the short-term?
   (b) In the long-term?

Answer:

   (a) In the short-term, Yes
       Most diets result in some weight loss in the short-term.
   (b) In the long-term, No
       Long-term (beyond one year) weight-loss diets do not work for the majority of individuals due to lack of compliance to the diet and the natural equilibrium of the body to return to a weight close to the pre-diet weight.

In discussing a healthy diet for healthy ageing, we reiterate outcomes from the previous Chapter 3:

- Fats in real food do not lead to weight gain
- Sugar from sugar-sweetened beverages, including energy drinks, sports drinks and fruit juices, comes in the form of liquid or empty calories
- Sugar (added or hidden sugar) in highly processed foods with few nutrients is a health hazard

A healthy diet should consist of real, natural food such as fruit, vegetables, nuts, legumes, whole grains, eggs, dairy, fish, poultry and meat. On that basis, what is the scientific evidence that real food is the best option?

The Really Good Stuff- Fruit and Vegetables

In the style of previous Chapters, only publications from recent years are discussed as it is recognized that scientific information, particularly on nutrition, is highly dynamic (translation: in the last decade, scientific studies have questioned long-held dogmas on human nutrition and health, particularly about fats and dairy).

There is consensus that, for a healthy diet profile, one should concentrate on an overall diet as in food groups rather than on a single or a few nutrients.

Thus, a recent systematic review of the scientific literature (data as of April 2017) concluded that a diet low in fruit, vegetables, whole grains and high in processed meats and sugar-sweetened beverages (SSBs) is a high risk factor for coronary heart disease (Micha et al., 2017). The authors quoted a 12 to 37% increased risk of coronary heart disease (CHD) for a diet based on unhealthy food groups and conversely 5 to 27% decreased risk for a diet based on healthy food groups.

In a similar systematic analysis (data as of March 2017) of food groups and risk factors for CHD, the authors provided statistical data for a range of food groups, comparing cases of highest intake with lowest intake (Bechthold *et al.*, 2017). In the case of fruit and vegetables, there were modestly lower risks of CHD of 11% and 8% respectively. Significantly larger differences were reported between highest and lowest intake of whole grains (15% decreased risk) and refined grains (11% increased risk). Similarly, for red meat and processed meat, at the highest intake there were a 16% and a 15% increased risks of CHD respectively. Interestingly, there was no association with high or low intake of dairy or eggs and risk of CHD.

In a large prospective cohort study (n = 135,335, mean 7.4 years of follow-up) in eighteen countries, a modest intake of fruit (one to two servings, 125-250 gm/day) was associated with a 14% and 21% decreased risk of cardiovascular and all-cause mortality respectively (Miller *et al.*, 2017). In the same study, consumption (> two servings/day) of raw vegetables lowered the risk (31%) of all-cause mortality significantly more than consumption (> two servings/day) of cooked vegetables (9%).

The very latest publications on fruit and vegetables emphasized the importance of healthy and unhealthy plant-based foods. In an impressive review of US health professionals (n = 209,298, 80% female, > 20 years of follow-up) it was concluded that a predominantly plant-based diet was inversely associated with modest risk (8% decreased risk) of coronary heart disease (Satija *et al.*, 2017). Most significantly, a healthy plant-based diet decreased risk by 25% as contrasted to an unhealthy plant-based diet which increased risk by 32%. The authors classified a healthy plant diet to consist of whole grains, fruit, vegetables, nuts and legumes (e.g. beans, lentils) and an unhealthy plant diet to consist of SSBs, fruit juices, refined grains (e.g. cereals, muffins, pasta) and desserts.

The research was based on self-reported food frequency questionnaires every two to four years over a twenty-year follow-up. It was also noted that participants on a healthy plant diet, as compared to those on an unhealthy plant diet, scored higher on socio-economic status, were more physically active, smoked less and had a lower BMI. The authors did adjust the statistics to allow for some of these confounders, nevertheless, it should be emphasized that the data demonstrated an association and not absolutely causal for risk of CHD.

The importance in the diet of dietary fibre and whole grains was emphasized in a recent review (n = 4,635, total participants), published in the Lancet, a top-ranked medical journal (Reynolds et al., 2018), of 185 prospective studies (data as of April 2017) and thirty-five clinical trials (data as of February 2018). In summary the authors reported, in comparing cohorts with the highest to lowest intake of dietary fibre, a 15% to 20% reduction in all-cause mortality and cardiovascular mortality and incidence of coronary heart disease, stroke, type 2 diabetes and colorectal cancer.

Pub Test 4.3:

Question:

Is dietary fibre important for healthy ageing?

Answer:

Yes

There is scientific consensus that dietary fibre from fruit, vegetables and whole grains is a key factor in healthy ageing. The quality of the dietary fibre is an important parameter, with fibre from low quality processed foods a negative factor. The latter foods are also likely to be high in sugar and salt.

Vegetarian Diet and Healthy Ageing

These observations lead to the obvious question, do individuals on a predominantly vegetarian diet live longer and, more importantly, have a longer healthier life, than those on non-vegetarian diets?

Support for this concept comes from early studies on Seventh Day Adventist (SDA) communities in the United States.

In a large cohort (n = 73,308, 6 years of follow-up) of SDAs, all-cause mortality risk of vegetarians and vegans as compared with non-vegetarians was decreased by 12% and 15% respectively (Orlich *et al.*, 2013). Diet was assessed by self-report food frequency questionnaires and adjustments were made for confounders including age, sex, exercise, smoking, alcohol and education.

A later review of eight studies (total participants n = 183,321) noted that the decreased risk of cardiovascular mortality in vegetarians as compared with non-vegetarians was only observed in studies on SDAs and not in other cohorts (Kwok *et al.*, 2014). In another study on SDAs, overall risk of cancers, as compared with non-vegetarians, was decreased by 8% and 16% in vegetarians and vegans respectively (Tantamango-Bartley *et al.*, 2013).

In a systematic review of the literature (until mid-2015), the authors concluded that the risk of all-cause mortality was not significantly different among vegans, vegetarians and non-vegetarians (Dinu *et al.*, 2017). However, a vegetarian diet decreased incidence and mortality from ischaemic heart disease (25% decrease) and incidence of total cancer (8% decrease).

The decreased risk of certain cancers in vegetarians was also noted in a large UK study (n = 60,310, approximately one-third vegetarians, 75% female, aged 40-50 at baseline) with a fifteen to thirty-four year follow-up (Appleby et al., 2016). Adjustments for confounders included smoking and BMI. It was noteworthy that this same study found no statistical difference in all-cause mortality risk among vegetarians, vegans and non-vegetarians.

Similarly, in a large population-based Australian cohort (n = 243,096, mean age of 62.3, mean 6.1 years of follow-up) there was no statistically significant difference in all-cause mortality risk between vegetarians and non-vegetarians (Mihrshahi et al., 2017). The authors acknowledged that although this was a very large cohort, only a relatively small number (n =1,523) of participants were classified as vegetarians.

In a 2019 study published in the *British Medical Journal*, a high-ranked medical journal, the risks of ischaemic heart disease and stroke in vegetarians, fish-eaters and meat-eaters with over eighteen years of follow-up were reported (Tong et al., 2019). This was a very large study of U.K. residents, consisting of vegetarians/vegans (n= 16,254, 75% female, mean age of 39.4), fish-eaters (n = 7,506, 82% female, mean age of 42.1, consumed fish but not meat) and meat-eaters (n = 24,428, 76% female, mean age of 49.0, consumed fish, dairy and eggs). Over the eighteen years of follow-up, 2,820 cases of ischaemic heart disease and 1,072 cases of stroke were recorded.

In comparison to meat-eaters, fish-eaters and vegetarians had a 13% and 22% decreased risk of ischaemic heart disease respectively. However, after adjustment for BMI, blood pressure, cholesterol and diabetes (all higher in meat-eaters, all risk factors for heart disease) the decreased risk in vegetarians was marginally significant at 10%.

On the other hand, in comparison to meat-eaters, vegetarians and fish-eaters had a 20% and 14% increased risk of stroke (ischaemic and haemorrhagic stroke) respectively. Adjustments for stroke risk factors (e.g. body mass index, blood pressure, diabetes) did not greatly influence these values.

Although the authors did appropriate adjustments for confounders, particularly age, it was noted that BMI, diabetes and blood pressure were lower and physical activity higher in fish-eaters and vegetarians in comparison to meat-eaters.

To make an informed decision about healthy ageing in vegetarians as compared with non-vegetarians, one has to appreciate that there are multiple vegetarian diets just as there are multiple non-vegetarian diets. Vegetarian diets range from vegans (strictly no animal products) to lacto-vegetarian (dairy) to lacto-ovo-vegetarian (dairy, eggs) to pesco-vegetarian (fish); non-vegetarian diets range from a healthy plant diet with dairy, fish and low-meat to an unhealthy plant diet with highly processed meat, low fish and a multitude of combinations involving processed foods, added sugars and SSBs.

In consulting the recent scientific references (as above) comparing vegetarian and non-vegetarian diets, the interested Reader may have noted that the diets of the non-vegetarian cohorts were not well defined. It is very likely that the latter would have included a substantial number of individuals with an unhealthy diet such as an unhealthy plant diet (processed grains, cereals), and high consumption of processed foods (including processed meat) plus sugar-sweetened beverages.

Moreover, the scientific literature (and common knowledge), frequently notes that vegetarians are more health conscious than non-vegetarians, for example, very aware of what they eat, more physically active, smoke and drink less. By default, a vegetarian diet is characteristically low in energy (calories), a positive outcome that translates into a lower BMI for individuals on a vegetarian diet as compared with those on a non-vegetarian diet (Rizzo et al., 2013; Appleby et al., 2016; Mihrshahi et al., 2017).

The lower BMI noted in vegetarians provides a plausible explanation for the reported lower incidence of certain cancers in vegetarians as compared with non-vegetarians given the well-established observation that risk of cancer increases with excess weight and obesity (Massetti et al., 2017).

Studies on health outcomes of vegetarian and non-vegetarian diets have taken into consideration different vegetarian diets but have failed to take into consideration different non-vegetarian diets and indeed different lifestyles. Thus, acknowledging the fact that vegetarians are particularly health conscious (e.g. consume less processed foods and sugar-sweetened beverages, smoke and drink less, are more physically active) then one needs to compare the long-term health outcomes of non-vegetarians and vegetarians with a *similar healthy lifestyle*, with diet (particularly meat) as the main difference between the two cohorts. The diet of healthy lifestyle non-vegetarians would consist of healthy plant foods (fresh fruit and vegetables, minimally processed carbohydrates), minimally processed foods, beverages low in sugar-sweetened drinks, fish, dairy and moderate amounts of red meat.

To the best of my knowledge, no study on comparing health outcomes in individuals classified as vegetarians (or vegans) and those classified as on a healthy non-vegetarian diet (including dairy, fish and meat) *and* with a healthy lifestyle has yet been published in a peer-reviewed scientific journal.

In summary, there is unequivocal scientific evidence that a healthy diet should incorporate fresh fruit and vegetables, fish, dairy, modest amounts of red meat and minimal amounts of highly processed foods and sugar-sweetened beverages. There is no scientific evidence, with the notable exception of studies on Seventh Day Adventists, that a vegetarian diet, including vegan, decreases risk of mortality (i.e. increases lifespan). On the other hand, there is evidence of a decreased risk of specific cancers in vegetarians as compared with non-vegetarians. However, this observation is debatable given the correlation of overweight and obesity with a wide range of cancers.

Vegetarians notably have lower BMIs than non-vegetarians and the latter cohort, at least in cohorts from the United States and Europe where the majority of studies have been conducted, would almost certainly consist of a large proportion (conservatively 20-30%) of individuals classified as overweight and obese individuals. Finally, one must take into consideration that a healthy diet is insufficient for healthy ageing without a healthy lifestyle, a topic that is further addressed in Chapters 5 and 6.

Pub Test 4.4:

Question:

Is a vegetarian or vegan diet better for *healthy* ageing than a healthy non-vegetarian diet?

Answer:

No

There is no published scientific evidence that a vegetarian or vegan diet is any better for healthy ageing than a *healthy* non-vegetarian diet that includes fruit, vegetables, dairy, fish and moderate intake of red meat (< two servings/week). Lifestyles (e.g. physical activity, social interactions, economic status) and not just a healthy diet play key roles in healthy ageing.

Fasting and Calorie Restriction

There is much hype on the benefits of fasting and calorie restriction (CR), but is there any meaningful scientific evidence that fasting or CR is truly beneficial for healthy ageing in humans?

Fasting has been practised by humans for thousands of years, either as part of a religious ritual (e.g. Ramadan, Lent) or in times of extreme hardship (e.g. drought). In recent times, numerous studies on rodents, the universal animal model system, have provided scientists with considerable data on the effects of fasting on animal physiology and behaviour (reviewed in Mattson *et al.,* 2017a). In general, the data indicate that fasting had positive health outcomes e.g. reduced weight, increased insulin sensitivity and improved parameters of cardiovascular health.

It is important to carefully and critically assess the various protocols adopted for animal studies by researchers, including methods for fasting that may include intermittent (extended periods of time with low or no calorie intake) and time-restricted feeding (e.g. calorie intake restricted to fixed times). The genetic strain and sex of the rodents, the selected diet and the degree of fasting all influence the data. The advantages of the rodent model system for the researcher are that experimental protocols can be strictly adhered to under laboratory conditions and the rodents do not provide feedback (e.g. are you happy?). This latter point is a key issue when one considers studies on long-term fasting and CR in free-living humans.

Scientific studies on fasting in humans in the past few decades have been largely confined to overweight and obese individuals and in general have proved to be relatively effective for weight loss. The long-term (> two years) benefits of fasting with respect to weight loss still awaits confirmation with compliance, as with all diets, a continuing issue. There have been very limited studies (certainly no large-scale and long-term) on the health effects of fasting in normal, healthy and non-overweight humans.

A variation of intermittent fasting in humans is the popular 5:2 weekly diet which refers to five days of normal diet and two days of very low-calorie diet (e.g. 500-750 calories/day). The two low-calorie days generally have at least one non-fasting day in between. Although the 5:2 diet is discussed at length in the popular media (e.g. magazines, newspapers and T.V.), there are simply no large-scale and long-term scientific studies on the health benefits or otherwise of the 5:2 diet.

There is no doubt that fasting results in stress to body metabolism (e.g. immune system, muscle loss) as well as requiring substantial disciplined adjustments to lifestyle (e.g. activity levels, when, what and how much to eat?).

The rodent (rats, mice) has also continued to be the animal model system of choice for CR studies ever since the original observations, over eighty years ago, demonstrating that laboratory rats feed a CR diet (30-50% less calories/day) lived significantly longer than rats feed a normal diet (McCay *et al.*, 1935).

One should be absolutely clear what a 'normal' diet is for a laboratory rat, as this is a key point in any critical analysis of CR studies on laboratory animals. The term *ad libitum* (Latin for 'according to pleasure') is used in reference to laboratory-fed animal studies and simply means animals are allowed to freely feed, an all-you-can-eat buffet in human terms. Thus, it is not unusual for laboratory animals, and rats and mice are no exception, to be overweight or approaching obesity.

By contrast, CR rats, at 30% to 50% less calories/day, are substantially smaller (translation: growth retarded) than *ad libitum* control rats (Ingram and Cabo, 2017). The CR rats may be clinically healthier (e.g. leaner, improved cardiovascular and insulin sensitivity parameters) but have lower fertility rates and are constantly hungry and cold (lower body temperature). Moreover, the smaller body weight means that they are easily dominated by larger males and females, a factor that can be controlled in an artificial laboratory environment but is a distinct disadvantage in the wild. More recent studies on rodents have indicated that lifespan can be increased on less drastic diets of between 10% and 25% CR (Ingram and Cabo, 2017).

To date, the most significant and relevant studies, with respect to humans, on CR and healthy ageing have been on non-human primates, namely the rhesus monkey. These long-term studies were commenced in the 1980s and conducted in the USA at the University of Wisconsin-Madison (UWM) and the National Institute of Aging-Baltimore (NIA). The rhesus monkey serves as an excellent model for human ageing, given their relatively long life-span (30 to 40 years), a similar anatomy and physiology to humans and with a 93% DNA similarity to humans (Gibbs, 2007).

Data from the UWM studies showed that CR (25% to 30% decreased daily calories, n = 23 male, n = 15 female) increased lifespan (two to four years) in rhesus monkeys as compared with *ad libitum* fed controls (n = 38, 23 male, 15 female) (Colman *et al.*, 2014). Both CR and controls (adults aged 7 to 14 at onset) were fed the same diet, just less for the CR, with the important difference that the CR animals received an additional dietary supplement of vitamins and minerals to prevent possible dietary deficiency.

However, there was considerable angst in the scientific community when the outcomes from the NIA studies were published; there was no statistically significant difference in survival between control and CR animals (Mattison et al., 2012). The NIA animals (n = 62 male, n = 59 female) at onset consisted of essentially three distinct groups: juvenile (aged 1 to 5), adult (aged 7 to 15) and old (aged 16 to 23).

A comprehensive reappraisal of these contradictory outcomes was published in 2017 in *Nature Communications*, a highly ranked journal, in which the authors critically analyzed the data from both studies and concluded that, overall, CR indeed had benefits that had application to human health (Mattison et al., 2017b).

The interested Reader is encouraged to read, and digest, the information provided in the publication (warning: it will take considerable time to thoroughly understand the data and a non-biased approach is essential).

The authors concluded that, in the NIA studies, the control animals were in fact somewhat calorie restricted in that the bodyweights of the controls were significantly lower (10% to 15%) than the average for captive rhesus monkeys (obtained from a comprehensive database). In the NIA studies both control and CR animals were fed exactly the same diets, including a vitamin and mineral supplement, except that the CR animals were simply fed less.

Moreover, and most importantly, the control animals were not *ad libitum* fed, and were instead fed according to a predetermined amount depending on age, sex and height. The NIA diet was higher in protein, higher in fibre and lower in fat than the UWM diet which was also much higher in sucrose (28.5% UWM, 3.9% NIA). In other words, the NIA animals (control and CR) were on a healthy diet, including the vitamin and mineral supplements.

In summary, in the NIA study both the controls and CR animals were 10% to 15% and 21% to 22% respectively lower in body weight than the average for captive rhesus monkeys. The latter may, in fact, be somewhat overweight, given that captive animals are generally fed *ad libitum* and thus favouring a tendency to overeat, a possible characteristic of boredom.

The authors, nevertheless, concluded that the NIA control animals were, in fact, partially calorie restricted and further calorie restriction, as in the test CR animals, provided no further benefit. However, one may apply a similar argument to the UWM studies in which the UWM controls were 18% to 19% more and the CR 11% to 12% less than the average body weight of captive rhesus monkeys.

Thus, one is comparing the health outcomes of CR animals with that of a cohort of overweight (a known health hazard) control animals. Indeed, the CR animals in this case may well represent a 'normal' weight, on the assumption, and it is only an assumption, that captive rhesus monkeys fed *ad libitum* may be somewhat overweight or at least not at optimum (read: healthy) weight.

It is noteworthy that in both the NIA and UWM studies, clinical parameters of age-related conditions (e.g. arthritis, cataracts) and, to a lesser degree, age-related diseases (e.g. cardiovascular, diabetes) in the CR animals were significantly positive as compared with the controls, although the NIA results were somewhat mixed. These observations were consistent with the longer survival of the UWM-CR animals but were inconsistent with the NIA experimental outcomes. The NIA data (on-going as of the end of 2017) also projected that the young/juvenile cohort (aged 1- 5 at onset of CR) was at a higher survival risk as compared to controls, thus indicating a potential negative effect of CR in these younger animals.

Early reports of CR in humans were not promising, given some of the side-effects e.g. constant hunger and cold (lower core body temperature), akin to the early studies on rodents. The more recent studies in which CR was set at less drastic levels of 25% less calories/day have provided more encouraging results.

Here again, the interested Reader will note that in essentially all human studies reporting a baseline of CR at 25%, as the studies progress, the actual CR levels drop dramatically, and generally equilibrated at around 15% after six months and 10% to 15% at twelve months. In other words, compliance, as in the case of all diets, is a major issue and humans are, after all, free-living individuals, unlike laboratory animal model systems.

There is solid scientific evidence that dieting in the form of fasting and CR is an effective way of losing weight and improving the health status of overweight and obese individuals (Trepanowski et al., 2018). The pattern of weight loss in these studies follows the classical changes noted in conventional dieting: upon adoption of the intervention (fasting or CR), there is an initial relatively rapid weight loss (three to six months), after which there is little weight loss (six to twelve months) followed by a period of gradual weight gain, frequently equilibrating at a weight close to the initial weight of the individual. This classic pattern, of course, depends on the motivation and self-determination of the individual to really make both diet and lifestyle changes.

However, we concentrate here on scientific studies on CR involving relatively non-obese individuals with respect to health and healthy ageing. In 2015, the first scientific study on long-term (twenty-four months) CR in non-obese and moderately overweight individuals was published (Ravussin *et al.*, 2015).

This study appeared in the *Journal of Gerontology-Medical Sciences*, the official journal of the Gerontological Society of America. Participants (at baseline, aged 21-51, 70% female, BMI 22-28 [mean of 25.1], dietary intake approximately 2,400 cals/day) were divided into a CR cohort (n = 117) and a cohort designated as *ad libitum* (AL) or normal diet (n = 71). At baseline, CR was set at 25% less calories/day as compared with the AL cohort.

At six months, the average CR was 19.5%, and this decreased to 12% at twelve months and <10% at eighteen to twenty-four months. There was little change in weight at twenty-four months in the AL cohort. By contrast, in the CR cohort, there was a relatively rapid weight loss, averaging 7.1 kg after six months, followed by little change in weight at eighteen to twenty-four months, stabilizing at 7.6 kg weight loss after twenty-four months.

In a follow-up study (Marlatt *et al.*, 2017) to test if weight loss was maintained beyond the original twenty-four months' trial, but without further monitoring of calorie intake, individuals (66% female) were allocated into an original CR cohort (n = 18, 11 of whom were designated as overweight) and an original AL cohort (n = 11). In the CR cohort that recorded an average weight loss of 9.1 kg at twenty-four months after the original CR trial, after a further twelve months (without monitoring of calorie intake), this reduced to an average weight loss of 5.1 kg and after a further twelve months, this was reduced to an average weight loss of 4.1 kg. Thus, although weight loss was maintained after twenty-four months follow-up (without monitoring of calorie intake), there was a gradual weight gain.

On the other hand, as the authors had stated, one could interpret these observations as a positive effect of CR given that there was a net weight loss of about 4.1 kg in the forty-eight months' time frame, a significantly long-term effect for a weight-loss program. In a further follow-up study (CR n = 34, AL n = 19, 70% female), clinical parameters related to cardiovascular health (e.g. lower total cholesterol and triglycerides) also improved in the CR cohort as compared with the AL cohort (Most et al., 2018).

In another phase of these studies, urine samples from participants in the twenty-four months' CR trial (remember these were highly motivated participants) were analyzed for F2-isoprostanes as a measure of oxidative stress (see this Chapter, Dietary Supplements). Levels of F2-isoprostanes were significantly lower in the CR cohort (n = 143) as compared with the AL cohort (n = 75), indicative of less oxidative stress (Il'yasova et al., 2018).

Oxidative stress has been proposed as a biological marker of ageing, the lower the value the slower the ageing process. However, it is known that weight loss in overweight or obese women, not on a CR diet, is also associated with lower F2-isoprostane levels (Duggan et al., 2016). Moreover, in the NIA ageing study on rhesus monkeys, significantly lower F2-isoprostane levels in CR animals, as compared with AL animals, did not translate into any advantage with respect to longevity or mortality (Mattison et al., 2012).

In all of these studies, participants were carefully supervised to monitor adherence to the CR diet and clinical parameters (e.g. weight, cardiovascular assessments, resting metabolic rate) were periodically measured. The researchers also noted that participants were highly motivated and self-disciplined in their approach to the CR protocol. Overall, compliance with the objective of 25% CR decreased with time, averaging 15% to 20% at six months, 10% to 15% at twelve months and < 10% at eighteen to twenty-four months.

It is highly unlikely that the general population will be motivated to adopt a 20% CR diet any time soon, requiring constant vigilance of calorie intake, given lifestyle (e.g. physical activity, career objectives) and lifelong commitments (e.g. family, friends, birthdays, weddings, funerals). However, a 10% CR diet may just be plausible (how about simply state 'eat less?').

To put this in perspective, and taking into account that commonly proposed calorie intakes for a moderately active male and female (e.g. aged 25-50) on a typical Western-style diet are 2,500 and 2,000 calories/day respectively, then this equates to 200 to 250 calories/day less for a 10% CR diet (double those calories for a 20% CR diet).

A 10% CR diet is feasible if one considers that a medium apple or banana is around 100 calories, a serving (375 ml) of a soft drink/soda or beer is approximately 140 calories, two large fried eggs around 160 calories, a blueberry or banana muffin 300 calories and a BigMac medium meal (burger, fries, coke) a whopping 1,000 calories.

These are simply examples, and keep in mind that calories from drinks (e.g. sugar-sweetened beverages [liquid calories]) or highly processed foods are quite different from calories from natural foods (e.g. eggs, fruit, vegetables) as discussed in the previous Chapter.

It is no secret that if you are overweight, then losing some weight will have health benefits, particularly if one maintains a long-term healthy weight, and thus a plus for healthy ageing.

I should state that in my (biased) opinion, *both fasting and calorie restriction are essentially extreme variations of diet protocols.*

I make no apologies for outlining at length a critique of studies on calorie restriction or fasting given that these topics are currently featured in the popular media. One finds it very difficult to understand why anybody wants to subject themselves to an extreme eating protocol in one of the pleasures of life, that is, eating good food in the company of family, friends and colleagues. This is one of the cornerstones of healthy ageing.

The following cautionary tale should be kept in mind when one is considering any nutritional diet for healthy ageing: be careful what you wish for.

Sharon (a retired nutritional scientist) and Kevin (a retired financial advisor) (real names withheld for privacy reasons) have lived a comfortable life in a spacious home with views of Sydney Harbour and the Opera House. Now in their mid-eighties, they finally decide to take that dream vacation, a luxury round-the-world cruise on the *Queen Mary* and then flying first class back to Sydney. Unfortunately, the plane crashes on the way home and they both end up in Heaven.

Their Guardian Angel, Jenny (real name withheld for privacy reasons), shows them their new home: a luxury mansion with swimming pool, sauna, home theatre etc. Kevin says: 'We can't afford it. Who is going to pay the mortgage?' The Guardian Angel replies: 'You're in Heaven. Nobody has a mortgage.'

The next morning, there is a sumptuous buffet breakfast laid out, and Sharon says: 'All that food. We'll put on weight.'

The Guardian Angel replies: 'Don't stress. After all you're in Heaven. You can eat as much as you like. Nobody puts on weight.'

Just then, Kevin looks out the window and sees a magnificent golf course and the clubhouse in the background. 'How much does it cost to join the club and play a round of golf?'

The Guardian Angel replies: 'Relax Kevin, you're in Heaven. It's free and won't cost you a cent.'

Kevin thinks for a minute, turns to Sharon and says: 'You and that 20% CR diet. To think we could have been here years ago!'

Pub Test 4.5:

Question:

Does a calorie restriction diet (20 to 25% decrease in daily calorie intake) add years to a healthy lifespan?

Answer:

No

The evidence is simply not there. Maintaining, for example, a 20% calorie restriction (CR) diet for more than six months is extremely difficult for even the most dedicated individual.

There are so many issues related to calorie restriction that to recommend it to maintain health and as a means for healthy ageing in free-living humans is non-sensible.

For example, at what age should one commence the CR diet? How long does it take to maintain the CR diet? What level of CR - 10%, 20% - is deemed beneficial? What can or can't you eat, and what about nutrient deficiency? What about physical activity and can one really fully participate in social and competitive sport? What are the social consequences of daily interactions with family, friends or work colleagues, especially in relation to eating and drinking?

And while on the topic of CR, please don't mention intermittent fasting. Similar issues as listed above also apply. *Simply eat less.*

Dietary Supplements

The previous topics on nutrition may have challenged the readers' biases but the topic of dietary supplements is perhaps even more challenging.

The term *dietary supplement* generally refers to vitamins, minerals, antioxidants, fish oil (omega-3 fatty acids) and herbal (primarily plant) products that are taken in the form of a tablet, capsule or liquid. These are commercial products classified as foods, not medicines, and are thus not regulated or subject to intense human clinical trials.

The only regulatory requirement is that the supplement is safe and does not cause harm, but even those requirements are loosely applied and dependent on consumer reports of any adverse effects to the appropriate regulatory body (e.g. the US Food and Drug Administration). A very readable (and freely available) overview of regulations in various countries and public health issues related to dietary supplements was recently published in *Annual Review of Public Health* (Binns et al., 2018).

Although the dietary supplements cannot claim to treat or cure a particular disease that has not deterred manufacturers to make claims about the efficacy of their supplements as in statements on the labels e.g. 'for healthy heart/brain/ immune function, for daily wellbeing and vitality, for stress reduction' or vague statements such as 'may relieve joint pain', 'reduces severity of colds' etc. without providing any proof for these statements.

Because the supplements are available in pharmacies and indeed in supermarkets, most consumers assume that the supplements have been clinically tested in human trials or at least regulated by medical bodies. This is simply not the case.

The most popular supplements are multivitamins and minerals (frequently taken as a mixture), with omega-3 fatty acids (commonly taken as fish oil supplements) and antioxidants also extremely widely used.

Vitamin and Mineral Supplements

The popularity of vitamin supplements is based, firstly, on the knowledge that vitamins are essential for human health. Notwithstanding that only small amounts are required, from a few micrograms (e.g. vitamin B12, 2.5 µg/day) to milligrams (e.g. vitamin B6, 1.5 mg/day), it is supposed that more is even better for health. Secondly, vitamin and mineral supplements (e.g. calcium, zinc, magnesium, selenium) are taken as an insurance policy based on the premise that a poor or unhealthy diet requires additional vitamins and minerals as supplements.

Thirdly, the ingenious and at times misleading advertising of these supplements have created a consumer market obsessed by the concept of eternal youth and anti-ageing therapies.

Perhaps most importantly, the decision to take dietary supplements also provides the individual the opportunity to take a more active role in their own health care and thus imposes a measure of individual responsibility and control as opposed to dependence on conventional medicine.

So, who actually takes dietary supplements? Reliable data are available for a number of countries. In Australia, the most recent data (n = 19,257) show that 50% of the female and 35% of the male adult population take daily supplements in some form or another, predominantly multivitamins and minerals with a relatively high 10% taking fish oil supplements (O'Brien *et al.*, 2017).

In the USA, a survey (n = 37,958, mean age of 46.4, 52% female) from 1999 to 2012 showed that approximately 60% of females and 50% of males take supplements, again predominantly multivitamins and minerals (Kantor *et al.*, 2016).

There was intriguing data from Europe which suggested a north/south divide in the taking of dietary supplements (Skeie *et al.*, 2009). The percentage of consumers taking supplements, predominantly multivitamins and minerals, in the adult UK population (n = 1,283, 60% female) was reported to be approximately 45% for both females and males. Supplement use in Denmark (n = 3,917) was reported as 66% of females and 51% of males and in Sweden (n = 6,050) it was 41% female and 31% male.

By contrast, supplement use in the south of Europe was substantially lower. In Greece (n = 2,684), only 2% of males and

7% of females were reported as taking supplements and in Italy (n = 3,953), 7% and 13% for males and females respectively with similar figures for Spain (n = 3,220). Supplement intake in France and Germany was somewhat in-between the north/south divide with 21% and 27% for males and females respectively in Germany (n = 4,415).

Given that the life expectancy and, importantly, the healthy life expectancy of individuals living in of all these European countries, Australia, the UK and the USA are very similar (see Table 1), one could conclude that taking dietary supplements of multivitamins and minerals may have little influence on healthy ageing.

The demographics of individuals taking dietary supplements are most intriguing. Numerous studies have reported that the typical profile is an individual of middle to high socio-economic status, of above-average education level, physically active, consuming a good quality diet and with a healthy BMI (Rock, 2007; Dickinson and MacKay, 2014). Females and the elderly are also more likely to be taking dietary supplements.

A large observational study (n = 37,193, aged ≥ 45, 16 years of follow-up) in women concluded no association between multivitamin use and major cardiovascular events, including stroke and mortality (Rautiainen *et al.*, 2015). An even larger observational study, the Nurses' Health Study (n = 86,142, women aged 34-59 at baseline, 32 years of follow-up), also concluded that multivitamin use was not associated with decreased risk of stroke or mortality (Adebamowo *et al.*, 2017).

Similarly, a large observational study of men, the Physicians' Health Study (n = 18,530, aged ≥ 40 with n = 3,790 taking multivitamins at baseline, 12 years of follow-up), concluded that there was no significant decrease in risk in major cardiovascular events with multivitamin use (Rautiainen et al., 2016). Interestingly, individuals who self-reported use of multivitamins for ≥ 20 years, had a decreased risk of major cardiovascular events. However, these observations were based on very small numbers (e.g. eighteen major cardiovascular events and nine cardiovascular-associated deaths) and hence this association may not be statistically strong.

In a 2016 Editorial (Cohen, 2016) entitled 'The supplement paradox: negligible benefits, robust consumption' in the official *Journal of the American Medical Association*, a summary was presented on the scientific consensus about the outcomes of decades of published research on dietary supplements.

Further confirmation of the minimal benefits of dietary supplements was recently published in the *Journal of the American College of Cardiology* (Jenkins et al., 2018). This was a comprehensive review of multivitamin and mineral supplements and their influence on all-cause mortality and cardiovascular disease. The review covered publications (initially 1,496 publications) in the period January 2012 to October 2017, from which the authors excluded e.g. duplications, small studies, studies of short duration (< six months), and others of low-quality evidence to eventually review 179 peer-reviewed publications of randomized controlled trials (RCTs) deemed to be of high quality.

In summary, it was concluded that multivitamin and mineral supplements (e.g. vitamins C and D, beta-carotene and calcium all taken alone or multivitamins taken generally with minerals,) had no effect on all-cause mortality or prevention of cardiovascular disease or stroke. On the other hand, there was a small increase in risk, 6% to 9%, of all-cause mortality in the case of antioxidant supplements. By contrast, folic acid alone or in combination with B-vitamins reduced risk of stroke, 20% and 10% decrease respectively.

However, it should be noted that the outcomes for folic acid alone was highly skewered by the observations of a large randomized clinical trial, the China Stroke Primary Prevention Trial (n = 20,702, mean age of 60, 59% female, 5 years of follow-up), in an area of China where there was no folic acid fortification of grain products (e.g. bread, flour, cereals) which by comparison was mandatory in > 80 countries including North America, Australia and New Zealand. It should be further noted that the trial specifically involved individuals who were hypertensive and on blood pressure lowering medication (Enalapril or Enalapril plus folic acid), and thus, the question remained if folic acid supplementation would decrease risk of stroke in non-hypertensive individuals.

A review covering the scientific literature published between 1970 and 2016 concluded that, for the general public, there was no benefit to cardiovascular health from multivitamin and mineral supplementation (Kim *et al.*, 2018). The authors included both observational studies as well as clinical trials involving a total of over two million participants with an average twelve year follow-up (eighteen studies included).

Two very recent (2019) publications, both published in *Annals of Internal Medicine*, one of the world's most cited medical journals, confirmed that dietary supplements had limited effects on cardiovascular health or mortality.

One study comprised data from 30,899 U.S. adults (mean age of 47, 6.1 years of follow-up) and compared nutrient intake from food versus dietary supplement (Chen *et al.*, 2019). The authors reported, for example, that a lower risk of cardiovascular disease was associated with nutrients (vitamin A, vitamin K and zinc) from foods not from supplements and lower risk of mortality associated with nutrients (vitamin K and magnesium) from foods not from supplements.

The second study (Khan *et al.*, 2019), an umbrella review of systematic reviews and randomized clinical trials, concluded that: '..nutritional supplements, such as vitamin B6, vitamin A, multivitamins, antioxidants, and iron and dietary interventions, such as reduced fat intake, had no significant effect on mortality or cardiovascular disease outcomes.'

Pub Test 4.6:

Question:

Does taking multivitamin and mineral supplements have benefits for healthy ageing?

Answer:

No

There is simply no good evidence that multivitamin and mineral supplements will extend healthy ageing lifespan. A healthy diet will provide all the necessary vitamins and minerals for good health.

[Footnote: It is well established that folate (B-type vitamin) is essential for proper health and development, particularly for babies during early pregnancy for the prevention of neural tube defects such as spina bifida].

Antioxidant Supplements

Two currently popular dietary supplements are antioxidants and fish oil supplements. The review by Jenkins *et al.* (2018) included antioxidant supplements and a recent analysis showed a small but significant increase in risk (6-9%) of all-cause mortality with antioxidant supplements which was in agreement with previous findings over a decade ago (Bjelakovic *et al.*, 2007).

A brief discussion of the background to the popularity of antioxidant supplements is presented here, and the interested Reader will readily find further information on this topic in a multitude of outlets, including books, magazines, newspapers and, of course, the internet. A word of caution here, with particular reference to the internet - many of these outlets are linked to commercial interests (translation: selling antioxidant products).

Claims about the efficacy of antioxidant supplements require application of rigorous scientific evidence and, frankly, the evidence is essentially non-existent. Statements such as 'clinically tested' and 'scientifically proven' are meaningless as much of the data are presented in leaflets produced commercially in-house or published in low-profile journals involving short-term trials with inadequate number of participants and controls with ill-defined outcomes. On the other hand, it should be noted that there is considerable high-quality scientific research on the characterization and mechanisms of action of antioxidant compounds in foods, particularly of plant origin.

However, their *efficacy as dietary supplements* in humans has proved to be extremely modest at best, with the scientific data actually indicating a negative effect. We return to the original theme (see opening paragraphs of this Chapter) that intake of antioxidants is best through healthy, natural and minimally processed foods.

The concept of antioxidants as protective to health is based on the original proposal on a mechanism for ageing by Harman (Harman, 1956) generally known as *'the free radical theory of ageing,'* or sometimes as *'the mitochondrial free radical theory of ageing.'*

Mitochondria are small (approximately 0.5 to 10 micrometers, about the same size of some bacteria) subcellular organelles found in the cells of all plants, fungi and animals. Mitochondria require oxygen to convert chemical energy from nutrients into biological energy in the form of adenosine triphosphate or ATP. Almost all (> 95%) of the energy requirements of human cells, in the form of ATP, is produced by the mitochondria in the process termed oxidative phosphorylation. Mitochondria are thus essential to all forms of life dependent on oxygen (note the previously mentioned test: try not breathing oxygen for five minutes).

Briefly, every time one breathes by taking in oxygen, the by-products of this process (an estimated 2% of the available oxygen) generates 'free radicals' in the form of superoxide radical, hydroxyl radical, or oxygen-derived reactive species e.g. hydrogen peroxide. In turn, these highly reactive free radicals and oxygen species may interact and damage our proteins, lipids, carbohydrates and DNA, the results of which may lead to cellular ageing, thus the concept of the *free radical theory of ageing*. The term *oxidative stress* is also frequently used to describe the potential for oxygen-derived reactive species to damage or stress biological systems.

Antioxidants are seen as the good guys in that they are capable of neutralizing and thus inactivating free radicals, and, *voila*, by taking antioxidant supplements we have no more ageing and thus eternal youth. At least that's how the advertising goes in the popular health magazines.

An inconvenient known fact is that the human body has a multitude of antioxidant defence systems that are tightly controlled to maintain a healthy equilibrium: the Goldilocks state, not too much antioxidant, not too little but just right. Another inconvenient known fact is that free radicals and oxygen-derived reactive species are essential for health such as in neutralizing and killing invasive bacteria via reactive oxygen species produced by defensive macrophages. Moreover, free radicals and reactive oxygen species act as key signalling molecules, termed redox signalling, to activate or inactivate essential metabolic pathways including the body's defences and the immune system.

Apart from mitochondria, the production of free radicals and reactive oxygen species also occurs in most cell types as part of normal metabolism. Importantly, biological cells maintain a fine equilibrium (termed homeostasis) by neutralizing excess reactive oxygen species by a complex network of enzymatic (e.g. superoxide dismutase, glutathione oxidase/reductase) and non-enzymatic (e.g. vitamins C and E, glutathione) systems.

Perturbation of this finely balanced system, as in taking antioxidant supplements, may lead to unforeseen health issues. On the other hand, consumption of antioxidants in the form of real food has not been scientifically demonstrated to be a health hazard. Antioxidant supplements may be chemically identical to the antioxidants in food, but the latter comes with the added bonus of a complex food matrix the nature of which significantly alters the way the digestive and metabolic systems process the antioxidants.

Pub Test 4.7:

Question:

Does taking antioxidant supplements provide positive health outcomes?

Answer:

No

Several decades of scientific studies clearly show that antioxidant supplements provide little health benefit and indeed may even have a negative health outcome. By comparison, intake of antioxidants via a healthy diet such as real, minimally processed food has substantial health benefits.

Fish Oil or Omega-3 Supplements

Fish oil supplements (also known as omega-3 fatty acids or DHA and EPA) are extremely popular. They have been advertised as essential for brain health, promoting a healthy heart, as anti-inflammatory agents, and even as treatment for depression and dementia. If all this sounds too good to be true, it is. So, what is the basis of these claims?

The scientific and public interest in fish oil supplements can be traced back to the 1970s in publications by Danish scientists in which it was reported that Inuits or Eskimos living in northern Greenland had a relatively low incidence of cardiovascular disease as compared with the general population (Fodor *et al.*, 2014, and references therein). This observation was attributed to the high intake of fatty fish, particularly whale and seal, by the indigenous population.

These observations have spawned an immense industry based on the hypothesis that fish oils have health benefits, particularly for cardiovascular health. Unfortunately, this hypothesis suffers from one simple, ugly fact, and that is that heart disease is just as prevalent, perhaps even more so, in the Inuit population living in the Arctic environment as compared to the general population (Fodor *et al.*, 2014, and references therein). Indeed, the life expectancy of the Inuit is substantially lower, about five to ten years lower, than for a comparable, non-indigenous population living in Denmark and Canada (Wilkins *et al.*, 2008; Ellsworth and O'Keeffe, 2012).

Moreover, studies on fish oil supplements over the past two decades have produced little evidence for health benefits with data showing no or at best a very modest positive effect. A recent Cochrane review (data as of April 2017) covering seventy-nine randomized controlled trials (total participants, n = 112,059) of at least twelve months' duration concluded that there was little or no effect of omega-3 fatty acid supplementation on all-cause mortality or cardiovascular health (Abdelhamid *et al.*, 2018).

In a 2018 comprehensive review of ten clinical trials (mean duration of 4.4 years) involving n = 77,917 high-risk individuals (mean age of 64, 38.6% female), the authors concluded that omega-3 fatty acid supplementation had no significant effect on cardiovascular mortality or any major vascular events (Aung *et al.*, 2018).

Similarly, claims for beneficial effects of omega-3 supplements on brain function, including Alzheimer's, had been proved to be unsubstantiated (reviews in Burckhardt *et al.*, 2016; Canhada *et al.*, 2017). For example, in an eighteen-month randomized controlled trial study of cognitive health in older adults (n = 390, mean age of 73.1), fish oil supplements, as compared with an olive oil placebo, did not maintain or improve cognitive performance (Danthiir *et al.*, 2018).

Let us now apply the same simple test, akin to that for the Mediterranean diet, and ask the question; do people living in countries (e.g. Iceland, Norway, Japan, South Korea) with a diet high in fish live longer and have a longer healthy lifespan than people living in countries (e.g. Germany, France, Australia) with a moderate intake of fish?

The answer is no (see Table 1). (Note: it is important that the comparison is made with countries of comparable economic status and with respect to levels of health care, education and welfare). Nevertheless, it is universally accepted that fish should be an integral part of a healthy diet.

Pub Test 4.8:

Question:

Does taking fish oil supplements (omega-3 fatty acids) have clear health benefits related to cardiovascular health and brain development or slow/prevent the onset of dementia/Alzheimer's?

Answer:

No

There is little evidence for health benefits of fish oil supplements despite many decades of scientific research. On the other hand, there is reasonable evidence that dietary intake of fish has positive health benefits.

Conduct Your Personal Pub Test on Dietary Supplements

In summary, research over the past few decades have provided little scientific evidence for the efficacy or health benefits of dietary supplements consisting of multivitamins, minerals, fish oil and antioxidants.

Nevertheless, if you take dietary supplements and feel strongly that they have a definite positive influence on your personal health, then by all means continue taking them. Clearly, they are beneficial to your health: the benefit may well be due to the well-known placebo effect, the strong belief that a certain intervention will have a positive effect.

There are several tests that one should perform in order to confirm the efficacy or otherwise of the dietary supplement in question.

Firstly, critically review all the individuals (family, friends, family doctor, social media etc) and information resources that you have consulted with respect to the dietary supplement(s) you are taking (apart from Google, you have consulted the scientific literature, haven't you?). Now, apply the *Pub Test* (ideally actually go to the pub or bar and explain to an interested group of associates why you are taking your favourite dietary supplement; this is most effective after a few drinks).

Secondly, what are the levels (before and after you take the supplements) in your body of the supplements in question? This is not always possible as determination of the concentrations of some dietary supplements require highly specialized technology. Nevertheless, concentrations of some vitamins (e.g. B12, B6, D [as 25-hydroxy vitamin D], E [as alpha-tocopherol] can all be readily determined (at a cost) from a blood sample as can omega-3 fatty acids (fish oil) and F2-isoprostanes (measure of oxidative stress/free radical activity).

Most individuals taking dietary supplements have no idea about their actual levels in their own body. For example, if you are a strict vegetarian (vegan) then it will be important to check out your levels of vitamin B12, as this essential vitamin is found predominantly in meat (also in fish, dairy and fortified cereals) and thus you may actually need a supplement of vitamin B12.

Thirdly, continue taking the supplement for three to four weeks, then stop taking the supplement for three to four weeks (termed the wash-out period) and then recommence the supplement for three to four weeks. Try to make an informed decision about your comparative wellness before the wash-out period, at the end of the wash-out period and after recommencement of the supplement. This is the crucial test and also the most difficult. It confronts our innermost biases, with the irresistible need to conclude that the supplement is essential for our wellness, indeed it may well be so. Again, ideally, your lifestyle and environment (e.g. diet, exercise, work, family, social engagements) should all be similar in all three phases of the test periods.

This is why scientists use laboratory animals, especially rodents, so that the experimental environment is kept constant before, during and after an experimental procedure. Humans, by contrast, are mostly free-living individuals and do not conform to strict (artificial) laboratory conditions. Welcome to the real world of human food nutrition research.

Table 1

Life Expectancy (LE) and Healthy Life Expectancy (HLE)

	Female		Male	
	LE	HLE	LE	HLE
Australia	85	74	81	72
Canada	85	74	81	72
Denmark	83	73	79	71
Finland	84	74	79	70
France	86	75	80	72
Germany	83	73	79	70
Greece	84	74	79	71
Iceland	84	74	81	72
Italy	85	74	81	72
Japan	87	77	81	73
Korea	86	75	80	71
Netherlands	83	73	80	71
Spain	86	75	80	72
Sweden	84	73	81	72
UK	83	73	80	70
USA	81	70	76	67

Data adapted from World Health Statistics, World Health Organization apps.who.int

Abdelhamid, AS, Brown, TJ, Brainard, JS, *et al.* 2018. Omega-3 fatty acids for the primary and secondary prevention of cardiovascular disease (Review). *Cochrane Database of Systematic Reviews* 7:CD003177. doi:10.1002/14651858.CD003177.pub3.

Adebamowo, SN, Feskanich, D, Stampfer, M, *et al.* 2017. Multivitamin use and risk of stroke incidence and mortality amongst women. *European Journal of Neurology* 24:1266-1273. doi:10.1111/ene.13358.

Appleby, PN, Crowe, FL, Bradbury, KE, *et al.* 2016. Mortality in vegetarians and comparable nonvegetarians in the United Kingdom. *American Journal of Clinical Nutrition* 103:218-230. doi:10.3945/ajcn.11.119461.

Aung, T, Halsey, J, Kromhout, D, *et al.* 2018. Associations of omega-3 fatty acid supplement use with cardiovascular disease risks. *JAMA Cardiology* 3:225-234. Doi:10.1001/jamacardio.2017.5205.

Bechthold, A, Boeing, H, Schwedhelm, C, *et al.* 2017. Food groups and risk of coronary heart disease, stroke and heart failure: a systematic review and dose-response meta-analysis of prospective studies. *Critical Reviews in Food Science and Nutrition* 59:1071-1090. doi:10.1080/10408398.2017.1392288.

Binns, CW, Lee, MK, Lee, AH. 2018. Problems and prospects: public health regulations of dietary supplements. *Annual Review of Public Health* 39:403-420. doi:10.1146/annurev-publhealth-040617-013638.

Bjelakovic, G, Nikolova, D, Gluud, LL, *et al.* 2007. Mortality in randomized trials of antioxidant supplements for primary and secondary prevention: systematic review and meta-analysis. *JAMA* 297:842-857. doi:10.1001/jama.297.8.842.

Burckhardt, M, Herke, M, Wustmann, T, et al. 2016. Omega-3 fatty acids for the treatment of dementia (Review). *Cochrane Database of Systematic Reviews* 4:CD009002. doi:10.1012/14651858. CD009002.pub3.

Canhada, S, Castro, K, Perry, IS, et al. 2017. Omega-3 fatty acids' supplementation in Alzheimer's disease: a systematic review. *Nutritional Neuroscience* 21:529-538. doi:10.1080/1028415X. 2017.1321813.

Chen, F, Du, M, Blumberg, JB, et al. 2019. Association among dietary supplement use, nutrient uptake, and among U.S. adults: a cohort study. *Annals Internal Medicine* 170:604-613. doi:10.7326/M18-2478.

Cohen, PA. 2016. The supplement paradox: negligible benefits, robust consumption. *JAMA* 316:1453-1454. doi:10.1001/jama. 2016.14252.

Colman, RJ, Beasley, TM, Kemnitz, JW, et al. 2014. Caloric restriction reduces age-related and all-cause mortality in rhesus monkeys. *Nature Communications* 5:3557. doi:10.1038/ncomms4557.

Danthir, V, Hosking, DE, Nettelbeck, T, et al. 2018. An 18-mo randomized, double-blind, placebo-controlled trial of DHA-rich fish oil to prevent age-related cognitive decline in cognitively normal older adults. *American Journal of Clinical Nutrition* 107:754-762. doi:10.1093/ajcn/nqx077.

Dehghan, M, Mente, A, Zhong, X, et al. 2017. Associations of fats and carbohydrate intake with cardiovascular disease and mortality in 18 countries from five continents (PURE): a prospective cohort study. *The Lancet* 390:2050-2062. doi:10.1016/ S0140-6736(17)32252-3.

Dehghan, M, Mente, A, Rangarajan, S. *et al.* 2018. Association of dairy intake with cardiovascular disease and mortality in 21 countries from five continents (PURE): a prospective cohort study. *The Lancet* 392:2288-2297. doi:10.1016/S0140-6736(18)31812-9.

Dickinson, A, MacKay, D. 2014. Health habits and other characteristics of dietary supplement users: a review. *Nutrition Journal* 13:14-21. doi:10.1186/1475-2891-13-14.

Dinu, M, Abbate, R, Gensini, GF, *et al.* 2017. Vegetarian, vegan diets and multiple health outcomes: a systematic review with meta-analysis of observational studies. *Critical Reviews in Food Science and Nutrition* 57:3640-3649. doi:10.1080/10408398.2016.1138447.

Dinu, M, Paglial, G, Casini, A, *et al.* 2018. Mediterranean diet and multiple health outcomes: an umbrella review of meta-analysis of observational studies and randomised trials. *European Journal of Clinical Nutrition* 72:30-43. doi:10.1038/ejcn.2017.58.

Duggan, C, Tapsoba, JD, Wang, CY, *et al.* 2016. Dietary weight loss, exercise, oxidative stress in postmenopausal women: a randomized controlled trial. *Cancer Prevention Research* 9:835-843. doi:10.1158/1940-6207.CAPR-16-0163.

Ellsworth, L, O'Keeffe, A. 2013. Circumpolar Inuit health systems. *International Journal of Circumpolar Health* 72:21402. doi:10.3402/ijch.v72i0.21402.

Fodor, JG, Helis, E, Yazdekhasti, N, *et al.* 2014. "Fishing" for the origins of the "Eskimos and Heart Disease" story: facts or wishful thinking? *Canadian Journal of Cardiology* 30:864-868. doi:10.1016/j.cjca.2014.04.007.

Gardner, CD, Trepanowski, JF, Del Gobbo, LC, et al. 2018. Effect of low-fat vs low-carbohydrate diet on a 12-month weight loss in overweight adults and the association with genotype pattern or insulin secretion. The DIETFITS randomized clinical trial. *JAMA* 319:667-679. doi:10.1001/jama.2018.0245.

Gibbs, RA, Rogers, J, Katze, MG, et al. 2007. Evolutionary and biomedical insight from the rhesus macaque genome. *Science* 316:222-234. doi:10.1126/science.1139247.

Harman, D. 1956. Aging: a theory based on free radical and radiation chemistry. *Journal of Gerontology* 11:298-300. doi:10.1093/geronj/11.3.298.

Il'yasova, D, Fontana, L, Bhapkar, M, et al. 2018. Effects of 2 years of caloric restriction on oxidative status assessed by urinary F2-isoprostanes: the CALERIE 2 randomized clinical trial. *Aging Cell* 17:e12719. doi:10.1111/acel.12719.

Ingram, DK, de Cabo, R. 2017. Calorie restriction in rodents: caveats to consider. *Ageing Research Reviews* 39:15-28. doi:10.1016/j.arr.2017.05.008.

Jenkins, DJA, Spence, JD, Giovannucci, EI, et al. 2018. Supplement vitamins and minerals for CVD prevention and treatment. *Journal of the American College of Cardiology* 71:2570-2584. doi:10.1016/j.jacc.2018.04.020.

Kantor, ED, Rehm, CD, Du, M, et al. 2016. Trends in dietary supplement use among US adults from 1999-2012. *JAMA* 316:1464-1474. doi:10.1001/jama.2016.14403.

Kim, J, Choi, J, Kwon, SY, et al. 2018. Association of multivitamin and mineral supplementation and risk of cardiovascular disease.

Circulation Cardiovascular Quality and Outcomes 11:e004224. doi:10.1161/CIRCOUTCOMES.117.004224.

Khan, SS, Ning, H, Wilkins, JT, *et al.* 2018. Association of body mass index with lifetime risk of cardiovascular disease and compression of morbidity. *JAMA Cardiology* 3:28-287. doi:10.1001/jamacardio.2018.0022.

Khan, SU, Khan, MU, Riaz, H, *et al.* 2019. Effects of nutritional supplements and dietary interventions on cardiovascular outcomes: an umbrella review and evidence map. *Annals of Internal Medicine* 171:190-198. doi:10.7326/M19-0341.

Kosite, D, Konig, LM, De-loyde, K, *et al.* 2019. Plate size and food consumption: a pre-registered experimental study in a general population sample. *International Journal of Behavioral Nutrition and Physical Activity* 16:75. doi:10.1186/s12966-019-0826-1.

Kwok, CS, Umar, S, Myint, PK, *et al.* 2014. Vegetarian diet, Seventh Day Adventists and risk of cardiovascular mortality; a systematic review and meta-analysis. *International Journal of Cardiology* 176:680-686. doi:10.1016/j.ijcard.2014.07.080.

Lassale, C, Tzoulaki, I, Moons, KGM, *et al.* 2018. Separate and combined associations of obesity and metabolic health with coronary heart disease: a pan-European case-cohort analysis. *European Heart Journal* 39:397-406. doi:10.1093/eurheartj/ehx448.

Malik, VS, Li, Y, Pan, A, *et al.* 2019. Long-term consumption of sugar-sweetened and artificially sweetened beverages and risk of mortality in US adults. *Circulation* 139:2113-2125. doi:10.1161/CIRCULATIONAHA.118.037401.

Marlatt, KL, Redman, LM, Burton, JH, et al. 2017. Persistence of weight loss and acquired behaviors 2 y after stopping a 2-y calorie restriction intervention. 2017. *American Journal of Clinical Nutrition* 105:928-935. doi:10.3945/ajcn.116.146837.

Massetti, GM, Dietz, WH, Richardson, LC. 2017. Excessive weight gain, obesity, and cancer. Opportunities for clinical intervention. *JAMA* 318:1975-1976. doi:10.1001/jama.2017.15519.

Mattison, JA, Roth, GS, Beasley, TM, et al. 2012. Impact of caloric restriction on health and survival in rhesus monkeys from the NIA study. *Nature* 489:318-321. doi:10.1038/nature11432.

Mattson, MP, Longo, VD, Harvie, M. 2017a. Impact of intermittent fasting on health and disease processes. *Ageing Research Reviews* 39:46-58. doi:10.1016/j.arr.2016.10.005.

Mattison, JA, Colman, RJ, Beasley, TM, et al. 2017b. Caloric restriction improves health and survival of rhesus monkeys. *Nature Communications* 8:14063. doi:10.1038/ncomms14063.

McCay, CM, Crowell, MF, Maynard, LA. 1935. The effect of retarded growth upon the length of life span and upon the ultimate body size. *The Journal of Nutrition* 10:63-79. doi:10.1093/jn/10/1/63.

Micha, R, Shulkin, ML, Penalvo, JL, et al. 2017a. Etiologic effects and optimal intakes of foods and nutrients for risk of cardiovascular diseases and diabetes: systematic reviews and meta-analyses from the Nutrition and Chronic Diseases Expert Group (NutriCoDE). *PLoS ONE* 12:e0175149. doi:10.1371/journal.pone.0175149.

Micha, R, Penalvo, JL, Cudhea, F, et al. 2017b. Association between dietary factors and mortality from heart disease, stroke, and type 2 diabetes in the United States. *JAMA* 317:912-924. doi:10.1001/jama.2017.0947.

Mihrshahi, S, Ding, D, Gale, J, *et al.* 2017. Vegetarian diet and all-cause mortality: evidence from a large population-based Australian cohort – the 45 and Up Study. *Preventive Medicine* 97:1-7. doi:10.1016/j.ypmed.2016.12.044.

Miller, V, Mente, A, Dehghan, M, *et al.* 2017 Fruit, vegetable, and legume intake, and cardiovascular disease and deaths in 18 countries (PURE); a prospective cohort study. *Lancet* 390:2037-2049. doi:10.1016/S0140-6736(17)32253-5.

Most, J, Gilmore, A, Smith, SR, *et al.* 2018. Significant improvement in cardiometabolic health in healthy nonobese individuals during caloric restriction-induced weight loss and weight loss maintenance. *American Journal of Physiology Endocrinology and Metabolism* 314: E396-E405. doi:10.1152/ajpendo.00261.2017.

O'Brien, SK, Malacova, E, Sherriff, JL, *et al.* 2017. The prevalence and predictors of dietary supplement use in the Australian population. *Nutrients* 9:1154-1163. doi:10.3390/nu9101154.

Orlich, MJ, Singh, PN, Sabate, J, *et al.* 2013. Vegetarian dietary patterns and mortality in Adventist Health Study 2. *JAMA Internal Medicine* 173:1230-1238. doi:10.1001/jamainternalmed.2013.6473.

Payne, C, Barnett, R. 2018. The Economists' Diet. Pan Macmillan Australia: Sydney.

Rautiainen, S, Rist, PM, Glynn, RJ, *et al.* 2016. Multivitamin use and the risk of cardiovascular disease in men. *The Journal of Nutrition* 146:1235-1240. doi:10.3945/jn.115.227884.

Ravussin, E, Redman, LM, Rochon, J, et al. 2015. A 2-year randomized controlled trial of human caloric restriction: feasibility and effects on predictors of health span and longevity. *Journals of Gerontology Series A Biological Sciences Medical Sciences* 70:1097-1104. doi:10.1093/gerona/glv057.

Rees, K, Takeda, A, Martin, N, et al. 2019. Mediterranean-style diet for the primary and secondary prevention of cardiovascular disease. *Cochrane Database of Systematic Reviews* 3:CD009825. doi:10.1002/14651858.CD009825.pub3.

Reynolds, A, Mann, J, Winter, N, et al. 2018. Carbohydrate quality and human health: a series of systematic reviews and meta-analyses. *The Lancet* 393:434-445. doi:10.1016/S0140-6736(18)31809-9.

Rizzo, NS, Jaceldo-Siegl, K, Sabate, J, et al. 2013. Nutrient profiles of vegetarian and non-vegetarian dietary patterns. *Journal of the Academy of Nutrition and Dietetics* 113:1610-1619. doi:10.1016/j.jand.2013.06.349.

Rock, CL. 2007. Multivitamin-multimineral supplement: who uses them? *American Journal of Clinical Nutrition* 85:277S-279S. doi:10.1093/ajcn/85.1.277S.

Satija, A, Bhupathiraju, SN, Spiegelman, D, et al. 2017. Healthful and unhealthful plant-based diets and the risk of coronary heart disease in U.S. adults. *Journal of the American College of Cardiology* 70:411-422. doi:10.1016/j.jacc.2017.05.047.

Skeie, G, Braaten, T, Hjartaker, A, et al. 2009. Use of dietary supplements in the European Prospective Investigation into Cancer and Nutrition calibration study. *European Journal of Clinical Nutrition* 63:S226-S238. doi:10.1038/ejcn.2009.83.

Sofi, F, Dinu, M, Pagliai, G, et al. 2018. Low-calorie vegetarian versus Mediterranean diets for reducing body weight and improving cardiovascular risk profile. *Circulation* 137:1103-1113. doi:10.1181/CIRCULATIONAHA.117.030088.

Tatamango-Bartley, Y, Jaceldo-Siegl, K, Fan, J, et al. 2013. Vegetarian diets and the incidence of cancer in a low-risk population. *Cancer Epidemiology, Biomarkers & Prevention* 22:286-294. doi:10.1158/1055-9965.EPI-12-1060.

Tong, TYN, Appleby, PN, Bradbury, KE, et al. 2019. Risks of ischaemic heart disease and stroke in meat eaters, fish eaters, and vegetarians over 18 years of follow-up: results from the prospective EPIC-Oxford study. *British Medical Journal* 366:l4897. doi:10.1136/bmj.l4897.

Trepanowski, JE, Kroeger, CM, Barnosky, A, et al. 2018. Effects of alternate-day fasting or daily calorie restriction on body composition, fat distribution, and circulating adipokines: secondary analysis of a randomized controlled trial. *Clinical Nutrition* 37:1871-1878. doi:10.1016/j.clnu.2017.11.018.

Wilkins, R, Uppal, S, Fines, P, et al. 2008. Life expectancy in the Inuit-inhabited areas of Canada 1989 to 2003. *Health Reports* 19:7-19. Statistics Canada Cat. No. 82-003.

Chapter 5
Alcohol and Coffee

Drinking to Your Healthy Ageing

In Chapter 2, we discussed longevity and healthy ageing as influenced by inherited DNA (familial DNA) and to a lesser, but significant, extent by the epigenome (epigenetic DNA). The latter referred to the modulation of inherited DNA by lifestyle and the environment. In Chapters 3 and 4, we discussed the importance of diet as a risk factor for age-related disorders such as cardiovascular disease, cancer and stroke.

In this Chapter, we consider the influence of two everyday lifestyle factors, both of which have been reported to influence as much as, if not more than, diet on health and ageing. The two lifestyle factors considered are alcohol and coffee, both of which could be classified as part of one's diet. Nevertheless, there are many individuals who do not consume either of these two items as part of their normal diet. We critically examine the evidence, as provided by publication in peer-reviewed scientific articles, for conclusions that consuming alcohol and coffee positively impacts health.

A Brief History of Alcohol

Humans have long been obsessed with drinking alcoholic beverages. Archaeological findings, including illustrated recipes written on clay tablets and charred residues in pots used for wine and beer, dating back six thousand years, have provided evidence of advanced knowledge of alcohol and its production.

If one enters into Google the question 'how often is the word *wine* mentioned in the Bible?' you will come across a reference stating 231 matches in 212 verses. The first miracle attributed to Jesus is that of turning water into wine at a marriage in Cana of Galilee (John 2: 1-11). Several particular quotes associated with wine are in relation to Noah:

'after the flood....Noah planted a vineyard' (Genesis 9: 20)

'and Noah lived after the Flood three hundred and fifty years..'
'and all the days of Noah were nine hundred and fifty years, and he died' (Genesis 9: 28-29)

These quotes are the first published references to the health benefits of alcohol and ageing, albeit in a non-peer reviewed or refereed publication.

One wonders if Methuselah drank wine or beer given that he lived to 969 years (Genesis 5: 27), the oldest human to have ever lived. On the other hand, the longevity of Noah and Methuselah may have nothing to do with alcohol given that Methuselah was Noah's grandfather and thus genes may have played the key role. Interestingly, a six-litre bottle (equivalent to eight standard bottles) of champagne or wine is called a Methuselah.

It was common practice even for children in medieval England and Europe to drink beer and wine in preference to just water, given that the latter was generally contaminated by pathogenic bacteria (e.g. agents for typhoid, cholera) although their presence was not formally identified until the late nineteenth to early twentieth century.

It was often safer and healthier to drink alcoholic beverages as the alcohol substantially decreased the numbers of pathogenic organisms which, at that time, were ubiquitous in drinking water. Indeed, it was not until the late nineteenth century that adequate sewage disposal followed by filtration and chlorination of water supplies, allowed relatively pathogen-free drinking water to be readily available to the general public. One should, therefore, not complain about the relatively small inconvenience of the smell and taste of chlorinated water as the alternative is widespread cholera and typhoid epidemics. Water, clean water, is one of three essentials for human life.

There has been and continues to be much debate about the health benefits of alcohol. Two of my favourite quotable quotes summarize the contradicting viewpoints presented as early as the sixteenth and seventeenth centuries:

'..moderately drunken, it doth quicken a man's wit, it doth comfort the heart, scour the liver....it doth nourish the brain and all the body...' (Andrew Boorde, physician,1592)

'...since leaving drinking, I do find myself much better, and so spend less money and less time lost in idle company...' (Samuel Pepys, author,1662)

The words 'moderately drunken' as used by Dr Boorde in 1592 remains, to this day, a term that is not widely understood by the general public and hotly debated by the scientific community with respect to the potential health benefits of alcohol consumption.

The other misunderstood term is 'a standard drink.' Just what constitutes a standard drink? It depends on which country you are referring to as this value ranges from eight grams (UK, Iceland), ten grams (Australia, France), fourteen grams (USA, Canada) to twenty grams (Austria) of alcohol (Kalinowski and Humphreys, 2016). I will totally avoid yet another confusing issue, and that is standard drinks as expressed in fluid ounces.

Scientific studies on alcohol consumption invariably refer to grams of alcohol and this is understandable as that is a precise quantitative measurement of alcohol consumed as compared with the volume of liquid consumed (expressed as millilitres, ml) containing the alcohol. The latter, of course, requires the concentration in grams (gm) of alcohol in 100 ml in order to calculate the amount of alcohol consumed. However, the alcohol content of drinks is generally given as, for example, 5% alcohol by volume (not weight). So, try this test: how many standard drinks are in a 355 ml bottle of beer of 4.8% alcohol by volume? (hint: assume a standard drink is ten gm of alcohol).

The required formula is simple, if you have a background in science and some basic maths:

Volume of the container (in litres)
Multiply by the % alcohol by volume
Multiply by the specific gravity of alcohol (weight/volume, 0.789)
Thus: 0.355 x 4.8 x 0.789 = 1.34 standard drinks

OR

Volume of container (in fractions of 100 ml, as % alcohol by volume refers to 4.8 ml of alcohol in a total of 100ml) 3.55 x 4.8 x 0.789 = 13.4 gm alcohol = 1.34 standard drinks

This then brings me to another issue - when was the last time you went to a friend's house or a pub/bar and was offered or asked for 13.4 gm of beer, wine or whisky? Almost certainly never. And another thing, the general public can relate to statements like 'I've had a couple of drinks.' (translation: two beers or two glasses of wine or two shots of whisky) as compared with 'I've had 26.8 grams of alcohol.'

It is not surprising, therefore, that the general public is totally confused with the meaning of the term 'a standard drink.' Most bottles of alcoholic drink state the number of standard drinks in that bottle, and this value is a useful guide on responsible drinking. Nevertheless, the general public more readily relates to the term a standard drink to mean a bottle/can of beer or a glass of wine or a shot of spirits as that is the way an individual actually drinks.

It is appreciated that the alcohol content of beer generally varies from 4.5% to 5% (by volume, meaning 4.5 to 5.0 ml alcohol per 100 ml) and a bottle or can varies from 330 to 375 ml. You simply need to note that a typical bottle or can of beer is 1 to 1.5 standard drinks, and thus, importantly, three beers are not three standard drinks but closer to between 4 and 4.5 standard drinks.

Now consider wine. In general, wine is packaged in 750 ml bottles, with an alcohol content of around 12% by volume (ranging on average from 11% to 14.5%). A bottle of wine is thus about seven to eight standard drinks. A medium glass (say 125 ml) of wine

(12% alcohol by volume) is almost 1.2 standard drinks and a large glass (250 ml) of wine is about 2.4 standard drinks. A shot (40 ml) of spirit (e.g. whisky, 40% alcohol) is about 1.3 standard drinks.

For the purposes of the present discussion, we simply consider a standard drink to be a bottle/can of beer (330-375 ml), a medium glass (125 ml) of wine and a shot (40 ml) of spirits. Although these amounts are above the concept of a standard drink based on 10 gm alcohol (see calculations above), they are in fact within the range of a standard drink in the USA and Canada, where a standard drink is defined as 13.6 and 14.0 gm alcohol respectively.

We can now move forward to considering the scientific studies on alcohol and health in a practical way, keeping in mind the concept of a standard drink as generally understood by the public.

The most important and obvious fact is that heavy drinking is a health (and wealth) hazard. It has long been recognized that excess alcohol intake can be highly destructive, leading to undesirable behaviour and social breakdown.

Alcohol is a leading cause of death world-wide, accounting for, directly or indirectly, 3.3 million deaths per year (World Health Organisation) and, conservatively, five times that number in serious injuries. These include motor vehicle accidents, criminal violence, domestic violence and health issues related to mental disorders, stroke, obesity and cancers. Thus, advocating that alcohol intake has positive health outcomes is a very hard sell. The key issues here are light to moderate alcohol consumption *plus a healthy lifestyle*.

In recent times, the initial interest in the potential health benefits of alcohol intake was attributed to a 1991 segment on the CBS-US TV show *60 Minutes* on the 'French paradox.' The latter term was first used in the 1980s by French researchers referring to the relatively low incidence of coronary heart disease in France as compared with other European countries and the USA, despite the high intake of fat-rich foods (e.g. butter, cheese, pate, animal fat) in France. The lower incidence of heart disease was attributed to the high intake of wine, especially red wine, in France. Needless to say, the airing of this program lead to an immediate and substantial increase in sales of Californian wines.

Drinking in Moderation Is Good for You? You've Got to be Kidding Me!

What is the scientific evidence for the potential health benefits of alcohol? In keeping with previous Chapters, we concentrate on the most recent publications and present a brief summary of previous observations.

Historically, there was considerable debate about the relative merits of different alcoholic beverages. Red wine was initially promoted as the beverage of choice. It was thought that the presence of antioxidants (as scavengers of free radicals, discussed in Chapter 4: Diets and Dietary Supplements), in the form of polyphenols, tannins, procyanidins, resveratrol etc was responsible for the health benefits. There was and continues to be much debate on this issue and, indeed, many scientific egos have to be accommodated.

The current consensus is that the amount and the pattern of drinking are the key issues and not the type of alcoholic beverage. Most importantly and, in my opinion (biased), *it is the lifestyle associated with the pattern of drinking that is the key factor relating to potential health benefits.*

A criticism of previous studies on alcohol and health concerned the details of the control or reference group which generally consisted of non-drinkers. However, the latter reference group frequently consisted of lifetime non-drinkers (termed abstainers) plus previous drinkers (but currently non-drinkers) who had given up drinking, presumably for health-related reasons. The reference group thus contained individuals who may have already been compromised with respect to health issues. A number of recent studies have addressed this issue as discussed in the next section.

Numerous studies over the past thirty years had demonstrated distinct J-shaped curves relating alcohol consumption with morbidity and mortality, the latter particularly associated with cardiovascular events. The lower part of the curve (lowest risk) represented light to moderate alcohol intake with an increased risk associated with non-drinkers (left of the curve) and heavy drinkers (right of the curve).

As mentioned above, a valid criticism of these observations was that the reference cohort of non-drinkers did not distinguish between lifetime non-drinkers or abstainers from former drinkers who had given up drinking, frequently for health issues.

In an article published in 2017 (Bell *et al.*, 2017), in the prestigious *British Medical Journal*, it was concluded that moderate drinkers (≤ 21 drinks/week for males, ≤ 14 drinks/week for females) were at reduced risk for cardiovascular disease as compared with lifetime abstainers The latter cohort served as the reference group that, importantly, excluded former drinkers.

This was a very large study (n = 1.93 million adults, 51% female, aged ≥ 30 at baseline, mean 6 years of follow-up) that identified twelve common symptomatic characteristics of cardiovascular disease. For example, moderate drinkers as compared with lifetime abstainers had a 32% and 24% decreased risk of myocardial infarction and heart failure respectively. On the other hand, heavy drinkers as compared with lifetime abstainers had an increased risk (22%) of presenting with a number of cardiovascular disease symptoms but a decreased risk of myocardial infarction (12%).

In a US-based study (n = 333,247 adults, 50.6% female, aged ≥ 18 at baseline, median 8.2 years of follow-up) moderate drinkers (≤ 14 drinks/week for males, ≤ 7 drinks/week for females) had a decreased risk of cardiovascular disease (29%) and all-cause mortality (22%) as compared with lifetime abstainers (Xi et al., 2017). Interestingly, the latter cohort was biased towards females (65.5%) while the moderate drinkers were biased towards males (74.3%). On the other hand, there was an increased (13%) risk of cancers in moderate drinkers and heavy drinkers (≥ 14 drinks/week for males, ≥ 7 drinks/week for females).

In one of the very few non-European-non-USA studies of a Japanese population (n = 102,849, 53% female, aged 40-69 at baseline, median 18.2 years of follow-up) a typical J-shaped curve was observed relating all-cause mortality with alcohol intake (Saito et al., 2018). Occasional drinkers, defined as drinking 1 to 3 days/month, and moderate drinkers (≤ 14 drinks/week) were reported to have a 25% and 20% decreased risk of all-cause mortality respectively as compared with non-drinkers. The latter, however, also included individuals classified as previous drinkers (sometimes termed 'sick-quitters') and thus these observations may have been biased towards positive health benefits of light to moderate drinking.

It is well-established that heavy drinkers (≥ 21 drinks/week) are at increased risk of cancers including liver, pharynx, oesophagus and breast cancer (female). A number of recent studies have confirmed these observations (Cao et al., 2015; Xi et al., 2017; Kunzmann et al., 2018). The obvious question is what about light to moderate drinking?

A large cohort study of US health professionals (n = 88,084 female, n = 47,881 male, aged 30-75 at baseline, 24-30 years of follow-up) concluded that a moderate increase (< 5%) of overall cancers was associated with light to moderate drinking (≤ 7 drinks/week for females; ≤ 14 drinks/week for males). However, the authors noted that for females there was an increased risk of cancers, in particular for breast cancer, above about 7 drinks/week (Cao et al., 2015). The study by Xi et al. (2017) also noted a modest increase (13%) in risk of cancers in moderate drinkers as compared with abstainers.

A study of older adults (n = 99,654, 68.7% female, aged 55-74 at baseline, mean 8.9 years of follow-up) concluded that heavy drinkers (≥ 21 drinks/week) had a significantly higher (21%) risk of overall mortality and cancer as compared with light drinkers (1 to 3 drinks/week). Interestingly, light-moderate drinkers (< 14 drinks/week) had a decreased (20%) risk of overall mortality as compared with lifetime abstainers (Kunzmann et al., 2018). In these studies, light drinkers as the reference cohort (< 3 drinks/week), had the lowest combined risk of all-cause mortality and cancer as compared with lifetime abstainers and moderate drinkers.

In a very large study (n = 599,912, 44% female, mean age of 57, median 7.5 years of follow-up) of current drinkers from nineteen high-income countries, the lowest risk of all-cause mortality and cardiovascular disease was observed at ≤ 10 drinks/week (Wood et al., 2018). The decrease in risk was extremely modest, < 10% for cardiovascular disease and < 5% for all-cause mortality.

The key point here was that light drinkers (< 3 drinks/week) served as the reference cohort. On the other hand, there also was a 10% decrease in risk of myocardial infarction (heart attack due to blocked coronary artery) at 10 drinks/week as compared with < 3 drinks/week. The downside was a 14% increase in risk of stroke at ≤ 10 drinks/week. Very heavy drinkers (> 36 drinks/week) at 40 years of age was estimated to have four to five years shorter life expectancy than drinkers consuming ≤ 10 drinks/week. Estimates for risk were adjusted for potential confounders, including smoking, physical activity and occupation, and alcohol consumption was assessed on multiple occasions, albeit self-reported by participants.

The relative merits of wine, beer and spirits with respect to health have often been debated, with the socio-economic status (SES) of the drinker as a key issue.

Recent studies in a Norwegian population had thrown some light on this issue. The study (n = 207,394, 50% female, mean age of 47 at baseline, mean 16.6 years of follow-up) investigated SES in relation to drinking patterns and cardiovascular mortality (Degerud *et al.*, 2018). The SES of the participants was obtained from census surveys between 1960 and 1990, plus additional data from 2011 on levels of education. A limitation of the study was that alcohol intake was mostly restricted to a single self-reported questionnaire. The results were adjusted for confounders that included age, sex, BMI, smoking status and physical activity but not dietary intake.

As compared with infrequent drinkers (< 1 drink/month) as the reference cohort, individuals classified as high SES and consuming 2 to 3 (light drinkers) or 4 to 7 drinks/week (moderate drinkers) had a 34% and 20% decreased risk of cardiovascular mortality respectively. A similar decrease (21%) in risk in the cohort classified as low SES was only observed at a lower alcohol consumption of 2 to 3 drinks/week, with higher consumption (4 to 7 drinks/week) actually increasing (42%) the risk of cardiovascular mortality. Furthermore, in the low SES cohort, binge drinking (> 5 drinks on a single session, ≥ 1 time/week) greatly increased (85%) risk of cardiovascular mortality. Binge drinking in the high SES cohort also increased (22%) the risk of cardiovascular mortality but the risk was significantly lower. The authors concluded that the lower risk of cardiovascular mortality associated with light to moderate drinking was more prevalent in individuals classified as high SES than those classified as low SES.

There are also studies indicating that alcohol consumption may influence the risk of diabetes. Previous epidemiological studies had provided evidence that light to moderate alcohol drinkers, as compared with abstainers, have a lower risk of diabetes.

These observations have been confirmed in a recent study of Danish adults (n = 70,551, 59% female, aged ≥ 18, median 4.9 years of follow-up) in which light-moderate drinkers (3 to 4 drinks/week) had a decreased risk of diabetes (27% decreased in males, 32% decreased in females) as compared with drinkers consuming 1 drink/week (Holst et al., 2017). In other words, more frequent moderate alcohol consumption appeared to be better than less frequent consumption. Data were adjusted for confounders including age, sex, physical activity, education and smoking. However, a limitation of this study (and most other studies) was that alcohol intake was monitored only once.

Despite continued reports on positive effects on health of light to moderate consumption of alcohol there is no advocacy for abstainers to commence drinking. Nevertheless, there is the unexplained and almost universal observation that lifetime abstainers are at increased risk of all-cause mortality and cardiovascular disease as compared with light to moderate drinkers. Perhaps it is some aspect or aspects, as yet unidentified, of the lifestyle of lifetime abstainers that is a factor in these observations. For example, lifetime abstainers may be more introverted or less social or may have some underlying health reasons for not drinking. It is quite noticeable that females are much more likely to be lifetime abstainers; certainly, this is seen in the scientific studies on alcohol and health.

Not Drinking Alcohol Is Good for You? You've Got to be Kidding Me!

Several recent studies have advised caution about the potential health benefits of alcohol intake.

In one study (Topiwala *et al.*, 2017) of British civil servants (n = 550, predominantly male, mean age of 43 at baseline, 30 years of follow-up), alcohol intake at moderate to high levels (14 to 21 drinks/week) was reported to be associated with a decrease in cognitive function (tested multiple times over the course of the study) and brain structural changes (tested once only) that included hippocampal atrophy (brain shrinkage). At these levels of alcohol intake, there was a threefold increase in the risk of hippocampal atrophy and at higher levels (> 21 drinks/week) there was almost a sixfold increase as compared with abstainers as the reference cohort.

In another study (Sabia *et al.*, 2018), also involving British civil servants (n = 9,087, 67% male, aged 35-55 at baseline, mean 23 years of follow-up) alcohol consumption (assessed multiple times over the course of the study) of > 14 drinks/week was associated with only a modest increase (8%) risk of dementia as compared with a reference cohort of moderate drinkers, defined in this study as drinking < 14 drinks/week. However, the risk of dementia more than doubled (17%) in the cohort consuming ≥ 21 drinks/week. Surprisingly, abstainers (lifetime abstainers plus former drinkers) were 47% more likely to develop dementia as compared with light-moderate drinkers (1 to 14 drinks/week). The authors adjusted their data for numerous confounders including age, sex, SES, smoking, physical activity and some dietary habits (fruit and vegetable consumption).

There is no doubt about the detrimental effects of heavy drinking on memory impairment and brain atrophy and a recent review of these issues makes for a sobering thought (Topiwala and Ebmeier, 2018).

A nationwide retrospective study of > 31 million adults discharged from French hospitals from 2008 to 2013, identified > 1 million with some type of dementia with 57,353 diagnosed with early-onset dementia (Schwarzinger et al., 2018). Approximately 56% of the latter cohort was attributed to alcohol-related use disorders. The authors concluded that alcohol use disorders were a major risk factor for all types of dementia, especially for early-onset dementia. Although the authors emphasized that heavy drinking was a high-risk factor, they also targeted the role of moderate drinking as a potential risk for alcohol use disorders associated with dementia.

In the most comprehensive review to date of the global burden of alcohol for 195 countries (GBD 2016 Alcohol Collaborations,1990-2016) it was concluded that 'the level of consumption that minimises health loss is zero.' The authors took into consideration the estimated 2.8 million annual deaths (3.3 million according to the World Health Organisation) attributed to alcohol plus the many more millions directly affected by alcohol-related trauma, e.g. road accidents and domestic violence.

The population aged < 50 years was particularly vulnerable with an estimated 3.8% female deaths and 12.2% male deaths attributable to alcohol use. The authors also reasoned that the modest health benefits (e.g. reduced risk of cardiovascular disease, diabetes) of light-moderate drinking were more than cancelled by the increased risk of cancers.

This latter point may not be valid given that the scientific evidence is actually the reverse: the modest increase in risk of cancers from light-moderate drinking is more than balanced by the decreased risk of CVD and diabetes (see above references). Moreover, their conclusion that 'no level of alcohol minimizes harm across health outcomes' may also not be valid and is certainly unrealistic.

Motor traffic accidents are estimated to be responsible for 1.3 million deaths world-wide, plus at least twenty times that number from accident-related trauma (www.who.int/news-room/fact-sheets/detail/road-traffic-injuries), 90% of which occur in low- to middle-income countries. A zero level of motor traffic would minimize these outcomes but is, again, totally unrealistic.

The authors also reported that in high-income and thus high SES countries, 72% of females and 83% of males were current drinkers. A zero alcohol consumption in these countries would lead to a lot of unhappy individuals (leading to increased health costs), high unemployment (leading to high economic costs) and, importantly, no more Pub Tests.

In reality, the take home message from these studies is that alcohol-related harm in the past has been substantially underestimated and the recommended, upper limit, guidelines for alcohol consumption such as in standard drink definitions should be significantly lowered.

The Verdict: To Drink or Not to Drink? That Is the Question

Overall, current scientific evidence favours light drinking (< 3 drinks/week for females, < 7 drinks/week for males) as the optimum for health benefits related to all-cause mortality, cardiovascular disease and cancers.

The modest increase in risk of cancers associated with moderate drinking in males and females (≤ 7 drinks/week for females, ≤ 14 drinks/week for males) is largely offset by the decreased risk of all-cause mortality and cardiovascular associated events. Heavy drinking (≥ 14 drinks/week for females, ≥ 21 drinks/week for males), on the other hand, is a definite health hazard.

There is some evidence (Degerud *et al.*, 2018) that SES is a factor for potential health benefits of light to moderate drinking. Additionally, individuals at a high SES, as compared with low SES, may well have a healthier diet, smoke less, be more physically active, have access to better health care and have a more supportive social network.

Lifestyle is the key issue. Thus, one should consider not only the amount of alcohol consumed but also where you consume it, with whom you consume it and why you consume it.

Consuming alcohol at home, at the pub or bar or elsewhere may depend on your family, social or work environment. Having a quiet, relaxing drink alone at home may suit some individuals but if depression is the reason for drinking, this environment could be a problem. In general, one has drinks with your friends, rarely with your enemies. You are more likely to be relaxed and less stressed in the former than the latter environment. Drinking is also associated with celebrations, such as birthdays, weddings and even at funerals.

As far as I am aware, there have been no large, long-term studies on the topic of 'where, with whom and why' in relation to alcohol intake and potential health benefits. Such studies are unlikely to be undertaken any time soon given the logistics involved. The best we can do is simply take the *Pub Test*.

Pub Test 5.1:

Question:

Does light to moderate drinking (1 to 2 standard drinks/day) have positive health effects?

Answer:

Yes

Light to moderate drinking is the key word, with females drinking less than males. However, your overall lifestyle and socio-economic status are key factors for health. Drinking in moderation has to be accompanied by having a healthy diet, not smoking, being physically active, maintaining a social network and having regular health checks. Cheers!

What about Coffee and Tea?

Excluding water (which is essential for life), coffee and tea are two of the most popular beverages consumed by humans. After decades of research, there is now consensus that individuals who drink coffee and/or tea are modestly healthier than those who do not drink these beverages.

This is not exactly a surprising outcome, after all drinking coffee and tea is integral to the culture of social interactions among humans. One does not need long-term randomized clinical trials to prove that positive social interactions play key roles in human health, happiness and welfare. We drink these beverages with friends and colleagues in our homes, workplaces and at cafes and restaurants. In these respects, drinking coffee and tea shares many similarities to the reported modest health benefits of light-moderate alcohol consumption.

Several recent publications summarised the current scientific evidence supporting the health benefits of coffee consumption.

The 2017 publication in the *Annals of Internal Medicine*, a highly prestigious medical journal, of a large (n = 521,330, 71% female, mean 16.4 years of follow-up) multicentre study of coffee drinking and mortality in ten European countries (Gunter *et al.*, 2017), generally confirmed previous studies in the USA and Japan of the health benefits of coffee drinking.

Compared with non-drinkers, individuals consuming ≥ 3 cups/day had a decreased risk of all-cause mortality of 18% and 8% for males and females respectively. These observations were consistent for both caffeinated and decaffeinated coffee. Interestingly, in this study, substantially lower mortality risks were associated with digestive and liver diseases as well as circulatory diseases. In particular, the latter, in terms of cerebrovascular disease, was more strongly associated with lower risk in females than in males. On the other hand, an increased (12%) risk of ovarian cancer was noted in females, however, a recent review of eight prospective cohort studies concluded that there was no association between consumption of coffee and risk of ovarian cancer (Berretta *et al.*, 2018).

A significant weakness of the Gunter et al. (2017) study was that coffee consumption was only assessed once, at baseline, by self-report questionnaire. Any changes with time in habitual coffee consumption were not further assessed.

A strength of this study was that data were adjusted for confounders, which included BMI, physical activity, education level, smoking and alcohol consumption. It was most notable that the cohort who consumed the highest amount of coffee also consumed the highest amount of alcohol. Moreover, this cohort also had the highest percentage of smokers.

For males, the cohort of non-coffee drinkers consumed on average ≤ 5 alcoholic drinks/week and consisted of 18% smokers. By contrast, the cohort of high coffee drinkers consumed ≤ 9 drinks/week and consisted of 41% smokers.

For females, the cohort of non-coffee drinkers consumed ≤ 1 drink/week and consisted of 11% smokers. The cohort of high coffee drinkers consumed ≤ 3 drinks/week and consisted of 31% smokers.

In other words, individuals consuming relatively high amounts of coffee also consumed relatively high amounts of alcohol and smoked more and *vice versa* for those classified as non-coffee drinkers. These characteristics further highlighted the importance of lifestyle factors as key parameters in assessing habitual drinking and health.

A comprehensive review of 201 meta-analyses of observational studies and seventeen controlled trials on coffee consumption and health was recently published in the *British Medical Journal* (Poole *et al.*, 2017).

You could term this review, up to date as of July 2017, as 'all you wanted to know about the scientific evidence for health outcomes and coffee drinking but were afraid to ask' with the detailed discussion section as required reading.

In summary, it was concluded that, as compared with none, drinking 3 to 4 cups of coffee/day decreased risk of all-cause mortality (17%), incident cancer (18%) and cardiovascular disease (15%). The authors also concluded that there were no definitive harmful effects of coffee consumption, with the notable exceptions of possible harmful effects related to pregnancy and modest increased risk of bone fracture in women. The important role of confounders (lifestyle) was raised, in particular smoking, alcohol consumption, age and BMI, all associated with habitual coffee drinking.

Not all coffees are created equal. Thus, any descriptive coffee containing combinations of words such as 'mocha, caramel, chocolate and Frappuccino' will almost certainly not be equivalent, in terms of sugar calories and healthy/unhealthy outcomes, to your regular black coffee. Nevertheless, if having one of these descriptive coffees at your favourite cafe lowers your stress levels, that is the key outcome.

Try this simple question: Do scientific studies on health and consumption of coffee take into consideration that some non-coffee drinkers may actually drink tea?

This then brings me to the issue of health and consumption of tea. Well, I am simply going to avoid this topic and leave you, the interested Reader, to do your own research. Consider this topic as an Assignment for *Tea 101 Potential Health Benefits*. (Hints: avoid simply doing a Google search, consult publications in high-quality peer-reviewed journals and critically assess the data [e.g. who the authors are, their associated institutions, long-term follow-up, number of participants, any commercial interests, confounders]). Good luck, come to a non-biased conclusion and submit to the *Pub Test*.

There is no substantiated scientific evidence of a specific compound(s) present in coffee and tea that explains the modest health effects of these beverages. There is considerable speculation, and speculation is the word, that polyphenols, acting as antioxidants, are responsible for the modest health effects.

Laboratory tests have certainly provided evidence of the efficacy of polyphenols in neutralizing free radicals. The point is that in the human body, levels of antioxidants and free radicals are critically balanced: not too much or not too little, the Goldilocks state. Chemical reactions that occur in the laboratory test-tube do not necessarily replicate themselves in relation to the complexity of the human body.

Pub Test 5.2:

Question:

Does drinking coffee or tea have any health benefits?

Answer:

Yes

The important concepts are the same as in the case of light-moderate alcohol consumption. It is where you drink, with whom you drink and why you drink. *It is the overall lifestyle of individuals who drink coffee, tea and alcohol (light-moderate) that influences their health.*

Bell, S, Daskalopoulou, M, Rapsomaniki, E, *et al.* 2017. Association between clinically recorded alcohol consumption and initial presentation of 12 cardiovascular diseases: population based cohort study using linked health records. 2017. *British Medical Journal* 356:j909. doi:10.1136/bmj.j909.

Berretta, M, Micek, A, Lafranconi, A, *et al.* 2018. Coffee consumption is not associated with ovarian cancer risk: a dose-response meta-analysis of prospective cohort studies. *Oncotarget* 9:20807-20815. doi:10.18632/oncotarget.24829.

Cao, Y, Willett, WC, Rimm, EB, *et al.* 2015. Light to moderate intake of alcohol, drinking patterns, and risk of cancer: results from two prospective US cohort studies. *British Medical Journal* 351:h4238. doi:10.1136/bmj.h4238.

Degerud, E, Ariansen, I, Ystrom, E, *et al.* 2018. Life course socioeconomic position, alcohol drinking patterns in midlife, and cardiovascular mortality: analysis of Norwegian population-based health surveys. *PLoS Medicine* 15:e1002476. doi:10.1371/journal.pmed.1002476.

GBD Alcohol Collaborations 2016. Alcohol use and burden for 195 countries and territories, 1990-2016: a systematic analysis for the Global Burden of Disease Study 2016. *The Lancet* 392:1015-1035. doi:10.1016/S0140-6736(18)31310-2.

Gunter, MJ, Murphy, N, Cross, AJ, et al. 2017. Coffee drinking and mortality in ten European countries – the EPIC study. *Annals Internal Medicine* 167:236-247. doi:10.7326/M16-2945.

Holst, C, Becker, U, Jorgensen, ME, et al. 2017. Alcohol drinking patterns and risk of diabetes: a cohort study of 70,551 men and women from the general Danish population. *Diabetologia* 60:1941-1950. doi:10.1007/s00125-017-4359-3.

Kalinowski, A, Humphreys, K. 2016. Government standard drink definition and low-risk alcohol consumption guidelines in 37 countries. *Addiction* 111:1293-1298. doi:10.1111/add.13341.

Kunzmann, AT, Coleman, HG, Huang, W-Y, et al. 2018. The association of lifetime alcohol use with mortality and cancer risk in older adults: a cohort study. *PLoS Medicine* 15:e1002585. doi:10.1371/journal.pmed.1002585.

Poole, R, Kennedy, OJ, Roderick, P, et al. 2017. Coffee consumption and health: umbrella review of meta-analysis of multiple health outcomes. *British Medical Journal* 359:j5024. doi:10.1136/bmj.j5024.

Sabia, S, Fayosse, A, Dumurgier, J, et al. 2018. Alcohol consumption and risk of dementia: 23 year follow-up of Whitehall II cohort study. *British Medical Journal* 362:k2927. doi:10.1136/bmj.k2927.

Saito, E, Inoue, M, Sawada, N, et al. 2018. Impact of alcohol intake and drinking patterns on mortality from all causes and major causes of death in a Japanese population. *Journal of Epidemiology* 28:140-148. doi:10.2188/jea.JE20160200.

Schwarzinger, M, Pollock, BG, Hasan, OS, et al. 2018. Contribution of alcohol use disorders to the burden of dementia in France 2008-13: a nationwide retrospective cohort study. The Lancet 3:e124-e132. doi:10.1016/S2468-2667(18)30022-7.

Topiwala, A, Allan, CL, Valkanova, V, et al. 2017. Moderate alcohol consumption as risk factor for adverse brain outcomes and cognitive decline: a longitudinal cohort study. British Medical Journal 357:j2353. doi:10.1136/bmj.j2353.

Topiwala, A, Ebmeier, KP. 2018. Effects of drinking on late-life brain and cognition. Evidenced-Base Mental Health 21:12-15. doi:10.1136/eb-2017-102820.

Wood, AM, Kaptoge, S, Butterworth, AS, et al. 2018. Risk thresholds for alcohol consumption: combined analysis of individual-participant data for 599,912 current drinkers in 83 prospective studies. The Lancet 391:1513-1523. doi:10.1016/S0140-6736(18)30134-X.

Xi, B, Veeranki, SP, Zhao, M, et al. 2017. Relationship of alcohol consumption to all-cause, cardiovascular, and cancer-related mortality in U.S. adults. Journal of the American College of Cardiology 70:913-922. doi:10.1016/j.acc.2017.06.054.

Chapter 6
Physical Activity

Keep Calm and Walk the Dog

There is overwhelming evidence and general consensus that lifelong physical activity has positive effects on health. By comparison with sedentary individuals, physically active individuals also tend to adopt healthier lifestyles, such as not smoking, maintaining social contacts and having a nutritious diet.

Physical activity leads to improved blood circulation and thus supplies oxygen to all body extremities including the brain. The latter constitutes about 2% of the body mass of the average adult but consumes 20% of the body's oxygen. The function of the brain is not only critically dependent on a continuous supply of oxygen but is also highly sensitive to changes in oxygen levels. Furthermore, physical activity improves heart function, bone health, sleep quality, reduces stress and depression and contributes to weight control. It is a no-brainer that one must 'keep moving' (and 'keep breathing') to achieve healthy ageing.

The most recent worldwide data (as of September 2017) on physical activity or lack thereof in 168 countries, including almost two million participants, provides sobering statistics. In this comprehensive review (Guthold *et al.*, 2018) in the *Lancet*, a highly prestigious medical journal, insufficient physical activity was defined as not meeting the World Health Organisation (WHO) recommendations of at least 150 min/week of moderate physical activity or 75 min/week of high intensity activity (or equivalent combinations).

Overall, the data showed that approximately 30% of adults worldwide did not meet these recommendations. There were substantial differences across countries, with adults in high-income countries less active (37% not meeting the recommendations) than in low-income countries (16%). Interestingly, women were substantially less active than men, particularly in Latin-America, the Caribbean, South-East Asia and high-income Western countries (< 40% not meeting the recommendations). It is no coincidence that these figures reflect the high incidence of obesity in these countries.

Given that physical activity is a key factor in healthy ageing, the data appears to be a contradiction of the fact that adults in high-income countries, in comparison with those in low-income countries, have a significantly longer life expectancy and, importantly, longer healthy life expectancy. This may simply be explained by the higher standard of living in high-income countries e.g. better health care, housing, education, social security and nutrition.

On the other hand, the significantly lower physical activity of women as compared with men in high-income Western countries, Latin-America, the Caribbean, and South-East Asia also does not correlate with the fact that women, irrespective of country of origin, live longer than men (see Table 1). Although there are plausible explanations for this phenomenon, there is continuing debate about the precise reasons (see Chapter 8: If We All Lived to a Healthy 100).

Recent studies have focused on the recommended levels of physical activity for optimum health. A large prospective US study examined the amount of walking activity in older adults in relation to all-cause mortality (Patel et al., 2017). The study, based on self-reported questionnaires, examined n = 62,178 men (baseline mean age of 70.7) and n = 77,077 women (baseline mean age of 68.9) with an average follow-up of thirteen years during which time approximately 40% and 25% of the male and female cohorts died respectively.

Individuals who were classified as physically inactive or sedentary at baseline had a 26% increased risk of all-cause mortality as compared with those who were walking at less than the WHO recommended levels of physical activity (see above). Individuals meeting or exceeding (twice) the recommended levels were associated with a 20% and 29% decreased risk of all-cause mortality respectively. The authors noted that their data related specifically to walking as a physical activity although similar trends were reported for other types of moderate to vigorous physical activities. Although the authors adjusted risk assessment for confounders, it was most notable that physically active individuals were less overweight, more educated, smoked less, adopted better diets and consumed more alcohol than individuals classified as physically inactive.

These outcomes confirmed an earlier report (n = 661,137, 56% female, median age of 62, median 14.2 years of follow-up, 18% deaths) in which individuals undertaking less than the minimum recommended, 1-2 times and 2-3 times the recommended amounts of physical activity had a 20%, 31% and 39% decreased risk of all-cause mortality respectively as compared with those reporting little leisure time physical activity (Arem et al., 2015).

In another study (Diaz et al., 2017) of US adults (n = 7,985, aged ≥ 45, median 4 years of follow-up) it was concluded that sedentary time, both long and short bouts, constituted a high risk for all-cause mortality. This study was notable in that physical activity was objectively measured by a waist-mounted accelerometer as a measure of duration and intensity of physical activity. On the other hand, only seven days of accelerometer data were collected and the relatively low number of deaths (340) was a weaknesses of this study.

The hazards of a sedentary lifestyle were also reported in a study (Patel et al., 2018) of a very large US cohort (n = 127,554, mean age of 62, 60% female, median 20.3 years of follow-up). Physical activity (self-reported questionnaire, min/week) was scored as a metabolic equivalent of task (MET) as a measure of energy expenditure with e.g. normal walking speed at 3.5 MET and jogging/running at 7.0 MET. Prolonged sedentary time (> 6 hr/day) was associated with 19% higher risk of all-cause mortality as compared with < 3 hr/day, independent of moderate to vigorous physical activity.

The benefits of improved clinical markers of cardiovascular health of light intensity and moderate-vigorous physical activity was recently published in the official journal of the American Heart Association (LaMonte et al., 2017). In this study of a large female cohort with low cardiovascular risk (n = 4,832, mean age of 78.9) physical activity was objectively measured by waist-attached accelerometer (4 to 7 days, > 10 hr/day awake wear time). Each thirty-min additional physical activity was associated with 18% decrease in risk factors associated with cardiovascular health (e.g. LDL-cholesterol, triglycerides, BMI, C-reactive protein). Importantly, results were adjusted for age, BMI, alcohol intake and smoking.

Similar results were reported in a UK study (n = 1,622, aged 60-64, 51% female) in which greater physical activity and lower sedentary time were associated with more favourable biomarkers of cardiovascular health (Elhakeem et al., 2018). Physical activity was monitored by accelerometer (five consecutive days) and biomarkers of cardiovascular health including inflammatory proteins (e.g. C-reactive protein, interleukin-6). Data were adjusted for confounders which included socioeconomic status, education, smoking history and a number of clinical parameters (e.g. diabetes, cardiovascular disease, blood pressure, medications).

The health benefits of physical activity in individuals with cardiovascular disease were well illustrated in a 2018 publication in the *Mayo Clinic Proceedings* (Kieffer et al., 2018). Patients classified as physically active as compared with those classified as physically inactive had a 24% and 36% decreased risk of all-cause mortality and mortality from cardiovascular disease respectively. In this study of n = 3,133 individuals (64% male, mean age of 67.6, mean 12.5 years of follow-up, 2,936 deaths), physical activity was assessed only at baseline by self-report questionnaire and data were appropriately adjusted for confounders (age, sex, smoking status, alcohol consumption, education level, hypertension and motion impairment). Although data were adjusted for these confounders, it was most noticeable that the cohort classified as physically active were younger (~ 6.5 years younger), had lower BMI, were more educated and consumed more alcohol.

There is continuing debate about the amount (min/week) and type (light, moderate, vigorous) of physical activity necessary for optimal health benefits. One hat fits all simply does not apply, and the type and amount of physical activity is very much dependent on individual lifestyle. Subscribing to a 'lifetime' gym membership may ease your conscience but does not constitute physical activity: one really has to regularly attend the gym. Simple regular brisk walking may actually achieve the same benefits.

The total amount of physical activity in terms of light, moderate or vigorous activity appears to be the key factor.

In a recent study of n = 4,840 adults (aged > 40, 50.3% female, mean 6.6 years of follow-up, 700 deaths) physical activity was objectively monitored (seven-day measurement) by waist-attached accelerometer (Saint-Maurice *et al.*, 2018a). Increasing amounts of light physical activity and comparing highest to lowest was associated with 31% decreased risk of all-cause mortality. Increasing amounts of moderate-vigorous physical activity and comparing highest to lowest was associated with a whopping 72% decreased risk, demonstrating the potential benefits of moderate-vigorous physical activity.

Note that the authors in one data set were comparing cohorts classified as high and low light physical activity and in another data set comparing cohorts classified as high and low moderate-vigorous physical activity. Their overall conclusion was that the duration of physical activity was more influential on outcomes than the intensity of the physical activity. Although the data were adjusted for confounders it was, nevertheless, notable that the most physically active participants were less obese, were more educated, consumed more alcohol and presented with fewer chronic diseases.

In a related publication (Saint-Maurice *et al.*, 2018b), the authors further reported that decreased risk of all-cause mortality was associated with the *total amount of physical activity* irrespective of how the activity was accumulated, that is, as long or short bouts of activity.

A similar conclusion was reached in a study (Jefferis et al., 2019) of older UK males (n = 1,181, aged 71-92, median 5 years of follow-up, 194 deaths) with physical activity objectively monitored by waist-attached accelerometer (seven-day measurement). Compared with sedentary behaviour, there was a 40% decreased risk of all-cause mortality in individuals attaining 150 min/week of moderate-vigorous physical activity accumulated in long or short bouts. Similar data were correlated with light physical activity with a 17% decrease for each additional thirty minutes of light physical activity. Data were adjusted for confounders which included socio-economic status, BMI, smoking history and alcohol consumption.

The outcomes of a two-year (longest to date) randomized controlled trial on the effects of a structured exercise program on the cardiac health of previously sedentary middle-aged adults were recently published in the high impact journal, *Circulation* (Howden et al., 2018).

The cohort consisted of n = 53 (mean age of 53, 55% female) with twenty-eight assigned to the exercise group and twenty-five as matched controls. Basically, the exercise group completed 300-360 min/week of moderate exercise with 1 session/week of intense exercise (4 x 4 min intense with 3 min recovery in between), and the control group completed a closely monitored program of balance and flexibility training, 3 times/week. Adherence to the exercise program over the two-year period lead to significantly improved cardiovascular structure and function as measured by increased maximal oxygen uptake and decreased cardiac stiffness. By comparison, there was little change in these two parameters in the control group.

This was an important observation in that one obvious issue with previous studies on physical activity and health was that individuals who were physically active were already healthy and had a healthier lifestyle than cohorts classified as sedentary or relatively physical inactive.

The physically active cohorts in the majority of the published scientific studies (see above) were less overweight, smoked less, were classified as of higher socio-economic status, were better educated, adopted more nutritious diets and, interestingly, consumed more alcohol than the cohorts classified as sedentary or relatively physically inactive.

To be fair, many of the recent studies had applied statistically valid adjustments to account for these differences, termed confounders, in these cohorts. But one would wonder if, in these same studies and using the same data, the goal was finding out not what are the effects of physical activity on health but, say, the effects of moderate alcohol consumption or a nutritious diet on health and then applying statistically valid adjustments for physical activity and the other confounders. Almost certainly, the same data would conclude that a nutritious diet or moderate alcohol consumption positively affects health, with data adjusted for appropriate confounders, including physical activity. A similar argument applied to the scientific studies on coffee (another potential confounder) and health.

In my opinion (biased), the positive impact of physical activity on health is also closely associated with the overall lifestyle of the individual. In other words, individuals who are physically active are likely to be more health conscious (e.g. adopt a nutritious diet, do not smoke, socially active) than sedentary individuals.

The above mentioned publication in *Circulation* is important in that it demonstrated that previously sedentary individuals can improve their health by adopting physical activity as part of their lifestyle. No doubt these same individuals would have adopted a healthier lifestyle as well.

A recent review (Oja et al., 2018) of randomized controlled trials (review of 37 trials, n = 2,100, 81% female) among previously inactive, healthy adults concluded that walking interventions led to improvements in clinical parameters of cardiovascular disease (decreased BMI, decreased blood pressure, lower fasting glucose levels, increased maximum oxygen uptake).

In a small study of healthy older adults (n = 20, female, mean age of 70.3 ; n = 8, male, mean age of 67.6), greater physical fitness was associated with less language processing decline (Segaert et al., 2018). Physical fitness was assessed by cycle ergometer to estimate maximal oxygen consumption and language processing assessed as inability to produce a word (tip-of-the-tongue) even though one knew the word. Although this was a very small study, it was important in that it was an exploratory study relating levels of physical activity to language processing. Maintaining language processing skills is an integral part of healthy ageing.

Physical Activity Update

A number of important publications in 2019 continued to endorse the link between physical activity and health.

In a study published in *JAMA Internal Medicine* (Lee et al., 2019), of older women (n = 16,741 individuals, mean age of 72.0, 4.3 years of follow-up, 504 deaths), physical activity (number of steps/day) was monitored by accelerometer (seven days, hip attachment). There was a decreased risk (0.42, measured as a hazard ratio) of all-cause mortality in the cohort with the highest number of steps/day (8,442) as compared with the cohort with the lowest steps/day (2,718). Data were adjusted for age, nutrition, smoking, alcohol and previous health status. The authors reported that there was a threshold of around 7,500 on the number of steps/day, above which there was a levelling-off with respect to benefits.

In a very large study (n = 315,059, 42% female, aged 50-61 at enrollment, 13.6 years of follow-up, 71,377 deaths) there was a 36%, 42% and 14% decreased risk of all-cause mortality, cardiovascular-disease-related mortality and cancer-related mortality respectively in individuals classified as participating in moderate-high leisure-time physical activity (2 - 8 hr/week, adolescence to adulthood) as compared with those classified as consistently inactive (Saint-Maurice *et al.*, 2019).

Interestingly, individuals who self-reported to be relatively inactive in early years but increased physical activity in adulthood (aged 40-61) also had decreased risk of mortality (all-cause mortality, cardiovascular related and cancer related) similar to those self-reported as physically active throughout adolescence to adulthood. In other words, it is never too late to 'keep moving.'

In another large study (n = 122,007, 40.8% female, mean age of 53.4, 8.4 years of follow-up, 13,637 deaths) physical fitness as objectively measured by exercise treadmill testing was associated with decreased risk of all-cause mortality (Mandsager *et al.*, 2019). Individuals were all patients at a medical centre and undergoing cardiorespiratory stress testing. Individuals rated as elite (highest physical fitness) had an impressive 80% decreased risk of all-cause mortality as compared with the lowest (adjusted for sex and age).

Even in comparison to individuals classified as having high physical fitness, elite individuals had a 23% decreased risk of all-cause mortality, leading the authors to concluded that, at least in the current studies, there appeared to be no upper limit of benefit of increased physical fitness. Moreover, reduced cardiorespiratory performance was a better predictor of all-cause mortality than conventional clinical markers of health (e.g. smoking, coronary heart disease).

A large study (n = 88,140, 51.4% female, approximately 80% aged 40-59, 20% aged ≥ 60, 9 years of follow-up) of US adults examined low and high doses of leisure time physical activity and health outcomes (Zhao et al., 2019). Individuals (self-reports) performing 10-59 min physical activity/week had an 18% decreased risk of all-cause mortality as compared with those classified as physically inactive. Individuals reporting high levels of physical activity, 150-299 min/week and ≥ 1,500 min/week, had 31% and 46% decreased risk of all-cause mortality respectively. Similar levels of decreased risks, for all three levels of physical activity, were noted for cardiovascular disease and cancer. Data were adjusted for a number of confounders, including age, sex, socio-economic status, smoking and drinking.

The significance of this study was the reported benefits of high (extreme) doses of leisure time physical activity. Individuals reporting 25 hr or more of leisure time physical activity/week are rare, although in this study there were 2,500 individuals (33.8% female) in this category with 141 deaths.

In a recent systematic review and meta-analysis (statistical analysis of similar scientific studies) on running and health outcomes (fourteen studies, n = > 230,000), the authors concluded that, even at modest amounts of running (e.g. 50 min/week), individuals had 27%, 30% and 23% reduced risk of all-cause, cardiovascular and cancer mortality, respectively (Pedisic et al., 2019). Although the authors found no evidence that high doses of running were even more beneficial than modest doses, they did propose that a larger number of participants at the higher doses may have improved the estimates.

Physical Activity and Cognitive Function

Recent studies had also confirmed earlier observations of a positive effect of physical activity on brain and cognitive function.

In a community-based study (n = 2,354, mean age of 53, 54.2% female) individuals attaining > 10,000 steps/day (measured by hip-accelerometer for eight days) were associated with a higher brain volume (measured by magnetic resonance imaging) as compared with those attaining < 5,000 steps/day (Spartano et al., 2019). Most interestingly, the authors were able to extrapolate their results to calculate that, in individuals meeting the physical activity guidelines (150 min/week), each additional hour of light physical activity was associated with approximately 1.1 years less brain ageing.

In a study (Opel et al., 2019) of healthy young adults (n = 1,206, mean age of 28.8, 54.5% female) the authors reported a strong correlation between physical fitness (walking endurance) and brain structure (magnetic resonance imaging, white matter microstructure) and cognitive function (e.g. memory, processing speed, cognitive flexibility). The data thus demonstrated that the relationship between physical fitness and brain structure and function was already established at an early age. Importantly, the data were adjusted for confounders including age, sex, BMI and education. Only the latter confounder weakened the association. One limitation of the study was that physical fitness was only measured as walking endurance (distance covered in two min), and overall regular physical activity of the participants was not accounted for.

In a very large study of relationships between physical activity and major depressive disorder (MDD) the authors concluded that physical activity, as objectively measured by an accelerometer (waist attachment) was protective for MDD (Choi *et al.,* 2019). In this study, physical activity was either self-reported (n =377,234) or by accelerometer (n = 91,084) with MDD from genome-wide association studies (n = 143,265). Interestingly, the association between physical activity and MDD was only valid when activity was objectively measured by accelerometer and not by self-report.

In a recent study, the Dunedin Multidisciplinary Health and Development Study (Rasmussen *et al.,* 2019), slower gait speed (walking speed) at midlife was a measure of accelerated ageing and was associated with cognitive impairment. In this study (n = 904, 49.7% female, aged 45, all born 1972-1973), gait speed (defined as usual, dual task and maximum) was assessed against nineteen biomarkers of clinical health (e.g. cardiovascular fitness, blood pressure, lipid biomarkers, BMI) and cognitive testing of brain health (e.g. brain volume, white matter hyperintensities). The authors were able to extrapolate their findings to conclude that impaired cognitive function as early as age 3 years (previously measured on all participants) was associated with slower gait speed at midlife (aged 45), a highly significant connection.

In the past decade, there had been numerous studies on the association between physical activity and depression, dementia and Alzheimer's.

In one early study, published in *Annals of Internal Medicine*, a highly ranked medical journal, the authors concluded that midlife fitness levels lowered the risk of developing dementia

(DeFina et al., 2013). In this study (n = 19,458, mean age of 49.8 at baseline, 21.1% female, median 25 years of follow-up) there was a 36% lower risk of all-cause dementia in comparing individuals at the highest fitness level to the lowest level.

Despite these earlier observations, there is clearly much ongoing debate on the issue of physical activity and cognitive function. The interested Reader should note that studies, to date, have not demonstrated a significant association between biomarkers of Alzheimer's and physical activity (Frederiksen et al., 2019), although a recent review reported a trend towards improvement in executive function (e.g. planning & reasoning, memory, attention) after physical exercise in individuals with Alzheimer's-type dementia (Guitar et al., 2018).

Why 10,000 Steps a Day?

Totally arbitrary. The much lauded 10,000 steps/day which has become the default standard for physical activity and health can be traced back to the 1964 Olympic Games held in Tokyo. There was a movement to get the Tokyo public involved in the games and to encourage physical activity. An early study by a university academic stated that the average Japanese person took 3,000 to 5,000 steps/day, and thus, an arbitrary 10,000 steps/day was proposed for increased physical activity. An enterprising Japanese company marketed a waist-attached pedometer under the name *Manpo-kei*, translated as '10,000 steps meter', and thus the concept of 10,000 steps/day for optimum health.

The current popular physical fitness trackers (Fitbit etc) commonly have the default setting or goal at 10,000 steps/day, equivalent to about 8 km/day for the average walker and

400-600 calories/day (depending on sex, age, BMI, walking speed). Although the 10,000 steps/day was purely arbitrary, the interested Reader may have noted that scientific studies have incorporated that figure in studies on physical activity and health (see references above).

For the exercise-adverse Reader, note that the average person burns around 40-60 calories/hr whilst asleep and 100-120 calories/hr working on the computer (dependent on sex, age, BMI). On the other hand, if one is using a lot of brain power (remember your brain consumes enormous amounts of oxygen and thus energy) you could be burning considerably more calories. For example, it has been estimated that a chess Grandmaster participating in a tournament may burn up to 6,000 calories/day.

Nevertheless, it is crucial to understand that physical activity is not just about burning calories. It also stimulates blood and oxygen flow to all parts of the body, critically to the brain. It can stimulate the body's defence systems, including the immune system, against infection and it positively affects our gut microbiota. It is beneficial in improving bone and muscle strength, sleep quality and cardiorespiratory fitness.

Furthermore, in the studies quoted in this Chapter, there is good quality scientific evidence that physical activity positively affects the brain in respect of mood, depression and cognitive function. The decreased risk in all-cause and cardiovascular mortality associated with increased physical activity is substantially higher than that reported for any other aspect of healthy ageing, including dietary studies. The latter studies are frequently compromised by lifestyle confounders and are often at the margin of significance at low to moderate decreased risk of all-cause and cardiovascular mortality.

Pub Test 6.1:

Question:

Is maintaining physical activity important for healthy ageing?

Answer:

Yes, most definitely Yes.

Physical activity or 'Keep Moving' is one of the most, if not the most, important criterion of successful healthy ageing. Individuals who are physically active also have healthy lifestyles, such as not smoking, maintaining social contact, adopting a healthy diet and having a positive attitude.

Do Competitive Athletes Have the Edge?

One obvious question is: do individuals who participate in moderate-vigorous physical activity as in leisure-time sports or sports at a competitive level gain additional benefits from their activities as compared with those participating in less active physical activities?

The associations between leisure-time sports and life expectancies were recently examined in a long-term (25 years of follow-up) prospective cohort study (n = 8,577, 4,448 deaths) of Danish adults (Schnohr et al., 2018).

Estimated life expectancy gains were highest for tennis (9.7 years) and badminton (6.2 years), followed by soccer, cycling, swimming and jogging (3 to 5 years), with the lowest for health club or gym activities (1.3 years). The authors noted that the leisure-time sports associated with the best longevity were also associated with high social interactions, for example comparing tennis/soccer with jogging or gym activities.

Limitations of this study were the self-report questionnaires at baseline and that most individuals also participated in sports other than the nominated major sport (at least 20% activity as the major sport). Data were adjusted for age, sex, education, income, smoking, drinking, diabetes and volume of physical activity. Nevertheless, it was striking that the various sports were mean age-dependent: 40-45 years for soccer, jogging, badminton and tennis; 45-60 years for swimming, cycling and gym activities; 60 years for the reference sedentary cohort.

The potential benefits of running/jogging for longevity and decrease risk of mortality were recently reviewed (Lee et al., 2017). Overall, the authors concluded that the published consensus was that regular running/jogging (e.g. ≥ 75 min/week) added 3.2 years to longevity and approximately 30% decreased risk of all-cause mortality with substantially greater decrease (43%) in all-cause mortality in runners who also participated in other forms of physical activity. The authors also discussed the issue that too much running may actually be detrimental to health outcomes with, for example, the increased risk of muscle and bone injury. The review considered potential mechanisms for the health outcomes of running and, in particular, noted studies on improved cardiorespiratory fitness (improved heart and lung function) in runners, thus the important concept of running/jogging contributing to healthy ageing and not just simply longevity.

If we now step up to competitive sports, one can recommend a very readable 2015 review on mortality and longevity in elite athletes (Lemez and Baker, 2015). Although the authors concluded that elite athletes generally have favourable lifespans, they did temper that conclusion by pointing out the many limitations associated with published data. For example, there is very limited data about how long the elite athletes maintained exercise levels later in life and limited knowledge about their level of holistic health (lifestyle health) in terms of not only mental health and social aspects but also to include diet.

An earlier study on longevity of Olympic medalists from 1896 to 2010 (n = 15,174) from Germany, France, Italy, U.K., Russia, Australia, New Zealand and Nordic countries concluded that medalists lived on average 2.8 years longer than appropriate matched controls (Clarke *et al.*, 2015). The authors proposed that, apart from physical activity, genetic factors, healthy lifestyle and social status may all have contributed to the increased longevity.

A study of French athletes (n = 2,814, 455 deaths) in the Olympics from 1912 to 2012 concluded that, for all sports, an average of 6.5 years of life expectancy was gained (Antero-Jacquemin *et al.*, 2018).

Another study of elite Finnish male athletes (n = 900) from the period 1920 to 1965 compared mortality with their age-matched brothers (n = 900). The risk for all-cause mortality was 25% lower in former athletes as compared with their age-matched brothers (Kontro *et al.*, 2018). Median age at death (combined death total of 1,296 from original n = 1,800) was approximately two years longer for former athletes. The authors concluded that former elite athletes were more physically active, smoked less and had better self-reported health than their brothers.

An intriguing study of Olympic athletes concluded that high jumpers and marathon runners had significantly longer life expectancies than sprinters and discus throwers (Lee-Heidenreich et al., 2017). In this study of athletes who competed in Olympics from 1928 to 1948, life expectancy (as compared with that expected for the general population) was highest for high jumpers (+7.1 years for females; +3.7 years for males) and marathon runners (+4.7 years for males; no Olympic marathons for females until 1984) and lowest for sprinters (-1.6 years for females; -0.9 years for males).

Interestingly, the authors raised the issue that substantial differences in weight (e.g. high jumpers versus discus throwers) largely explained the differences in survival, with the heavier athletes at lower survival. Nevertheless, it was noted that female, but not male, discus throwers lived longer than the general population.

Pub Test 6.2:

Question:

Do elite athletes live longer than the general population?

Answer:

Yes and No.

This is the only Yes/No answer to a Pub Test Question.

All studies, to date, have not fully addressed the issue of lifestyle (both pre- and post-competitive) of elite athletes. More importantly, the reference cohort, i.e. the general population, should include both healthy and unhealthy individuals from the same country of origin as the elite athlete. In other words, a truly comparable reference cohort will be individuals who are not elite athletes but with a healthy lifestyle akin to that of many (but not all) of the elite athletes (particularly post-competitive), including not smoking, physically active, nutritious diet and socially engaged. The differences in all-cause mortality and life expectancy between healthy and unhealthy lifestyles more than accounts for the reported differences between elite athletes and the general population.

In a pioneering 1986 study, published in the *New England Journal of Medicine*, a highly prestigious medical journal, Harvard male alumni (n = 16,936, 12 to 18 years of follow-up, 1,413 deaths) were assessed for physical activity (self-reported questionnaire) in relation to all-cause mortality and longevity. The authors concluded that, relative to sedentary individuals, physically active individuals lived on average two years longer (Paffenbarger *et al.*, 1986). Interestingly, if one exercises for one hour every day for fifty years, this equates to almost exactly two years.

More recent data (Lee *et al.*, 2017) have indicated that moderate-vigorous physical activity of around 120 min/week (2 hr/week) adds around 3.2 years to life expectancy; 2 hr/week equates to 0.6 years' exercising, thus a net benefit of around 2.6 years or ~ 4.4 min additional life expectancy per 1 minute of exercise over 50 years of exercising at 2 hr/week, a reasonable trade off. But of course, it is healthy ageing or healthy life expectancy that really matters, and this is the key take-home message that needs to be emphasized with respect to physical activity and health, not so much the life expectancy.

Physical activity improves cardiorespiratory fitness and that is the key parameter of healthy ageing. There is compelling evidence that physical activity, even as assessed simply by walking speed and gait or more objectively by exercise treadmill testing, is the key parameter of healthy ageing.

Keep Calm and Walk the Dog

It is important to note that physical activity may include simple leisure-time activities such as shopping, gardening, walking and walking the dog. The latter may provide additional benefits as there is anecdotal evidence that pet ownership, and not just dogs, has a positive influence on health outcomes, not least of which include companionship and reduced levels of stress.

A nationwide (Sweden) cohort study concluded that dog ownership, particularly in single-person households, was associated with lower risk of cardiovascular mortality (23% decrease) and all-cause mortality (20% decrease). In this 12-year follow-up study (n = 3,432,153, 52% female, mean age of 57) data were adjusted for confounders including age, sex, marital status, income and socio-economic status (Mubanga *et al.*, 2017). In this large cohort, 13.1% of households were identified as dog owners and ownership of hunting-breed dogs and single-person households were important variables for positive health outcomes.

In a follow-up study (Mubanga *et al.*, 2019) in a sub-cohort of patients (n = 181,696, 26.1% female, mean age of 71, 12-year of follow-up) with prior cardiovascular disease, dog ownership was reported to decrease risk of mortality in individuals living with a partner or child (15% decrease) and particularly in single-person households (33% decrease). Similar observations were reported for patients with prior ischaemic stroke (n = 154,617, 45% female, mean age of 73). Dog ownership was exceptionally low in these cohorts, 5.7% (cardiovascular studies) and 4.8% (ischaemic stroke) given that the average household dog ownership in Sweden is 15% and is close to a remarkable 40% in Australia and the USA (just Google those data).

The potential health benefits of dog ownership in single-person households (14% lower risk of all-cause mortality) as compared with individuals living with a spouse (2% decrease) were also recently reported in a study (n = 24,214 dog-owners, 42.4% female, mean age of 68.7) of Danish citizens (Sorensen *et al.*, 2018).

In another nationwide (Norway) study, no association was reported between dog ownership and all-cause mortality (Torske *et al.*, 2017; includes an excellent overview of previous studies). In this 18.5-year follow-up study of dog owners (n = 10,668, 52.8% female, mean age of 46.7, 1,586 deaths) and non-dog owners (n = 42,760, 54.5% female, mean age of 51.2, 11,112 deaths) no association was found between dog ownership and all-cause mortality. However, the authors noted that their cohort was largely a rural population with many dogs classified as working dogs rather than simply as household pets. Furthermore, physical activity was relatively high in this rural population irrespective of dog ownership.

So, what about dog ownership in non-Scandinavian countries and in households with predominantly non-working dogs, i.e. household pets?

A large 11.5-year follow-up study of dog ownership in an English population (n = 59,352, mean age of 46.5, 8,169 deaths) found no association between dog ownership and all-cause mortality or mortality due to cardiovascular disease (Ding *et al.*, 2018), and this was after adjusting for confounders (age, sex, education and socio-economic status).

It is apparent that issues related to single-person households, type of dog, duration of dog ownership, physical activity and overall lifestyle (coffee anyone?) of dog owners and non-dog owners all have to be taken into consideration in studies on potential health benefits of dog ownership. Really, just a dog's breakfast, but keep calm and walk the dog!

Pub Test 6.3:

Question:

Do dog owners have longer life expectancies (healthy life expectancies) than non-dog owners?

Answer:

Yes

(One has to declare a conflict of interest [bias] here as an owner of a Labrador that requires attention and long walks).

Large and long-term studies on dog ownership have provided conflicting results due to the complexities of confounders. Physical activity such as walking the dog (how long a walk, slow, moderate or brisk walking), breed of dog, how long the individual has owned the dog and providing companionship as in single-person households are all key confounders. On the other hand, on a positive note, there is no large, long-term study that concludes that dog owners have shorter life expectancies than non-dog owners. And just one more thing, do not even attempt to research potential health benefits of ownership of other types of pets (did someone say cats?).

Antero-Jacquemin, J, Rey, G, Marc, A, *et al*. 2015. Mortality in female and male French Olympians: a 1948-2013 cohort study. *American Journal of Sports Medicine* 43:1505-1512. doi:10.1177/0363546515574691.

Arem, H, Moore, SC, Patel, A, *et al*. 2015. Leisure time physical activity and mortality: a detailed pooled analysis of the dose-response relationship. *JAMA Internal Medicine* 175:959-967. doi:10.1001/jamainternmed.2015.0533.

Choi, KW, Chen, CY, Stein, MB, *et al*. 2019. Assessment of bidirectional relationships between physical activity and depression among adults: a 2-sample Mendelian randomization study. *JAMA Psychiatry* 76:399-408. doi:10.1001/jamapsychiatry.2018.4175.

Clarke, PM, Walter, SJ, Hayen, A, *et al*. 2015. Survival of the fittest: retrospective cohort study of the longevity of Olympic medallists in the modern era. *British Journal of Sports Medicine* 49:898-902. doi:10.1136/bjsports-2015-e8308rep.

DeFina, LF, Willis, BL, Radford, NB, *et al*. 2013. The association between midlife cardiorespiratory fitness levels and later-life dementia. *Annals of Internal Medicine* 158:162-168. doi:10.7326/0003-4819-158-3-201302050-00005.

Diaz, KM, Howard, VJ, Hutto, B, *et al*. 2017. Patterns of sedentary behaviour and mortality in U.S. middle-aged and older adults: a national cohort study. *Annals of Internal Medicine* 167:465-475. doi:10.7326/M17-0212.

Ding, D, Bauman, AE, Sherrington, C, *et al*. 2018. Dog ownership and mortality in England: a pooled analysis of six population-based cohorts. *American Journal of Preventive Medicine* 54:289-293. doi:10.1016/j.amepre.2017.09.012.

Elhakeem, A, Cooper, R, Whincup, P, *et al*. 2018. Physical activity, sedentary time, and cardiovascular disease biomarkers at age 60 to 64 years. *Journal of the American Heart Association* 7:e007459. doi:10.1161/JAHA.117.007459.

Frederiksen, KS, Gjerum, L, Waldemar, G, et al. 2019. Physical activity as a moderator of Alzheimer pathology: a systematic review of observational studies. *Current Alzheimer Research* 16:362-378. doi:10.2174/1567205016666190315095151.

Guitar, NA, Connelly, DM, Nagamatsu, LS, et al. 2018. The effects of physical exercise on executive function in community-dwelling older adults living with Alzheimer's-type dementia: a systematic review. *Ageing Research Reports* 47:159-167. doi:10.1016/j.arr.2018.07.009.

Guthold, R, Stevens, GA, Riley, LM, et al. 2018. Worldwide trends in insufficient physical activity from 2001 to 2016: a pooled analysis of 358 population-based surveys with 1.9 million participants. *The Lancet Global Health* 6:PE1077-E1086. dOI:10.1016/S2214-109X(18)30357-7.

Howden, EJ, Sarma, S, Lawley, JS, et al. 2018. Reversing the cardiac effects of sedentary aging in middle age – a randomized controlled trail. 2018. *Circulation* 137:1549-1560. doi:10.1161/CIRCULATIONAHA.117.030617.

Jefferis, BJ, Parsons, TJ, Sartini, C, et al. 2019. Objectively measured physical activity, sedentary behaviour and all-cause mortality in older men: does volume of activity matter more than pattern of accumulation? *British Journal of Sports Medicine* 52:1013-1020. doi:10.1136/bjsports-2017-098733.

Kieffer, Sk, Zisko, N, Coombes, JS, et al. 2018. Personal activity intelligence and mortality in patients with cardiovascular disease: the HUNT Study. *Mayo Clinic Proceedings* 93:1191-1201. doi:10.1016/j.mayocp.2018.03.029.

Kontro, TK, Sarna, SS, Kaprio, J, et al. 2018. Mortality and health-related habits in 900 Finnish former elite athletes and their brothers. *British Journal of Sports Medicine* 52:89-95. doi:10.1136/bjsports-2017-098206.

LaMonte, MJ, Lewis, CE, Buchner, DM, *et al.* 2017. Both light intensity and moderate-to-vigorous physical activity measured by accelerometry are favourably associated with cardiometabolic risk factors in older women: the Objective Physical Activity and Cardiovascular Health (OPACH) Study. *Journal of the American Heart Association* 6:e007064. doi:10.1161/JAHA.117.007064.

Lee, D, Brellenthin, AG, Thompson, PD, *et al.* 2017. Running as a key lifestyle medicine for longevity. *Progress in Cardiovascular Diseases* 60:45-55. doi:10.1016/j.pcad.2017.03.005.

Lee, I-M, Shiroma, EJ, Kamada, M, *et al.* 2019. Association of step volume and intensity with all-cause mortality in older women. *JAMA Internal Medicine* 179:1105-1112. doi:10.1001/jamainternalmed.2019.0899.

Lee-Heidenreich, J, Lee-Heidenreich, D, Myers, J. 2017. Differences in life expectancy between Olympic high jumpers, discus throwers, marathon and 100 meter runners. *BMC Sports Science Medicine and Rehabilitation* 9:3. doi:10.1186/s13102-017-0067-z.

Lemez, S, Baker, J. 2015. Do elite athletes live longer? A systematic review of mortality and longevity in elite athletes. *Sports Medicine - Open* 1:18. doi:10.1186/s40798-015-0024-x.

Mandsager, K, Harb, S, Cremer, P, *et al.* 2018. Association of cardiorespiratory fitness with long-term mortality among adults undergoing exercise treadmill testing. *JAMA Network Open* 1:e183605. doi:10.1001/jamanetworkopen.2018.3605.

Mubanga, M, Byberg, L, Nowak, C, et al. 2017. Dog ownership and the risk of cardiovascular disease and death – a nationwide cohort study. *Scientific Reports* 7:15821. doi:10.1038/s41598-017-16118-6.

Mubanga, M, Byberg, L, Egenvall, A, et al. 2019. Dog ownership and survival after a major cardiovascular event. *Circulation Cardiovascular Quality and Outcomes* 12:e005342. doi:10.1161/CIRCOUTCOMES.118.005342.

Oja, P, Kelly, P, Murtagh, EM, et al. 2018. Effects of frequency, intensity, duration and volume of walking interventions on CVD risk factors: a systematic review and meta-regression analysis of randomized controlled trials among inactive healthy adults. *British Journal of Sports Medicine* 52:769-775. doi:10.1136/bjsports-2017-098558.

Opel, N, Martin, S, Meinert, S, et al. 2019. White matter microstructure mediates the association between physical fitness and cognition in healthy, young adults. *Scientific Reports* 9:12885. doi:10.1038/s41598-019-49301-y.

Paffenbarger, RS, Hyde, RT, Wing, AL, et al. 1986. Physical activity, all-cause-mortality, and longevity of college alumni. *New England Journal of Medicine* 314:605-613. doi:10.1056/NEJM198603063141003.

Patel, AV, Hildebrand, JS, Leach, CR, et al. 2017. Walking in relation to mortality in a large prospective cohort of older U.S. adults. *American Journal of Preventive Medicine* 54:10-19. doi:10.106/j.amepre.2017.08.019.

Patel, AV, Maliniak, ML, Rees-Punia, E, et al. 2018. Prolonged leisure time spent sitting in relation to cause-specific mortality in a large US cohort. *American Journal of Epidemiology* 187:2151-2158. doi:10.1093/aje/kwy125.

Pedisic, Z, Shrestha, N, Kovalchik, S, *et al.* 2019. Is running associated with a lower risk of all-cause, cardiovascular and cancer mortality, and is more the better? A systematic review and meta-analysis. *British Journal of Sports Medicine* 0:1-9. doi:10.1136/bjsports-2018100493.

Rasmussen, LJH, Caspi, A, Ambler, A, *et al.* 2019. Association of neurocognitive and physical function with gait speed in midlife. *JAMA Network Open* 2:e1913123. doi:10.1001/jamanetworkopen.2019.13123.

Saint-Maurice PF, Troiano, RP, Berrigan, D, *et al.* 2018a. Volume of light versus moderate-to-vigorous physical activity: similar benefits for all-cause mortality? *The Journal of the American Heart Association* 7:e008815. doi:10./1161/JAHA.118.008815.

Saint-Maurice, PF, Troiano, RP, Matthews, CE, *et al.* 2018b. Moderate-to-vigorous physical activity and all-cause mortality: do bouts matter? *Journal of The American Heart Association* 7:e0077678. doi:10.1161/JAHA.117.007678.

Saint-Maurice, PF, Coughlan, D, Kelly, SP, *et al.* 2019. Association of leisure-time physical activity across the adult life course with all-cause and cause-specific mortality. *JAMA Network Open* 2:e190355. doi:10.1001/jamanetworkopen.2019.0355.

Schnohr, P, O'Keefe, JH, Holtermann, A, *et al.* 2018. Various leisure-time physical activities associated with widely divergent life expectancies: the Copenhagen City Heart Study. *Mayo Clinic Proceedings* 93:1775-1785. doi:10.1016/mayocp.2018.06.025.

Segaert, K, Lucas, SJE, Burley, CV, et al. 2018. Higher physical fitness levels are associated with less language decline in healthy aging. *Scientific Reports* 8:6715. doi:10.1038/s41598-018-24972-1.

Sorensen, IK, Bidstrup, PE, Rod, NH, et al. 2018. Is dog ownership associated with mortality? A nationwide registry study. *The European Journal of Public Health* 28:1169-1171. doi:10.1093/eurpub/cky164.

Spartano, NL, Davis-Plourde, KL, Himali, JJ, et al. 2019. Association of accelerometer-measured light-intensity physical activity with brain volume. The Framingham Heart Study. *JAMA Network Open* 2:e192745. doi:10.1001/jamanetworkopen.2019.2745.

Torske, MO, Krokstad, S, Stamatakis, E, et al. 2017. Dog ownership and all-cause mortality in a population cohort in Norway: the HUNT study. *PLoS ONE* 12:e0179832. doi:10.1371/journal.pone.0179832.

Zhao, M, Veeranki, SP, Li, S, et al. 2019. Beneficial associations of low and large doses of leisure time physical activity with all-cause, cardiovascular disease and cancer mortality: a national cohort study of 88,140 US adults. *British Journal of Sports Medicine* 53:1405-1411. doi:10.1136/bjsports-2018-099254.

Chapter 7

The Gut Microbiota

It's a Small World After All

The most important organisms on Earth are *Microbes*. This is a fact, not a hypothesis, and is a reality check for us humans. So, what is the evidence that microbes are the most important organisms on Earth?

Consider the topical issue of climate change. A very recent review in *Nature Reviews Microbiology*, a high-ranking scientific journal, emphasizes the key role of microorganisms in climate change (Cavicchioli *et al.*, 2019). This will come as a total surprise to most humans given that our dependence on fossil fuels for energy has been the focal issue in respect of global warming. There is little appreciation that microorganisms play a key role in climate control and thus climate change.

Pub Test 7.1 :

Question:

If all human life on Earth were eliminated, would other forms of life such as animals, plants, insects and microbes, still exist?

Answer:

Yes

In fact, non-human life will most likely thrive in the absence of humans. This experiment has already been conducted on planet Earth. Anatomically modern human-like individuals have been present on Earth for only a few million years (< 2 million years). By contrast, microorganisms have been around for a few billion years (< 4 billion years), plants < 600 million years ago, followed much later by marine organisms, insects and animals. And what about the dinosaurs?

There is scientific consensus that Earth is about 4.5 billion years old as determined by radioisotope analysis (Dalrymple, 2001). The earliest evidence (in the form of stable radioisotope ratios as measures of biological activity) for life forms has been dated at 3.4 – 4.0 billion years ago.

Several recent publications in *Nature*, one of the world's premier scientific journals, had presented data for microbial-biological activity in (a) sub-marine hydrothermal environments dated at 3.77 billion years old (Dodd *et al.*, 2017) and (b) sedimentary rocks from Labrador, Canada dated at 3.95 billion years old (Tashiro *et al.*, 2017). In a very recent publication in *Nature Communications* (Sim *et al.*, 2019), researchers applied stable sulphur (an essential element for life) radioisotope ratios as measurements of biological activity, and concluded that microbes were active in ancient oceans at least as far back as 3.5 billion years ago. An earlier publication (Tice and Lowe, 2014), also in *Nature*, provided evidence that photosynthetic microbial mats were active in carbonaceous matter in ocean sedimentary rocks dated at 3.416 billion years old.

These observations logically prompt the question, just how long have humans roamed the Earth? There is irrefutable evidence that the dinosaurs (think dinosaur bones) last roamed the Earth some 66 million years ago, after which time they became extinct. As far as I am aware, no human, dead or alive, has ever seen a live dinosaur for the simple reason that humans were not around 66 million years ago.

To date, the oldest anatomically modern human fossils have been dated at 315,000 years old, in remains found at an archaeological site in Morocco (Hublin *et al.*, 2017).

Although the direct ancestors of modern humans (Latin: *Homo sapiens*, meaning 'wise man'; a questionable definition for humans as this excludes 50% of the human population and, moreover, who has ever met a wise man?) are subject to much debate, there is substantial evidence from fossilized ape skulls that in the Miocene epoch (5 – 23 million years ago), Earth really was the planet of the apes. The divergence of extant hominoids (apes and humans) into the great apes (chimpanzee, gorilla and orangutan) and modern humans is estimated at 4 – 7 million years ago (Encyclopaedia Britannica). This divergence was followed (< 2 million years ago) by the evolution of the genus *Homo* as in *H. heidelbergenesis* and *H. erectus*, both potentially and controversially assigned as early ancestors of anatomically modern-day humans. The nomenclature of *H. erectus* refers to the genus *Homo* (Latin, for man) and species *erectus* (Latin, for upright) as capable of bipedal locomotion (translation: walking freely upright on two legs).

The simple point made here, in which we so briefly summarize decades of scientific studies, is that anatomically modern human-like individuals have been present on Earth for only a few million years (< 2 million years). By contrast, microorganisms have been around for a few billion years (< 4 billion years).

Pub Test 7.2:

Question:

If all microbes on Earth were eliminated, would humans still be around?

Answer:

No

In fact, there will be no life of any kind: no humans, animals, plants or insects. All these life forms are dependent on oxygen (mitochondria) and photosynthesis (chloroplasts). Both mitochondria and chloroplasts have their origins in ancestral microbes. Microbes are the essence of life.

Three Essentials for Human Life

If one still remains unconvinced that microbes have been and continue to be the most important organisms on Earth (and thus greatly influencing your healthy ageing), we can approach this issue another way by asking the question: what are the *three essentials for human life*?

Well, no, as previously alluded to in Chapter 4, your mobile phone is not essential for life and, surprisingly, neither is Facebook, Google, Instagram or Twitter.

We also have previously suggested the simple test of not breathing for five minutes. This simple test really does bring home the message that clean air, as in *oxygen*, is absolutely necessary for human life. The air we breathe is 20.9% oxygen with nitrogen (78.1%) as the main gas together with trace amounts of other gases including argon, helium, neon and carbon dioxide. Now consider the origin of the oxygen.

Photosynthetic microorganisms (ancestors of cyanobacteria) in the ocean surfaces first produced whiffs of oxygen as early as 3 billion years ago (Planavsky *et al.*, 2014). The well-defined Great Oxidation Event, about 2.45 billion years ago, raised atmospheric oxygen levels to about 0.1-0.2% of the current 20.9% (Holland, 2006). Recent models (Edwards *et al.*, 2017) of atmospheric oxygen had shown levels of 12% to 15% by 475 million years ago with fluctuations up to 30% before reaching the current 20.9% around 200-300 million years ago.

The oxygenation of the oceans, resulting in a massive increase of marine biodiversity, followed by the evolution of terrestrial plants around 400-500 million years ago (Lenton *et al.*, 2016), has been proposed as the origins of the current level of atmospheric oxygen. It is totally incorrect, as frequently described in biology textbooks, to assign photosynthesis (absorption of carbon dioxide and oxygen production) as primarily the activity of terrestrial plants (especially the tropical rainforests).

At best, terrestrial photosynthesis accounts for 50% of atmospheric oxygen levels with the other 50% (and possibly up to 80%; the oceans cover 71% of the Earth's surface) due to marine environments (marine phytoplankton which include dinoflagellates, diatoms and cyanobacteria; the former two are marine algae).

The current atmospheric oxygen concentration (20.9%) is essentially a balance between *photosynthesis (absorption of carbon dioxide* and production of oxygen) and respiration (absorption of oxygen and production of carbon dioxide). However, this topic is beyond the scope of the present discussion. Suffice it to note that microorganisms are the key players in photosynthesis not only in the marine environment but also in terrestrial plants.

The fundamental photosynthetic apparatus of the latter, the *chloroplast*, has its origin in the microbial ancestors of cyanobacteria which formed endosymbiotic associations with primitive eukaryotic cells (cells containing a nucleus) very early in the evolution of photosynthetic algae and plants. And finally, the fundamental organelles of respiration, the *mitochondria*, also find their origin as bacterial (sometimes termed proteobacteria) endosymbiotic associations with eukaryotic cells in the early evolution of all aerobic organisms, including humans.

Although these associations are most fascinating, they are much beyond the scope of the present discussions and the interested reader is referred to the scientific literature for in-depth analyses of these issues (e.g. Timmis *et al.,* 2004; Gray, 2012; both references require some prior knowledge of biology for comprehension).

Water and food, explicitly *clean water* and *clean food*, are the other essential requirements for human life. Humans can survive without water for about one week and without food for several weeks.

It is estimated that one-third (~ 2.5 billion) of the world's population, particularly in rural areas of sub-Saharan Africa and South-East Asia, do not have access to clean water and proper sanitation (https://www.cdc.gov/healthywater/global/wash_statistics.html). Unsafe drinking water is associated with epidemics of cholera and diarrhoea leading to preventable deaths (e.g. > 2,000 children/day in developing countries). Drinking water suitable for human consumption is dependent on filtration and chlorination of raw dam water, for example, and water is also required for personal hygiene (e.g. washing) and proper sanitation (e.g. flush toilets).

Food suitable for human consumption is dependent on best practice agriculture, crop harvesting, transport, storage, processing and consumer awareness of food hygiene.

Drinking contaminated water or food has serious outcomes for humans (e.g. death, to be absolutely avoided if one wishes to age healthily). The word *contaminated*, of course, refers to pathogenic microorganisms. Thus, we recognize the importance of microorganisms in their negative roles with respect to clean water and clean food.

These negative effects of microbes on the quality of the water and food we consume may be balanced in also recognizing that without the products of microbial metabolism (e.g. bread, wine, beer, cheese, yoghurt) our drinking and eating habits will be extremely boring. And we haven't even considered the important roles microorganisms play in agriculture (e.g. soil and rumen microbes), in industry (e.g. antibiotics, enzymes, chemicals), in the environment (e.g. clean-up of toxic wastes, sewage and water treatment) and in biotechnology (e.g. vaccines, human insulin, human growth hormone, gene technology).

Seeing Is Believing – The Invisible World of Microbes

Why is it that microorganisms are simply not recognized by the general public and, indeed, even by many of the scientific professions as the key organisms for all life on Earth?

Seeing is believing. Basically, we see humans, animals, plants, insects and other living organisms and we can thus relate to their significance.

Microorganisms are invisible to the human eye. For example, approximately 500 *Escherichia coli* bacteria (*E. coli*, typically found in our gut flora) will fit into the full stop at the end of this sentence. Many thousands of a typical virus (10-100 times smaller than bacteria) will fit into the same full stop. Bacteria can be visualized in a quality light microscope (up to 1,000 x magnification compared to the human eye) but one requires an electron microscope (50,000 and upwards x magnification of the human eye) to visualize a typical virus.

Are We Really 100% Human?

Consider these estimates. You consist of only 50% human cells, the other 50% are microbial cells (Sender, 2016). Your human DNA that codes for around 20,000 genes (see Chapter 2: Genes and Healthy Ageing) is outnumbered, conservatively, 100 x by your microbial genes (Gilbert *et al.,* 2018). Your average weight includes about one kg of microbes (variable but going on a diet will not greatly change your microbial biomass and getting rid of all your microbes will result in death). There are 40-100 trillion microbes on and in the human body, with estimates of distinct species from many hundreds to several thousand (Bilen *et al.,* 2018).

Microbes occupy key niches on and in the human body, and these include the skin, the oral cavity, the genitals and the intestinal tract or gut. The latter hosts the highest concentration of microbes ($\sim 40 \times 10^{12} = \sim 40$ trillion) and in the last few years it is the *gut microbiota* (the microorganisms present in the gut) that has attracted the most attention with respect to human health.

A recent review (Cani et al., 2018) estimated that > 80% of all scientific publications on human gut microbiota have been published just in the past five years with > 4,000 journal papers alone in 2017. Perhaps a much better gauge of interest in gut microbiota comes from an estimated US$37 billion world-wide market for probiotic supplements (Editorial, the Lancet 2019). A probiotic, usually taken as a food supplement (e.g. yoghurt), normally contains a single or two to six specific strains of viable bacteria (see following section on Probiotics).

Alterations in the human gut microbiota have been associated with a multitude of health- and age-related disorders, including obesity, cardiovascular disease, gastrointestinal inflammatory diseases (inflammatory bowel disease, Crohn's disease, ulcerative colitis, irritable bowel syndrome) and neurological disorders such as mood disorders, depression, Alzheimer's and Parkinson's. Furthermore, the importance of the gut microbiota is well illustrated by studies relating the acquisition of gut microbiota at birth through to early childhood as critical steps towards the proper development of the adult immune system.

This is a remarkable list of gut microbiota associations with health-related issues. In this Chapter we critically assess the most recent scientific publications with respect to these associations.

However, before we examine these issues in more detail, it is necessary to provide basic background information as to the methodology behind these studies and, notwithstanding the remarkable progress in technology in the past few years, state a few of their limitations.

What Is the Meaning of the Terms Microbiota and Microbiome?

When reading an article in a scientific publication or in a glossy magazine, it is important to appreciate what is meant by the terms *microbiota* and *microbiome*. In the majority of these articles, the terms *microbiota* or *microbiome* refers only to the bacteria. The term *gut microbiota* refers to all the microbes present in the human gut and in most articles refer only to the bacteria. Similarly, the term *gut microbiome* refers to all the microbial DNA or genes present in the gut and, again, generally refers only to the bacteria. The term gut microbiome is sometimes, erroneously, used as synonymous with the gut microbiota.

It is important to recognize that humans are also colonized by microbes other than bacteria, and these include archaea (a type of bacteria), viruses and fungi. The latter numbers are small by comparison with the bacteria and the archaea are estimated (and it is only an estimate) to be around 10% of the total intestinal bacterial microbial population (Pike and Forster, 2018). On the other hand, the viruses may well exceed, by an order of magnitude, the number of bacteria.

By comparison with the bacterial microbiota very few studies have focused on the health significance of the human mycobiota (the term *human mycobiota* refers to the fungal organisms and the term *human mycobiome* refers to the fungal DNAs and genes).

The most common fungi colonizing the human body (e.g. skin, vagina, oral cavity) are the *Saccharomyces*, *Candida* and *Malassezia* yeast genera with some disorders of the lung linked with the filamentous fungi *Aspergillus, Penicillium* and *Cladosporium* genera (Nash *et al.,* 2017; Kong and Morris, 2017; Laforest-Lapointe and Arrieta, 2018). Outbreaks of *Candida* yeast infection sometime occur after antibiotic use, the action of which may eliminate key bacterial species thus facilitating opportunistic growth of *Candida* (antibiotics do not target fungi). The above publications and references therein can be consulted for further details on the current status of the human mycobiota: the most recent update is published in *Nature Reviews* (Richard and Sokol, 2019)

The viruses colonizing the human body have attracted considerable attention in the past few years, particularly the *gut bacteriophages* (the term *bacteriophage* is used to describe viruses associated with bacteria). The characterization of viruses colonizing the human body is technologically challenging, to say the least. For example, there is no common genetic marker among viruses as in the case of bacteria (see section below on Methodology) and a significant number of viruses in the human gut do not show a significant match to that of any known viruses.

Further complicating the situation is that bacteria and viruses interact essentially in two ways:

(a) The virus (also termed *phage*) infects the bacterial cell, causing lysis (translation: burst open) with the death of the bacterium and release of viruses which can then go on to infect another bacterial cell and so on. This type of virus is scientifically termed a *lytic phage*.
(b) The virus infects the bacterial cell and specific sections of the viral DNA are able to integrate into the bacterial genome (DNA) to the extent that when the bacteria

replicate (divide) the integrated phage DNA also gets replicated. This type of virus is termed a *lysogenic phage* and the *integrated phage* is known as a *prophage*. Importantly, lysogenic phages can become activated in response to specific triggers and revert to a lytic stage, resulting in lysis of the bacterial cell and release of virus particles.

In both these scenarios, viruses are capable of influencing not only the total numbers of gut microbiota but also, and perhaps more significantly, the actual species or types of gut microbiota. A critical property of many viruses is their ability to target, in an extremely efficient manner, specific species (even down to the strain) of bacteria.

In summary, viruses may be viewed as the keepers or regulators of the gut microbiota in that they are capable of influencing the numbers, the species and thus the function of the gut microbiota.

For example, a large number of a particular species of bacteria may be present but have little influence on health outcomes or may even be functionally inactive. By comparison, a small number of a particular species of bacteria may be functionally very active and provide metabolites (e.g. short-chain fatty acids, see later section) known to be associated with a healthy gut microbiota.

As previously mentioned, bacteriophages (viruses capable of infecting bacteria) can be very specific in their ability to infect only certain strains of bacteria. Thus, specific pathogenic or non-functional bacteria may be targeted leaving intact the functionally useful bacteria. Thus, the key question is not so much as 'who's there?' but rather 'what are they doing?'

The balance between health and disease in relation to gut microbiota may well be governed by the human bacteriophages. At this point, despite substantial progress in our understanding of human bacteriophages (recently reviewed in Manrique *et al.*, 2017), we have much to learn about their role in regulating gut microbiota.

We look forward to the next few years in which advances in our understanding of human bacteriophages will greatly enlighten our (biased) concepts of the significance in human health and disease of these smallest of all living organisms (strictly speaking, viruses are not free-living organisms as they require a living host in order to replicate).

Pub Test 7.3:

Question:

Are bacteria the only microorganisms on or in the human body that have an influence on human health and disease?

Answer:

No

Although bacteria are the most abundant of the microbes associated with humans (with the possible exception of the viruses), other microbes include the archaea (a type of bacteria), the fungi (substantially lower numbers than bacteria) and the viruses. The latter, in particular, may be the key regulators of the number and types of bacteria present in the human gut. These two properties greatly influence the function of the gut microbiota and thus the overall health of the human host.

The rest of this Chapter will cover recent studies on the gut microbiota and health as this is the area that has been the most intensely studied in the past few years. Unless specifically mentioned, these studies refer to the gut microbiota as meaning the gut bacteria.

How Do We Know 'Who's There?' and 'What Are They Doing?'

The human gut is an extreme environment characterized by large sections of little or no oxygen (anaerobic) and harbouring trillions of microbes. Identifying what microbes were present initially involved analyses of faecal samples by modification of developed methods of culturing (translation: growing microbes on a Petri dish) that attempted to mimic the human gut environment. However, it was realized very early on that many of the gut microbes were unculturable by conventional methodology. The availability of large numbers of microbes by culturing would have allowed a more definitive identification of the gut microbiota. A recent estimate of > 80% non-culturable gut microbiota (with current technology) indicated the challenges of identifying members of the gut microbiota (Lagier *et al.*, 2018).

A method that does not require culturing the bacteria is extracting the DNA from an appropriate sample (generally a faecal sample) and the sample screened for a biomarker of bacteria. The biomarker of choice is the gene (DNA) for *16S ribosomal RNA* which is an essential gene found in all bacteria and is required for protein synthesis. A comprehensive reference data bank of 16S ribosomal RNA gene sequences is then screened to identify specific bacterial genera (which differ in their gene sequence code for 16S ribosomal RNA and can thus be identified).

The major limitation of this method is that it relies on a single bacterial biomarker gene and many species (and specific strains) are not definitively identified or not identified at all.

Nomenclature – What's in a Name? Everything

We'll have a short digression at this point to explain the concept of nomenclature as applied to microorganisms. Microorganisms, in common with all living organisms (e.g. *Homo sapiens*), are assigned Latin names in keeping with the long tradition that Latin was the language of the educated and of science. The binomial nomenclature system (generally attributed to Linnaeus, a Swedish naturalist from the mid-eighteenth century) consists of a first part generic name which identifies the genus (first letter capitalized, italicized) and the second part which identifies the species (not capitalized, italicized). A specific example clarifies these points.

The manufacture of yoghurt, highly popular these days as a probiotic (see later section), requires the input of microorganisms such as *Lactobacillus acidophilus*. Here, *Lactobacillus* is the genus and *acidophilus* the species. The full binomial name is used when first mentioned in the text; thereafter, it is convention that the name can be abbreviated as the first letter (capitalized) of the genus followed by the species, thus *L. acidophilus*.

An important additional concept here is that in the manufacture of yoghurt one has to use *specific strains* of *L. acidophilus*, depending on their specific properties and the product requirement for, say, a slightly more acidic (sharp) yoghurt or a creamier yoghurt; thus, we may have for example, *L. acidophilus* strain YG1 for a more acidic yoghurt and *L. acidophilus* strain YG2 for a creamier yoghurt. The strains are frequently commercial-in-confidence (as in patents) and are closely guarded by the manufacturers. A similar situation applies to the manufacture of beers, which require specific strains of yeast; not every strain of *Saccharomyces cerevisiae* or *S. carlsbergensis* is going to produce the required beer with its distinctive flavour.

One final example illustrates this key point of the significance of microbial strains. There are thousands of strains (including laboratory generated strains) of the common gut inhabitant *Escherichia coli*; some are highly pathogenic (e.g. *E. coli* O157) and most others are non-pathogenic. Thus, it is important to be able to identify the *specific strain* of a given microorganism and not just the genus and species.

Gut Microbiota Methodology

Recently, *shotgun metagenomics*, that is, the analyses of all the DNA ('metagenomics') in a sample, including that of the human host, is applied to examine gut microbiota.

This methodology has greatly expanded our knowledge of what microbes are present in the human gut ('who's there?') as it is capable of identification to the bacterial strain level. The extracted DNA is broken up into small segments ('shotgun'), individually sequenced and then reconstructed (like a jigsaw puzzle) into whole genomes (entire DNA of an organism, in this case a microbe) or parts thereof, if complete reconstruction is not feasible.

A comprehensive database(s) of known microbial (bacteria and archaea) genomes (DNA) can then be screened to identify specific genera, species and, importantly, strains. As reference databases are updated regularly, unknown organisms may be identified at a later date or a new organism may be assigned an appropriate name (Latin binomial nomenclature, as is the scientific tradition). Moreover, many microbial genes (segments of DNA which code for proteins, see Chapter 2) have known functions and this enables scientists to predict what the different microbes may actually be doing in the gut ('what are they doing?').

It should be noted that the mere presence of a microbe and its DNA in a sample does not equate to functionality. That is the microbe may be in a dormant or even dead state, and thus, some or all of its genes may not be activated (see Chapter 2; genes may be switched on or off).

Current research seeks to address this issue by looking for microbial gene products, such as amino acids and short-chain fatty acids, in the sample under investigation. Development of this type of methodology will greatly assist in answering the key question of 'what are they doing?'

A recent publication in the high-impact journal, *Nature Genetics*, highlighted this type of functional (termed metabolomic) analysis (Zierer *et al.*, 2018). In this study (n = 786, TwinsUK study, mean age of 65.2, predominantly female), faecal samples were analyzed for metabolites (products of biological metabolism), and the authors reported that visceral-fat-associated (abdominal fat) metabolites were associated with products of bacterial metabolism, adding further to the data linking gut microbiota and obesity (see later section).

The interested Reader can consult a number of recent publications for details of current metagenomic methodologies (Quince *et al.*, 2017; Allaband *et al.*, 2019; Pasolli *et al.*, 2019) [warning: a PhD in molecular biology is a prerequisite to fully comprehend the technology].

Pub Test 7.4:

Question:

Do we fully know what microbes are present in the human gut and therefore, what constitutes a 'standard' or healthy human gut microbiota?

Answer:

No

What constitutes a 'standard' or healthy human gut microbiota composition is currently unknown. Although there are reference data bases on microbes (thousands of microbes) which have been identified in the human gut, there are many unidentified microbes. Moreover, there is incomplete knowledge about the function of these microbes, how they interact among themselves and, most importantly, how they interact with the human host.

Origins of the Human Microbiota

Less than a decade ago, knowledge on the origin, composition and development of the human microbiota, that is, the microbes on and in our body, has been relatively limited. Thanks to advances in DNA technology and computational data analysis, there is now a large body of evidence that supports that the human gut microbiota is a key player in health and disease.

Although there is on-going debate about the degree of sterility (absence of microbes) of the foetal environment (Perez-Munoz et al., 2017; D'Argenio, 2018; Shao et al., 2019), there is absolutely no doubt that the mother-infant relationship is the key with respect to the very earliest acquisition of the microbiota of the new-born infant. The nature of the microbiota has been shown to be dependent on the maternal microbiota, the birth mode (vaginal or caesarean delivery) and the duration of breast feeding or infant-formula feeding.

In the case of vaginal birth, the infant is inoculated with microbes from the birth canal and intestine of the mother and then exposed to the immediate environment. A characteristically high diversity of infant gut microbiota is observed in the first few days post-natal and this rapidly decreases in the following weeks before increasing and stabilizing in the following months. These changes correspond to those in the infant's feeding routine, interactions with the environment and contact with other humans. Moreover, the nature of the gut microbiota which initially is in the aerobic and semi-anaerobic class, rapidly changes to semi-anaerobic and anaerobic as the gut adjusts to its natural environment of very low to no oxygen.

In the case of caesarean birth, the primary inoculation is via the mother's skin and the immediate environment. Importantly, the infant gut microbiota is initially less diverse than via vaginal birth and may also be greatly influenced by post-natal time in hospital and, if antibiotics have been used, either pre- and/or post-natal. Both of the latter two environments tend to be more common in caesarean births than vaginal births. These observations are consistent with the longer time required for the establishment of a 'normal' gut microbiota in caesarean-born infants. Early studies have provided evidence, albeit modest, that caesarean-born infants have a compromised immune system, with increased risk of allergy associated conditions such as asthma (Houghtelling & Walker, 2015; Tamburini et al., 2016 and references therein).

The importance of the development of the infant gut microbiota in early life in relation to future health outcomes had been emphasized in recent studies.

In a study of a Norwegian Birth Cohort (n = 165 children and their mothers) the authors were able to correlate the gut microbiota in the first two years of life (longitudinal study, samples at six time points) with BMI at age 12 (Stanislawski *et al.*, 2018). For example, bacterial species in the genera *Bacteroides* in the one- to two- year gut microbiota were predictive of BMI at age 12. Moreover, the subset of gut microbiota up to two years, which predicted later life BMI, showed an overlap with the maternal microbiota. The authors did state that the data could also be indicative of diet and environmental influences. It was notable that high BMI at age 12 was also related to mothers who were overweight, had higher rates of smoking and who shortened the duration of breastfeeding.

The key role of the mother in early life gut microbiota was also highlighted in several recent studies in which specific strains (i.e. not just genera and species) of bacteria were traceable from mother to infant.

In a cohort which included n = 139 infants (twenty-five born by caesarean section) the authors showed that only specific bacterial strains from the classes Actinobacteria and Bacteroidia, both essential components of the infant gut microbiota, were transmitted from mother to infant and persisted up to one year (Korpela *et al.*, 2018a). Interestingly, infants born by caesarean section failed to receive specific maternal bacterial strains in early life and only acquired maternal specific strains postnatally from the environment. In another study (n = 25, mother-infant pairs, vaginal delivery, 96% breast-fed at one month, 56% at four months) specific bacterial strains from the mother proved more persistent and better adapted in the infant gut microbiota than from other human or environmental sources (Ferretti *et al.*, 2018).

There is considerable scientific support that early-life gut microbiota is integral to the development of a functional immune system into adulthood, earlier reviewed (Tamburini *et al.*, 2016) in *Nature Medicine*, a very high- impact journal.

Altered gut microbiota (termed dysbiosis) in early-life is known to increase the risk of immune-related diseases including allergies, asthma, eczema and inflammatory gut disorders. As noted above, the gut microbiota of vaginal-delivered infants differs from caesarean-delivered infants, but this difference is less evident after three to four months. By ages 2 to 3, both delivery types approach the adolescent gut microbiota composition, and this is related to lifestyle and environmental influences, including commencement of solid food intake.

In a very detailed longitudinal (four blood samples in the first three months of birth) study of term (n = 50) and pre-term (n = 50) infants published in the very high-impact journal *Cell*, the authors reported that differences were noted in the formation of immune-related proteins (n = 267 proteins) and cell types (n = 58 types) related to the immune system (Olin *et al.*, 2018). Interestingly, and somewhat surprisingly, the authors noted that by three months, there was a convergence of immune development of term and pre-term infants (even in those that had been in hospital the entire three months). The authors also proposed that alterations (dysbiosis, lower bacterial diversity) in gut microbiota in the first few weeks of life adversely influence the development of the immune system.

In a long-term, longitudinal study of gut microbiota in faecal samples of children (n = 903, regular samples from 3 to 46 months) from three European countries (Finland, Germany and Sweden) and three US states (Colorado, Georgia and Washington), the authors (Stewart et al., 2018) were able to identify distinct phases of gut microbiota development using 16S ribosomal RNA gene sequencing and metagenomic sequencing. Three distinct gut microbiota phases were identified: a developmental phase (at ages 3 to 14 months), a transitional phase (at ages 15 to 30 months) and a stable phase (at ages 31 to 46 months).

Infants born vaginally had, comparatively, higher levels of *Bacteroides* species and breast-fed infants' higher levels of *Bifidobacterium* species. The authors reported that maturation of the infant gut microbiota (as measured in faecal samples) towards increased levels of bacteria belonging to the Firmicutes phylum (as a measure of maturation) tended to coincide with cessation of breast-feeding rather than introduction of solid food. Increase rates of microbiota maturation were also associated with infants living with siblings and in households with furry pets.

There is absolutely no doubt that gut microbiota, from early-life and into adulthood, is essential for the proper development and functioning of the immune system. However, there is far-from-complete understanding of what combination and, more significantly, their functionality, of early-life gut microbiota that is required for the development of a healthy immune system.

Studies on germ-free mice have shown that their highly impaired immune system can be restored, at least partially and depending at what developmental stage, upon exposure to microbes from the diet and environment (Durack and Lynch, 2019).

In summary, it is known that early-life gut microbiota plays a key role in future health outcomes of the individual and is critical for the development of a healthy immune system.

Acquisition of early-life microbiota is dependent on mother-infant transfer, which is further dependent on mode of delivery (vaginal or caesarean) and gestation period (full or pre-term). Add the additional variables of breast-feeding (how long?), infant-formula (how long?), antibiotic use (particularly caesarean and pre-term infants), interaction with family, lifestyle and the environment and we have a multitude of variables influencing early-life microbiota and health outcomes.

The very latest scientific research on early-life microbiota clearly favours full-term, vaginal-birth and breastfeeding for at least three months for proper immune development and positive health outcomes into adulthood. Interestingly, that's exactly what grandmother had figured out many years ago.

Given that there is general agreement that the mother-infant relationship plays a key role in early-life gut microbiota, the question then is does the human host genetics also determine the composition of the adult gut microbiota or does the environment and lifestyle of the individual also play a key factor?

Studies on the gut microbiota in twins (n = 416 twin pairs, average age of 60.6, predominantly female, Goodrich *et al.*, 2014) had shown that bacteria from the taxon Christensenellaceae were more highly heritable in monozygotic twins (identical) than dizygotic twins (non-identical). In a larger population follow-up study (n = 1,126 twin pairs), a similar conclusion about heritability (8.8% heritable) of specific bacterial gut taxa was reported (Goodrich *et al.*, 2016).

In a recent USA study (Brooks *et al.*, 2018) on gut microbiota diversity in four ethnic groups (African-American, Asian-Pacific Islander, Caucasian and Hispanic, total individuals n = 1,673), the authors reported that twelve microbial genera varied by ethnicity with the most heritable bacterial family being the Christensenellaceae taxon. In these studies, gut microbiota differences were consistently related to ethnicity and at least comparable to that of physiological traits such as BMI, age and sex. In another study, published in the high-ranking journal *Nature Medicine* (Deschasaux et al., 2018), the authors determined gut microbiota differences across six ethnic groups (total individuals n = 2,084), all living in the same urban environment (Amsterdam). Three main groups were characterized with microbiota classified as *Prevotella* (Moroccans, Turks, Ghanaians), *Bacteroides* (African-Surinamese, South-Asian Surinamese) and Clostridiales (Dutch).

The authors concluded that ethnicity explained differences in gut microbiota significantly better than other traits (e.g. lifestyle, diet, socio-economic status). Nevertheless, one has to consider that ethnicity includes not just ancestral genetics but clearly also cultural, environmental, lifestyle and social issues.

Although these and other studies have provided evidence of a heritable (genetic) component for gut microbiota diversity, it does appear that lifestyle and environment impose the predominant influences on the diversity of the adult gut microbiota. This is the clear conclusion of a recent study published in 2018 in the high-ranking journal, *Nature* (Rothschild et al., 2018).

The authors confirmed the genetic ancestry, as initially self-reported by participants (n = 1,046, mean age of 42.6, 61% female), of six distinct ancestries, all based in Israel: Ashkenazi (n = 508), North African (n = 64), Middle Eastern (n = 34), Sephardi (n = 19), Yemenite (n = 13) and other/mixed ancestries (n = 408). The authors reported that there was a significant similarity in the gut microbiota composition of genetically unrelated individuals living in the same household environment. In contrast, there was no significant similarity in gut microbiota composition among genetically related individuals not living in the same household environment. Furthermore, the authors reported a microbiome-association index of 22% to 36% with host physiological traits including BMI, waist circumference and levels of fasting glucose and HDL-cholesterol.

These estimates were comparable to values reported in the literature for heritability of these traits. Importantly, height, which is a highly heritable trait (literature values 33% to 68% heritability), was not associated with host gut microbiota composition.

The authors also reported that combining the microbiome-association index with the contribution assigned to host genetics improved the accuracy of prediction with respect to physiological traits (e.g. BMI, HDL-cholesterol, fasting glucose levels) of the participants. The fact that the two data sets were essentially additive strongly suggested that the gut microbiota and host genetics were independent of each another.

It is known that there are substantial differences in gut microbiota composition between individuals living in different geographic locations and consuming different diets (Fragiadakis *et al.*, 2018; Makki *et al.*, 2018), further emphasizing the key role of lifestyle and the environment in structuring the gut microbiota. A change in diet can rapidly (24 to 48 hr) alter gut microbiota composition as reported in a short-term (five consecutive days) limited study on humans (n = 10, ages 21 to 33, 40% female) consuming either a plant-based (herbivorous) diet or animal-based (carnivorous) diet, with the changes reflecting the two contrasting diets (David *et al.*, 2014).

Two recent publications have emphasized the key role of diet and lifestyle in gut microbiota composition. The publication in the BioMed Central journal, *Microbiome*, examined the gut microbiota composition of healthy individuals (n = 1,000, 50% female, ages 20 to 70, equal numbers in each decade) of Western European ancestry (Scepanovic *et al.*, 2019). The authors reported that host genetics had little influence on the gut microbiota composition (at least as identified by 16S ribosomal RNA; see above section on Gut Microbiota Methodology). In contrast, a number of non-genetic variables were associated with diversity of the gut microbiota. These included age, diet, clinical profiles, lifestyle and socio-economic status.

In a related study (n = 862) of the same cohort of healthy individuals, published in the *American Journal of Clinical Nutrition* (Partula *et al.*, 2019), the authors reported that a diet of foods considered as healthy (fish, fruit) contributed to greater microbiota diversity in contrast to decreased diversity on a diet of foods considered as less healthy (soft drinks, processed foods).

The fact that diet is the key factor influencing gut microbiota can simply be demonstrated by feeding your pet dog either a high plant-based or a high meat-based diet for several days and visually observing the form and texture of stool, with no need for high-tech shotgun metagenomic and metabolomic analyses.

The central role of diet in formulating the gut microbiota composition is illustrated by a number of novel studies in populations having distinct ethnicities and consuming a non-Western-style diet.

The gut microbiota community in children (n = 14, ages 2 to 8), consuming a high-fibre complex carbohydrate diet (primarily polysaccharides from vegetables), from a rural village in Africa (Burkina Faso) showed rich bacterial diversity with characteristics of ability to ferment fibre and polysaccharides (De Fillippo *et al.*, 2010).

By contrast, in children (n = 11, ages 2 to 8) living in an European urban environment (Florence), there was less gut bacterial diversity and with characteristics associated with metabolism of food rich in animal protein, sugars and fat but low in fibre. In an extension of the previous study, it was reported that children (n = 5) living in an urban (capital city) area of Burkina Faso had a gut bacterial diversity approaching that of children living in an European urban environment (Florence), thus illustrating the key role of diet, irrespective of ethnicity, in structuring the gut microbiota (De Fillippo et al., 2017).

In another novel study of the Hadzar hunter-gatherers of Tanzania, the high levels of gut microbial diversity were related to a diet rich in fibre (complex carbohydrates) from consumption of plant foods (Schnorr et al., 2014). In these individuals (n = 27, mean age of 32) the gut microbiota had increased levels of *Bacteroidetes* and low levels of *Firmicutes* bacteria, which was opposite to that of individuals consuming a typical Western-style diet (low fibre, high protein, fats and simple carbohydrates).

The key role of diet in structuring the gut microbiota was clearly demonstrated in these traditional Hadza hunter-gatherers by observations on alterations in gut microbiota linked with seasonally associated food sources (Smits et al., 2017). The authors were able to demonstrate that certain bacterial species were undetectable in specific seasons and then reappeared at the appropriate season concurrent with the availability of particular food sources.

The origins of the human microbiota are initially dependent on early-life mother-infant interactions, particularly the concept that specific strains appear to be transferrable, in a stable manner, from mother to infant. Shortly thereafter (days to weeks), the environment and human interactions play an increasing role in the acquisition of microbiota. Into adulthood, the environment and lifestyle of the individual are the key parameters about a stable gut microbiota. What microbes constitute a healthy gut microbiota is still far from resolved except that the scientific literature insists that there is a core gut microbiota composition, as yet undefined.

One underlining issue is that having a different gut microbiota composition ('who's there?') does not necessarily equate to the gut microbiota having a different behaviour or function, the latter is the core issue here ('what are they doing?'). It is not uncommon for different microbes to have similar or even identical functions (e.g. production of microbial metabolites such as short-chain fatty acids). Moreover, we have little understanding on how the communities of microbes, as opposed to individual microbes, interact within the gut. For example, some microbes produce metabolites which are essential for the growth and maintenance of other microbes or, conversely, produce metabolites which inhibit the growth and maintenance of other microbes. And if one considers the role of viruses, particularly the bacteriophages which can target and kill specific bacterial species and strains, then we begin to appreciate the complexity of the gut microbiota.

There are claims that every individual has a unique gut microbiota composition. However, there is no likelihood that a gut microbiota fingerprint is capable of positively identifying any individual, certainly not anywhere near as accurate as a hand fingerprint, a DNA fingerprint from a blood sample or mouth swab or by using face recognition technology. Simply consider that your gut microbiota profile is highly dependent on your diet.

Despite many unresolved issues, there is considerable optimism that understanding the form and function of the human microbiota will positively contribute towards key health outcomes related to obesity, heart disease, the immune response (e.g. allergies, asthma) and neurological disorders. In the next section we will discuss some recent research in these and other areas.

Pub Test 7.5:

Question:

Is the composition of the adult gut microbiota largely dependent on the genetics of the human host?

Answer:

No

The composition of the adult gut microbiota is largely dependent on diet, lifestyle and the environment. Although at birth there is initially a significant (especially in the future development of the immune system) contribution from the mother, the infant gut microbiota composition rapidly changes until, at around ages 6 to 18 months, it reflects the microbiota of the diet, lifestyle and the environment of the individual. The adult gut microbiota is relatively stable given a stable diet, lifestyle and environment.

Faecal Microbiota Transplants

In a publication in the *New England Journal of Medicine*, a leading medical journal, it was estimated that in 2011, the bacterium *Clostridium difficile* caused 29,000 deaths in the United States (Lessa et al., 2014). A more recent estimate showed that the number of hospital fatalities due to *C. difficile* infections actually decreased in the decade 2004-2014 although the number of infections increased (Shrestha et al., 2018).

The global burden of *C. difficile* infections (covering the period 2005-2015) has recently been reviewed (Balsells *et al.*, 2018) and a systematic review of randomized controlled trials (n = 657 patients, ten trials) of faecal microbiota transplantation for *C. difficile*-associated diarrhoea has been published in the *Medical Journal of Australia* (Moayyedi *et al.*, 2017).

To date, the most successful application of human microbiota research has been in faecal microbiota transplants for the treatment of chronic diarrhoea due to *C. difficile* infections, in particular for recurring and antibiotic-resistant infections. The elderly (aged > 65) and compromised individuals (e.g. hospital inpatients) are typically the most prone to these types of infections.

Guidelines for faecal microbiota transplants in the UK have recently been published (Mullish *et al.*, 2018). Briefly, suitable donors are rigorously screened (e.g. in good health, no family history of heritable diseases, faecal microbiota free of potential pathogenic organisms) and recipients required to have detailed documentation of their disease history including antibiotic usage. Depending on the expertise of the medical team and patient suitability, transplants can be administered via upper gastrointestinal tract (e.g. endoscopy, nasogastric tube), lower gastrointestinal tract (e.g. colonoscopy, enema) or capsule (frozen or freeze-dried faecal microbiota).

The above guidelines indicated that the latter (capsule) procedure provided outcomes comparable to the former two procedures. The bottom line was a high success rate for faecal microbiota transplants for treatment of antibiotic-resistant recurrent *C. difficile* infections.

By way of illustration, a high success rate (87.4%) was recently reported in treatment of recurrent *C. difficile* infections in a nationwide cohort of individuals (n = 111, median age of 70, 58% female) residing in Israel (Greenberg et al., 2018). Equal success was reported for administration via upper gastrointestinal tract (n = 24), lower gastrointestinal tract (n = 50) or capsule (n = 37). The authors noted that severe *C. difficile* infection was less likely to respond to transplants.

A high success rate (78%) was also reported in a small-scale trial in which faecal microbiota transplant was used as a first treatment (as opposed to the conventional antibiotic treatment) for primary acute *C. difficile* infection (Juul et al., 2018). In this trial, seven out of nine patients (78% success) responded to transplant treatment (five transplants only; two transplants followed after four days by antibiotic) and five out of eleven patients (45% success) responded to antibiotic treatment.

Intriguingly, it has recently been reported that filtered and sterile (bacteria-free) faecal extracts were effective in treatment of recurrent antibiotic-resistant *C. difficile* infections, thus raising the issue that intact bacterial cells may not be a pre-requisite for successful treatment (Ott et al., 2017). In this preliminary small-scale trial (n = 5; three females aged 59, 73 and 75; two males aged 49 and 72) symptoms of *C. difficile* infection were eliminated at least up to the six months' trial period. The authors speculated that bacterial components (e.g. cell walls, DNA fragments) could have stimulated host gut responses in a positive way. Alternatively, viruses, as bacteriophages, may have altered the microbiota composition of the recipients.

Note that many bacterial components and viruses (both small enough to pass through the filters, experimental size of 0.22 µm) would not have been entirely filtered out of the extracts used in the treatments. Support for the concept that bacteriophages may play a role in the efficacy of faecal transplants comes from two recent publications in which the relative success rate of treatment for recurrent *C. difficile* infection was associated with the gut viral diversity of both the donor and recipient (Zuo *et al.*, 2018; Park *et al.*, 2019).

Further studies will be required to confirm these early reports on the potential role of viruses and bacteriophages in faecal microbiota transplants.

The success of faecal microbiota transplants in the treatment of recurring antibiotic-resistant *C. difficile* infections has raised expectations that similar outcomes will be forthcoming for other gut-associated dysfunctions, including inflammatory bowel disease, ulcerative colitis and Crohn's disease. These disorders are known to be multifactorial; including not just gut microbiota dysbiosis (e.g. lack of bacterial diversity) but also a dysfunctional host immune system. To date, faecal microbiota transplant outcomes for gut microbiota disorders have been mixed. A review of four randomized controlled trials (n = 277, total number of patients) for inflammatory bowel disease has reported a 38% success rate in patients receiving a faecal microbiota transplant, as compared with 9% with patients treated with a placebo (reviewed by Levy and Allegretti, 2019).

The most recent studies on ulcerative colitis had reported around a 30% success rate for microbiota transplants (generally requiring multiple transplants) as compared with around 15% for conventional immunosuppressive treatments (Editorial, *the Lancet*, 2019). In a randomized controlled trial (n = 73, mean age of 39, 45% female), remission was achieved in 32% of recipients (twelve out of thirty-eight patients) who received donor transplants as compared with 9% of recipients (three out of thirty-five patients) who received autologous (self) transplants (Costello et al., 2019).

Faecal microbiota transplants have also been applied to studies on obesity, currently a world-wide epidemic and a major health issue. Although host (human) genetics has been proposed as a possible factor, this is most unlikely. Increases in obesity was first noted around sixty years ago, with an estimated 40% of the adult population and 20% of children under 12 now classified as overweight or obese. The approximate sixty years period is simply not long enough for changes in human genes to have occurred, changes which typically require thousands of years to occur.

The time-frame from, say, 1960 to 2020, coincides with dramatic changes in human lifestyle, particularly the marked decrease in physical activity (e.g. modern transport, sedentary/passive entertainment, workplace environment) and the availability of large quantities of relatively cheap, highly processed calorie-dense food. It is surely the latter that is the main cause for the obesity epidemic, which leads to the logical association of obesity, diet and the human gut microbiota.

Furthermore, diet can rapidly (within 24 to 48 hr) alter the composition and hence genetics of the gut microbiota. Sixty years is an immense time for microorganisms to adjust to a given environment. Consider that, at 37^0C and provided with appropriate nutrients (e.g. in the human gut), many bacteria can rapidly divide multiple times in 24 hr. However, we shouldn't completely exclude a role in obesity for the host (human) DNA as there is likelihood of interaction (complex) between host DNA and the rapidly changing genetics of the gut microbiota brought about by the present-day diet and lifestyle.

Associations between obesity and gut microbiota were first suggested in studies on mice. Faecal microbiota transplants from obese mice into germ-free lean mice resulted in a 47% increase in body fat as compared with a 27% increase in body fat when faecal microbiota from lean mice were transplanted into germ-free lean mice (Turnbaugh *et al.*, 2006). These experiments were over a two-week feeding cycle and experimental animals consumed essentially the same number of calories. These observations in rodents have been confirmed in recent studies including a study on faecal microbiota transplants using human twins discordant for obesity (Ridaura *et al.*, 2013).

Microbiota transplants from obese or lean individuals into lean germ-free mice resulted in an obese or lean phenotype respectively, at least for the fifteen days of follow-up. Studies on microbiota transplants in humans involving lean donors and recipients with metabolic syndrome (symptoms include a high BMI) had provided evidence of improved insulin-sensitivity in recipients but minimal change in symptoms of metabolic syndrome (Vrieze *et al.*, 2012; Kootte *et al.*, 2017).

There are complex issues associated with human microbiota transplants and obesity studies. These include the wide variation of microbiota diversity of both donor and recipient. These differences are dependent on age, sex, lifestyle, environment and diet as well as genetic components. Moreover, there are no long-term (> two years) studies on outcomes of microbiota transplants and obesity. Nevertheless, there is consensus that gut microbiota composition plays an important role in obesity. For example, it is reported that, in comparison with lean individuals, there is less microbial diversity in the gut microbiota of obese individuals and a higher proportion of *Firmicutes* to *Bacteroidetes*; the reverse is true for gut microbiota in lean individuals (Ley et al., 2006; Hartstra et al., 2015). However, these variations are dependent on study cohorts, again a reflection of diet and lifestyle.

Individuals who are overweight have increased risk of type 2 diabetes and cardiovascular disease. It is, therefore, not surprising that type 2 diabetes and cardiovascular disease have also been associated with alterations in gut microbiota. As in the case of obesity, this is an on-going area of research with considerable debate about what is and what is not a healthy gut microbiota composition.

A current issue is the reported association of the compound trimethylamine-N-oxide (TMAO) with increased risk of cardiovascular disease, recently reviewed in the high-impact journal, *Nature Reviews Cardiology* (Tang et al., 2019). Select microbiota in the gut produce trimethylamine (TMA) which can then be enzymatically oxidized in the liver to TMAO.

In a study of patients (n = 4,007) at risk of cardiovascular disease, there was a 2.5-fold increased risk of an adverse cardiovascular event in individuals with the highest plasma levels of TMAO (Tang et al., 2013). In animal model systems, microbiota transplantation from donor mice with high TMA-TMAO-generating gut microbiota into appropriate recipient mice (Gregory et al., 2015; Zhu et al., 2016), produced a pro-atherogenic phenotype (fatty deposit or hardening of the arteries, a prelude to cardiovascular disease).

The critical Reader will note a number of paradoxical facts that require explanation. Note that reports to date have found an association between high plasma levels of TMAO and increased risk of an adverse cardiovascular event in individuals with pre-existing or at high potential risk of coronary heart disease. There are no studies linking levels of TMAO and risk of cardiovascular disease in individuals not at high risk.

Fish is a major source of TMAO and there is consensus that a diet rich in fish has positive cardiovascular effects. A possible explanation is that omega-3-fatty acid (the 'good' polyunsaturated fat, see Chapter 3) in fish mitigates the negative effects of TMAO. However, one should note that not all fish have high levels of TMAO and/or omega-3-fatty acid. Now try making a logical conclusion from these observations and the fact that in individuals at risk of cardiovascular disease there is a correlation with high levels of plasma TMAO.

A recent critique of the association between TMAO and cardiovascular disease has been published in the open-access journal *Open Heart* (DiNicolantonio *et al.*, 2019), an official publication of the British Cardiovascular Society.

And just one more thing - significant dietary sources for precursors of TMAO include choline (e.g. eggs, fish, poultry, meat, beans) and carnitine (e.g. meat, poultry, fish, dairy). Both choline (e.g. for nerve function, biological membranes) and carnitine (for energy metabolism) are essential metabolic components and are popular as dietary supplements (ask yourself, where is the scientific evidence for the efficacy of these supplements?).

Furthermore, the metabolic pathways for utilization of TMAO from gut microbiota activity (TMAO formed by oxidation in the liver of the TMA generated by gut microbiota, see above), are quite different from pathways for the metabolism of TMAO from the diet. Thus, it is not surprising to note that, at this point, there is considerable debate about the efficacy of plasma TMAO levels as a biomarker for cardiovascular disease, at least for individuals at low risk.

Pub Test 7.6:

Question:

Are faecal microbiota transplants effective for the treatment of health issues associated with obesity, cardiovascular disease and inflammatory bowel disorders?

Answer:

No

Faecal microbiota transplants have been relatively successful only in the treatment of the specific case of recurring diarrhoea associated with antibiotic resistance due to *Clostridium difficile*. There are insufficient high quality studies to conclude that faecal microbiota transplant is effective for other inflammatory gut disorders.

Probiotics, a Gut Feeling

A milder form of microbiota transplant or transformation is by the use of probiotics which is defined as 'live microorganisms that, when administered in adequate amounts, confers a health benefit on the host' (Hill *et al.*, 2014).

Probiotics are most commonly taken as foods or beverages, dietary supplements or as pharmaceuticals. They are extremely popular, with one market research analysis (Zion market research) estimating the global market by 2024 to be at a remarkable US$66 billion a value very similar to the projected global market value for antibiotics (just Google that). Ironically, the high demand for probiotics is closely related to the high demand for antibiotics in that it is almost routine to be recommended, not just by friends but also by medical organizations, to take probiotics after taking a course of antibiotics.

The rationale is that antibiotics target (eliminate) both bad and good bacteria and the probiotics then assist in recovery of your normal gut microbiota. Simple : but is that rationale really true?

The former is essentially true, that is, antibiotics target both good and bad bacteria, but the jury is still out whether probiotics assist in the recovery of normal gut microbiota.

A similarity is that probiotics are over-used (no medical prescription required) and antibiotics are over-prescribed (medical prescription required), even in highly regulated countries like the U.K. (Smieszek *et al.,* 2018) and certainly in the less developed countries (readily available without prescription). The popularity of probiotics is reminiscent of the situation with dietary supplements in that broad claims of efficacy for health can be made without evidence-based outcomes.

Probiotics: An Update

As in previous Chapters and given the massive literature in the past few years on health and microbiota, only the most recent scientific publications on probiotics are citied.

The interested Reader can consult two very readable (and freely available to download) articles, the authors of which have declared commercial ties but nevertheless present a reasonably non-biased review of the current status of probiotics and gut health (Sanders *et al.,* 2018; Sniffen *et al.,* 2018). Overall, there have been modest outcomes for probiotics in the treatment of antibiotic-associated diarrhoea and infant acute diarrhoea with mixed outcomes for gut disorders such as irritable bowel disease, inflammatory bowel disease, ulcerative colitis and Crohn's disease.

In a recent study, probiotic supplementation was tested as a means to improve the gut microbiota composition and function in antibiotic-treated and in caesarian-born infants (Korpela et al., 2018b). This was a high quality randomized study (three months, double-blind, placebo controlled) in which mothers and infants (n = 168 breastfed, n = 31 formula-fed) were provided with a four-strain probiotic consisting of known amounts of specific strains of *Bifidobacterium breve* Bb99, *Propionibacterium freundenreichii* subspecies *shermanii* JS, *Lactobacillus rhamnosus* Lc705, and *L. rhamnosus* GG, or a placebo supplement (n = 201 breastfed, n = 22 formula-fed). Overall, the study concluded that probiotic supplementation in mothers and infants, in conjunction with breast-feeding, effectively restored healthy gut microbiota composition in antibiotic-treated and in caesarian-born infants.

Probiotics are frequently recommended for treatment of acute diarrhoea or gastroenteritis in young children. Two high quality randomized, double-blind and placebo-controlled studies have recently been published in the *New England Journal of Medicine* (Schnadower et al., 2018; Freedman et al., 2018). In essence both trials concluded that probiotics do not significantly reduce the clinical severity of the patients within a fourteen-day trial period. These were clinical trials of the highest quality and involved close to 2,000 infants aged 3 to 48 months and two commonly available probiotics (five-day course) based on strains of *L. rhamnosus* and *L.helveticus*.

However, the predominant users of probiotics are the 'worried healthy adults,' akin to users of dietary supplements (see Chapter

4). A review, covering publications (forty-five studies) up to August 2017 (Khalesi et al., 2019), on the use of probiotics in healthy adults concluded there was some evidence for short-term improvement of immune responses and a number of gastrointestinal issues (e.g. bowel consistency). Although fifteen of the forty-five publications involved gut microbiota colonization studies, only three actually reported diversity and composition of the gut microbiota as determined in faecal samples.

The interest in probiotics for the promotion of a healthy gut microbiota can be gauged by numerous publications with commentary and results of clinical trials in medical and scientific journals of the highest standard.

A recent study, published in the high-impact journal *Cell*, had challenged the assumption that probiotics assisted in the restoration of normal gut microbiota after antibiotic treatment in adults (Suez et al., 2018). Although the study involved only forty-six healthy adults (n = 25 controls, n = 21 antibiotic), this was the most comprehensive study to date on the influence of probiotics on post-antibiotic treatment in humans (six months of follow-up with detailed [genus, species and strain] microbiota analyses of 337 luminal, 702 mucosal and 557 stool samples together with 362 regional biopsies).

In summary, after antibiotic treatment, the test probiotic (eleven-strain bacterial probiotic, all strains commonly used as commercial probiotics) rapidly colonized the gut but prevented normal gut microbiota recolonization up to five months. In contrast, normal gut microbiota composition was restored, within days, in individuals (post-antibiotic) who received faecal microbiota transplants (autologous, sampled before antibiotic treatment). The authors concluded that, at least for their eleven-strain probiotic, application of probiotic after antibiotic treatment may, in fact, hinder recolonization of normal gut microbiota.

In a related study, using the same eleven-strain probiotic, several key observations were made (Zmora et al., 2018). Firstly, colonization by probiotics was characterized by individual and regional (within the gastrointestinal tract) specific patterns, with dependence upon composition of the host gut microbiota. Secondly, the composition of probiotics in faecal microbiota (non-colonizing probiotics as in wash-out) only partially corresponded to the actual microbiota composition *within* the host gut, particularly the gut mucosal layer. It also followed that microbiota composition in faecal samples did not truly reflect microbiota composition in the gut mucosal layer. This was an important observation given that gut microbiota studies most commonly quote faecal microbiota analysis and, rarely, the microbiota composition at the gut mucosal layer, the latter requiring invasive biopsy procedures such as endoscopy.

A recent review in *Nature Medicine* (Suez et al., 2019) provides the current (as of mid-2019) state of scientific research on probiotics with emphasis on evidence-based studies on clinical efficacy, mechanisms of activity, safety issues and future directions.

There is no doubt that probiotics will continue to be widely used by the general population; indeed, the public and commercial interests have already voted on their efficacy, given the 2024 projected global market of US$66 billion. The scientific community has a lot of catching up to do; it has recently been estimated that, in the past decade (2007-2016), the total research funding on the human microbiome was < US$2 billion (Proctor, 2019). One final point: no probiotic has, to date, been approved for medical use by government bodies responsible for regulating drug licences in the United States, Europe and Australia. You may want to ask yourself why not?

Pub Test 7.7:

Question:

Are probiotics effective for restoration of normal gut microbiota after a course of antibiotics?

Answer:

No

There is no definitive evidence that probiotics restore normal gut microbiota after a course of antibiotics. Some studies have indicated that taking probiotics may actually inhibit or delay the restoration of normal gut microbiota. Furthermore, we currently do not know the microbiota composition and function of a typical or 'standard' healthy human gut.

In the Mood for Bugs

It has long been known, largely based on behavioural studies in germ-free mice, that there is a gut-brain axis bidirectional communication system involving the gut microbiota. Hence, the term microbiota-gut-brain axis has been adopted to signify that gut microbiota play a key role in influencing behaviour and cognitive function (Rhee *et al.*, 2009; Fung *et al.*, 2017). Neurological, immunological and endocrinological (hormonal) communication lines link the gut microbiota via the enteric and central nervous systems to the human host brain (Heiss and Olofsson *et al.*, 2019).

It is not difficult to relate the consumption of tasty (translation: food high in sugar, salt, fat and flavour) calorie-rich, highly processed, low-nutrient junk foods to reward systems in the brain. In this respect, a direct link between the gut and the brain, via vagal neurons (the vagal nerve connects the brain to the lower intestines) and glutamate as a neurotransmitter, has recently been demonstrated in a mouse model system (Kaelberer *et al.*, 2018).

In the past two decades, scientific studies have established that gut microbiota produce numerous compounds, directly or indirectly, known to influence mood, emotion and cognitive functions of the human brain (Clarke *et al.*, 2014). These include serotonin, dopamine, gamma-amino butyric acid (GABA) and short-chain fatty acids (SCFAs as in acetate, propionate and butyrate). The former three compounds are well-known neurotransmitters and the latter SCFAs are end-products of bacterial gut fermentation of complex carbohydrates from the diet. Importantly, there is increasing evidence that SCFAs play key roles in mediating signalling along the gut-brain axis via the immune, neural and hormonal pathways (Dalile *et al.*, 2019).

There is much hype in the media and commercial sectors about reports of altered gut microbiota associated with autism spectrum disorder (ASD), Alzheimer's and Parkinson's. Although these disorders are quite distinct, they are commonly associated with gastrointestinal and inflammatory issues, thus implying involvement of gut microbiota. Several recent publications (with references therein) serve to illustrate current research in this area.

A two-year follow-up study of n = 18 children (ages 7 to 17) with ASD and gastrointestinal symptoms reported long-term benefits of a modified microbiota transfer therapy (Kang *et al.*, 2019). Outcomes reported included improvements in gastrointestinal and ASD symptoms and increased gut microbiota diversity. The difficulties with such experiments included the open nature of the studies (participants were aware of the treatment, no placebo), and participants were on medication, with changes in medication and diet (twelve out of the eighteen participants) during the two-year follow-up.

Altered gut microbiota associated with Alzheimer's disease (AD) had been reported in a study of n = 25 (mean age of 71.3, 68% female) individuals diagnosed with Alzheimer's and a control group (n = 25, mean age of 69.3, 72% female) matched for age, sex and BMI (Vogt et al., 2017). Overall, a decrease in gut microbiota diversity was noted, together with decreased abundance in Firmicutes, increased Bacteroidetes and decreased abundance in the genus *Bifidobacterium*. In the same studies, a correlation was also reported (nine individuals) between gut microbiota composition and cerebrospinal fluid biomarkers of AD.

On the other hand, decreased abundance in Bacteroidetes was reported in a cross-sectional study (Saji et al., 2019) in Japan of individuals diagnosed with dementia (n = 34, mean age of 77, 85% female) as compared with those diagnosed without dementia (n = 94, mean age of 76, 49% female). Ethnic, dietary and lifestyle differences as compared with the Vogt *et al.* (2017) studies were proposed to account for the contrasting results. However, both studies were unable to identify the microbiota down to the species and strain level which may have clarified these discrepancies.

A very recent study on AD was able to identify faecal microbiota at least to the species level (Haran *et al.*, 2019). In this study (n = 51, control, mean age of 83.0, 84% female; n = 24, with AD, mean age of 84.7, 83% female; n = 33, other non-AD dementia, mean age of 87.9, 82% female), the authors reported that they were able to identify in individuals with diagnosed AD a higher abundance of bacterial species in faecal samples known to cause pro-inflammatory states (in the gastrointestinal tract) as compared with controls and individuals identified with other non-AD dementia.

At this stage, suffice it to note that much of the research on gut microbiota and neurophysiology refers to studies on animal model systems, including mouse models for autism spectrum disorder, Alzheimer's and Parkinson's. There is a wealth of difference between the mouse and human. Apart from the obvious, there are fundamental differences in gut anatomy and microbiota composition.

These publications appear in high-quality scientific journals and thus the interested Reader may find them challenging to fully comprehend. Nevertheless, the fact that there are publications in quality scientific journals demonstrates the current interest and acceptance that gut microbiota play key roles in human health and disease.

The next decade of research will provide much needed clarification about how (i.e. mechanisms) and exactly which strains of gut microbiota do what, when and why. The what refers to identifying the chemical compounds produced by specific strains of gut bacteria. The when refers to the growing evidence that gut microbiota respond to a biological clock (Nobs *et al.*, 2019), akin to the well-recognized circadian rhythm in humans. The why refers to the issue of manipulation of host behaviour (e.g. mood) by microbiota, including for their own advantage (e.g. survival, parasitic) as recently reviewed (Johnson and Foster, 2018).

Allaband, C, McDonald, D, Vazquez-Baeza, Y, *et al.* 2019. Microbiome 101: studying, analysing, and interpreting microbiome data for clinicians. *Clinical Gastroenterology Hepatology* 17:218-230. doi:10.1016/j.cgh.2018.09.017.

Balsells, E, Shi, T, Leese, C, et al. 2019. Global burden of *Clostridium difficile* infections: a systematic review and meta-analysis. *Journal of Global Health* 9:010407. doi:10.7189/jogh.09.010407.

Bilen, M, Dufour, J-C, Lagier, J-C, et al. 2018. The contribution of culturomics to the repertoire of isolated human bacterial and archaeal species. *Microbiome* 6:94-105. Doi:10.1186/s40168-018-0485-5.

Brooks, AW, Priye, S, Blekhman, R, et al. 2018. Gut microbiota diversity across ethnicities in the United States. *PLoS Biology* 16:e2006842. doi:10.1371/journal.pbio.2006842.

Cani, PD. 2018. Human gut microbiome: hopes, threats and promises. *Gut* 67:1716-1725. doi:10.1136/gutjnl-2018-316723.

Cavicchioli, R, Ripple, WJ, Timmis, KN, et al. 2019. Scientists' warning to humanity: microorganisms and climate change. *Nature Reviews Microbiology* 17:569-586. doi:10.1038/s41579-019-0222-5.

Clarke, G, Stilling, RM, Kennedy, PJ, et al. 2014. Minireview: gut microbiota: the neglected endocrine organ. *Molecular Endocrinology* 28:1221-1238. doi:10.1210/me.2014-1108.

Costello, SP, Hughes, PA, Waters, O, et al. 2019. Effect of fecal microbiota transplantation on 8-week remission in patients with ulcerative colitis: a randomized clinical trial. *JAMA* 321:156-164. doi:10.1001/jama.2018.20046.

Dalile, B, van Oudenhove, L, Vervliet, B, et al. 2019. The role of short-chain fatty acids in microbiota-gut-brain communication.

Nature Reviews Gastroenterology & Hepatology 16:461-478. doi:10.1038/s41575-019-0157-3.

Dalrymple, GB. 2001. The age of the Earth in the twentieth century: a problem (mostly) solved. *Geological Society, London, Special Publications*. 190:205-22. doi:10.1144/GSL.SP.2001.190.01.14.

D'Argenio, V. 2018. The prenatal microbiome: a new player for human health. *High-Throughput* 7:38-48. doi:10.3390/ht7040038.

David, LA, Maurice, CF, Carmody, RN, *et al*. 2014. Diet rapidly and reproducibly alters the human gut microbiome. *Nature*: 505:559-563. doi:10.1038/nature12820.

De Filippo, C, Cavalieri, D, Di Paola, M, *et al*. 2010. Impact of diet in shaping gut microbiota revealed by a comparative study in children from Europe and rural Africa. *Proceedings of the National Academy of Sciences* 107:14691-14696. doi:10.1073/pnas.1005963107.

De Filippo, C, Di Paola, M, Ramazzzotti, M, *et al*. 2017. Diet, environments, and gut microbiota. A preliminary investigation in children living in rural and urban Burkina Faso and Italy. *Frontiers in Microbiology* 8:1979. doi:10.3389/fmicb.2017.01979.

Deschasaux, M, Bouter, KE, Prodan, A, *et al*. 2018. Depicting the composition of gut microbiota in a population with varied ethnic origins but shared geography. *Nature Medicine* 24:1526-1531. doi:10.1038/s41591-018-0160-1.

DiNicolantonio, McCarty, M, OKeefe, J. 2019. Association of moderately elevated trimethylamine N-oxide with cardiovascular risk: is TMAO serving as a marker for hepatic insulin resistance? *Open Heart* 6:e000890. doi:10.1136/openhrt-2018-000890.

Dodd, MS, Papineau, D, Grenne, T, *et al.* 2017. Evidence for early life in Earth's oldest hydrothermal vent precipitates. *Nature* 543:60-64. doi:10.1038/nature21377.

Durack, J, Lynch, SV. 2018. The gut microbiome: relationships with disease and opportunities for therapy. *Journal of Experimental Medicine* 216:20-40. doi:10.101084/jem.20180448.

Editorial, *the Lancet* 2019. Probiotics: elixir or empty promise. *The Lancet Gastroenterology & Hepatology* 4:81. doi:10.1016/S2468-1253(18)30416-1.

Edwards, CT, Saltzman, MR, Royer, DL, *et al.* 2017. Oxygenation as a driver of the Great Ordovician Biodiversification Event. *Nature Geoscience* 10:925-929. doi:10.1038/s41561-017-0006-3.

Ferretti, P, Pasolli, E, Tett, A, *et al.* 2018. Mother-to-infant microbial transmission from different body sites shapes the developing infant gut microbiome. *Cell Host & Microbe* 24:133-145. doi:10.1016/j.chom.2018.06.005.

Fragiadakis, GK, Smits, SA, Sonnenburg, ED, *et al.* 2018. Links between environment, diet, and the hunter-gatherer microbiome. *Gut Microbes* 10:216-227. doi 10.1080/19490976.2018.1494103.

Freedman, SB, Urquhart, SW, Farion, KJ, *et al.* 2018. Multicenter trial of a combination probiotic for children with gastroenteritis. *New England Journal of Medicine* 379:2015-2026. doi:10.1056/NEJMoa1802597.

Fung, TC, Olson, CA, Hsiao, EY. 2017. Interactions between the microbiota, immune and nervous systems in health and disease. *Nature Neuroscience* 20: 145-155. doi:10.1038/nn.4476.

Gilbert, JA, Blaser, MJ, Caporaso, JG, *et al.* 2018. Current understanding of the human microbiome. *Nature Medicine* 24: 392-400. doi:10.1038/nm.4517.

Goodrich, JK, Waters, JL, Poole, AC, *et al.* 2014. Human genetics shape the gut microbiome. *Cell* 159:789-799. doi:10.1016/j.cell.2014.09.053.

Goodrich, JK, Davenport, ER, Beaumont, M, *et al.* 2016. Genetic determinants of the gut microbiome in UK twins. *Cell Host & Microbe* 19:731-743. doi:10.1016/j.chom.2016.04.017.

Gray, MW. 2012. Mitochondrial evolution. *Cold Spring Harbor Perspectives in Biology* 4:a011403. doi:10.1101/cshperspect.a011403.

Greenberg, SA, Youngster, I, Cohen, NA, *et al.* 2018. Five years of fecal microbiota transplantation – an update of the Israel experience. *World Journal of Gastroenterology* 24:5403-5414. doi:10.3748/wjg.v24.i47.5403.

Gregory, JC, Buffa, JA, Org, E, *et al.* 2015. Transmission of atherosclerosis susceptibility with gut microbial transplantation. *Journal of Biological Chemistry* 290:5647-5660. doi:10.1074/jbc.M114.618249.

Haran, JP, Bhattarai, SK, Foley, SE, *et al.* 2019. Alzheimer's disease microbiome is associated with dysregulation of the anti-inflammatory P-glycoprotein pathway. *mBio* 10e00632-19. doi:10.1128/mBio.00632-19.

Hartstra AV, Bouter, KEC, Backhed, F, *et al.* 2015. Insights into the role of the microbiome in obesity and type 2 diabetes. *Diabetes Care* 38:159-165. doi:10.2337/dc14-0769.

Heiss, CN, Olofsson, LE. 2019. The role of the gut microbiota in development, function and disorders of the central nervous system and the enteric nervous system. *Journal of Neuroendocrinology* 31: e12684. doi:10.1111/jne.12684.

Hill, C, Guamer, F, Reid, G, et al. 2014. Expert consensus document. The International Scientific Association for Probiotics and Probiotics consensus statement on the scope and appropriate use of the term probiotic. *Nature Reviews Gastroenterology & Hepatology* 11:506-514. doi:10.1038/nrgastro.2014.66.

Holland, HD. 2006. The oxygenation of the atmosphere and oceans. *Philosophical Transactions of the Royal Society* B 361:903-915. doi:10.1098/rstb.2006.1838.

Houghtelling, PD, Walker, WA. 2015. Why is initial bacterial colonization of the intestine important to the infant's and child's health? *Journal of Pediatric Gastroenterology and Nutrition* 60:294-307. doi:10.1097/MPG.0000000000000597.

Hublin, J-J, Ben-Ncer, Bailey, SE, *et al*. 2017. New fossils from Jebel Irhoud, Morocco and the pan-African origin of *Homo sapiens*. *Nature* 546:289-292. doi:10.1038/nature.2017.22114.

Johnson, KV-A, Foster, KR. 2018. Why does the microbiome affect behaviour? *Nature Reviews Microbiology* 16:647-655. doi:10.1038/s41579-018-0014-3.

Juul, FE, Garborg, K, Bretthauer, M, *et al*. 2018. Fecal microbiota transplantation for primary *Clostridium difficile* infection. *New England Journal of Medicine* 378:2525-2536. doi:10.1056/NEJMc1803103.

Kaelberer, MM, Buchanan, KL, Klein, ME, *et al*. 2018. A gut-brain neural circuit for nutrient sensory transduction. *Science* 361: eaat5236. doi:10.1126/science.aat5236.

Kang, DW, Adams, JB, Coleman, DM, *et al*. 2019. Long-term benefit of microbiota transfer therapy on autism symptoms and gut microbiota. *Scientific Reports* 9:5821. doi:10.1038/s41598-019-42183-0.

Kelly, CR, Ananthakrishnan, AN. 2019. Manipulating the microbiome with fecal transplantation to treat ulcerative colitis. *JAMA* 321:151-152. doi:10.1001/jama.2018.20497.

Khalesi, S, Bellissomo, N, Vanderlanotte, C, *et al*. 2019. A review of probiotic supplementation in healthy adults: helpful or hype? *European Journal of Clinical Nutrition* 73:24-37. doi:10.1038/s41430-018-0135-9.

Kong, HH, Morris, A. 2017. The emerging importance and challenges of the human mycobiome. *Virulence* 8:310-312. doi:10.1080/21505594.2017.1279780.

Kootte, RS, Levin, E, Salojarvi, J, *et al*. 2017. Improvement of insulin sensitivity after lean donor feces in metabolic syndrome is driven by baseline intestinal microbiota. *Cell Metabolism* 26:611-619. doi:10.1016/j.cmet.2017.09.008.

Korpela, K, Costea, P, Coelho, LP, *et al*. 2018a. Selective maternal seeding and environment shape the human gut microbiome. *Genome Research* 28:561-568. doi:10.1101/gr.233940.117.

Korpela, K, Salonen, A, Vepsalainen, O, *et al*. 2018b. Probiotic supplementation restores normal microbiota composition and function in antibiotic-treated and in caesarean-born infants. *Microbiome* 6:182-193. doi:10.1186/s40168-018-0567-4.

Laforest-Lapointe, I, Arrieta, M-C. 2018. Microbial eukaryotes: a missing link in gut microbiome studies. *mSystems* 3:e00201-17. doi:10.1128/mSystems.00201-17.

Lagier, J-C, Dubourg, G, Million, M, *et al*. 2018. Culturing the human microbiota and culturomics. *Nature Reviews Microbiology* 16:540-550. doi:10.1038/s41579-018-0041-0.

Lenton, TM, Dahl, TW, Daines, SJ, *et al*. 2016. Earliest land plants created modern levels of atmospheric oxygen. *Proceedings of the National Academy of Sciences* 113:9704-9709. doi:10.1073/pnas.1604787113.

Lessa, FC, Mu, Y, Bamberg, WM, *et al*. 2014. Burden of *Clostridium difficile* infection in the United States. *New England Journal of Medicine* 372:825-834. doi:10.1056/NEJMoa1408913.

Levey, AN, Allegretti, JR. 2019. Insights into the role of fecal microbiota transplantation for the treatment of inflammatory bowel disease. *Therapeutic Advances in Gastroenterology* 12:1-0. doi:10.1177/1756284819836893.

Levy, RE, Turnbaugh, PJ, Klein, S, *et al*. 2006. Microbial ecology: human gut microbes associated with obesity. *Nature* 444:1022-1023. doi:10.1038/4441022a.

Makki, K, Deehan, EC, Walter, J, *et al*. 2018. The impact of dietary fiber on gut microbiota in host health and disease. *Cell Host & Microbe* 23:705-7i5. doi:10.1016/j.chom.2018.05.012.

Manrique, P, Dills, M, Young, MJ. 2017. The human gut phage community and its implications for health and disease. *Viruses* 9:141-160. doi:10.3390/v9060141.

Moayyedi, P, Yuan, Y, Baharith, H, *et al*. 2017. Faecal microbiota transplantation for *Clostridium difficile*-associated diarrhoea: a systematic review of randomized controlled trials. *Medical Journal of Australia* 207:166-172. doi:10.5694/mja17.00295.

Mullish, BH, Quraishi, MN, Segal, JP, *et al*. 2018. The use of faecal microbiota transplant as treatment for recurrent or refractory *Clostridium difficile* infection and other potential indications: joint British Society of Gastroenterology (BSG) and Healthcare Infection Society (HIS) guidelines. *Gut* 67:1920-1941. doi:10.1136/gutjnl-2018-316818.

Nash, AK, Auchtung, TA, Wong, MC, *et al*. 2017. The gut mycobiome of the Human Microbiome Project health cohort. *Microbiome* 5:153-166. doi:10.1186/s40168-017-0373-4.

Nobs, SP, Tuganbaev, T, Elinav, E. 2019. Microbiome diurnal rhythmicity and its impact on host physiology and disease risk. *EMBO Reports* 20:e47129. doi:10.15252/embr.201847129.

Olin, A, Henckel, E, Chen, Y, *et al*. 2018. Stereotype immune system development in newborn children. *Cell* 174:1277-1292. doi:10.1016/j.cell.2018.06.045.

Ott, SJ, Waetzig, GH, Rehman, A, *et al*. 2017. Efficacy of sterile filtrate transfer for treating patients with *Clostridium difficile* infection. *Gastroenterology* 152:799-811. doi:10.1053/j.gastro.2016.11.010.

Park, H, Laffin, MR, Jovel, J, *et al.* 2019. The success of fecal microbial transplantation in *Clostridium difficile* infection correlates with bacteriophage relative abundance in the donor: a retrospective cohort study. *Gut Microbes* 10:676-687. doi:10.1080/19490976.2019.1586037.

Partula, V, Mondot, S, Torres, MJ, *et al.* 2019. Associations between usual diet and gut microbiota composition: results from the *Mileur Interieur* cross-sectional study. *American Journal of Clinical Nutrition* 109:1472-1483. doi:10.1093/ajcn/nqz029.

Pasolli, E, Asnicar, F, Manara, S, *et al.* 2019. Extensive unexpected human microbiome diversity revealed by over 150,000 genomes from metagenomes spanning age, geography, and lifestyle. *Cell* 176:1-14. doi:10.1016/j.cell.2019.01.001.

Perez-Munoz, ME, Arrieta, M-C, Ramer-Tait, AE, *et al.* 2017. A critical assessment of the "sterile womb" and "in utero colonization" hypotheses: implications for research on the pioneer infant microbiome. *Microbiome* 5: 48-67. doi:10.1186/s40168-017-0268-4.

Pike, LJ, Forster, SC. 2018. A new piece in the microbiome puzzle. *Nature Reviews Microbiology* 16:186. doi:10.1038/nrmicro.2018.24.

Planavsky, NJ, Asael, D, Hofmann, A, *et al.* 2014. Evidence for oxygenic photosynthesis half a billion years before the Great Oxidation Event. *Nature Geoscience* 7:283-286. doi:10.1038/ngeo2122.

Proctor, L. 2019. What's next for the human microbiome? *Nature* 569:623-625. doi:10.1038/d41586-019-01654-0.

Quince, C, Walker, AW, Simpson, JT, et al. 2017. Shotgun metagenomics, from sampling to analysis. *Nature Biotechnology* 35:833-844. doi:10.1038/nbt.3935.

Rhee, SH, Pothoulakis, C, Mayer, EA. 2009. Principles and clinical implications of the brain-gut-enteric microbiota axis. *Nature Reviews Gastroenterology & Hepatology* 6:306-314. doi:10.1038/nrgastro.2009.35.

Richard, ML, Sokol, H. 2019. The gut mycobiota: insights into analysis, environmental interactions and role in gastrointestinal diseases. *Nature Reviews Gastroenterology & Hepatology* 16:331-345. doi:10.1038/s41575-019-012-2.

Ridaura, VK, Faith, JJ, Rey, FE, et al. 2013. Cultured gut microbiota from twins discordant for obesity modulate adiposity and metabolic phenotypes in mice. *Science* 341:1241214. doi:10.1126/science.1241214.

Rothschild, D, Weissbrod, O, Barkan, E, et al. 2018. Environment dominates over host genetics in shaping human gut microbiota. *Nature* 555:210-215. doi:10.1038/nature25973.

Saji, N, Niida, S, Murotani, K, et al. 2019, Analysis of the relationship between the gut microbiome and dementia: a cross-sectional study conducted in Japan. *Scientific Reports* 9:1008. doi:10.1038/s41598-018-38218-7.

Sanders, ME, Merenstein, D, Merrifield, CA, et al. 2018. Probiotics for human use. *Nutrition Bulletin* 43:212-225. doi:10.1111/nbu.12334.

Sender, R, Fuchs, S, Milo, R. 2016. Revised estimates for the number of human and bacterial cells in the body. *PLoS Biology* 14:e1002533. doi:10.1371/journal.pbio.1002533.

Scepanovic, P, Hodel, F, Mondot, S, *et al.* 2019. A comprehensive assessment of demographic, environmental, and host genetic associations with gut microbiome diversity in healthy individuals. *Microbiome* 7:130. doi:10.1186/s40168-019-0757-x.

Schnadower, D, Tarr, PI, Casper, TC, *et al.* 2018. *Lactobacillus rhamnosus* GG versus placebo for acute gastroenteritis in children. *New England Journal of Medicine* 379:2002-2014. doi:10.1056/NEJMoa1802598.

Schnorr, SL, Candela, M, Rampelli, S, *et al.* 2014. Gut microbiome of the Hadza hunter-gatherers. *Nature Communications* 5:3654. doi:10.1038/ncomms4654.

Shao, Y, Forster, SC, Tsaliki, E, *et al.* 2019. Stunted microbiota and opportunistic pathogen colonization in caesarean-section birth. *Nature* 574:117-121. doi:10.1038/s41586-019-1560-1.

Shrestha, MP, Bime, C, Taleban, S. 2018. Decreasing *Clostridium difficile*-associated fatality rates among hospitalized patients in the United States: 2004-2014. *The American Journal of Medicine* 131:90-96. doi:10.1016/j.amjmed.2017.07.022.

Sim, MS, Ogata, H, Lubitz, W, *et al.* 2019. Role of APS reductase in biogeochemical sulfur isotope fractionation. *Nature Communications* 10:44-49. doi:10.1038/s41467-018-07878-4.

Smieszek, T, Pouwels, KB, Dolk, FCK, *et al.* 2018. Potential for reducing inappropriate antibiotic prescribing in English primary care. *Journal of Antimicrobial Chemotherapy* 73: Suppl 2: ii36-ii43. doi:10.1093/jac/dkx500.

Smits, SA, Leach, J, Sonnenburg, ED, *et al*. 2017. Seasonal cycling in the gut microbiome of the Hadza hunter-gatherers of Tanzania. *Science* 357:802-806. doi:10.1126/science.aan4834.

Sniffen, JC, McFarland, LV, Evans, CT, *et al*. 2018. Choosing an appropriate probiotic product for your patient: an evidence-based practical guide. *PLoS ONE* 13:e0209205. doi:10.1371/journal.pone.0209205.

Stanislawski, MA, Dabelea, D, Wagner, BD, *et al*. 2018. Gut microbiota in the first 2 years of life and association with body mass index at age 12 in a Norwegian birth cohort. *mBio* 9:e01751-18. doi:10.1128/mBio01751-18.

Stewart, CJ, Ajami, NJ, O'Brien, JL, *et al*. 2018. Temporal development of the gut microbiota in early childhood from the TEDDY study. *Nature* 562:583-588.doi:10.1038/s41586-018-0617-x.

Suez, J, Zmora, N, Zilberman-Schapira, G, *et al*. 2018. Post-antibiotic gut mucosal microbiome reconstitution is impaired by probiotics and improved by autologous FMT. *Cell* 174:1406-1423. doi:10.1016/j.cell.2018.08.047.

Suez, J, Zmora, N, Segal, E, *et al*. 2019. The pros, cons, and many unknowns of probiotics. *Nature Medicine* 25:716-729. doi:10.1038/s41591-019-0439-x.

Tamburini, S, Shen, N, Wu, HC, *et al*. 2016. The microbiome in early life: implications for health outcomes. *Nature Medicine* 22:713-721. doi:10.1038/nm.4142.

Tang, WHW, Wang, Z, Levison, BS, et al. 2013. Intestinal microbial metabolism of phosphatidylcholine and cardiovascular risk. *New England Journal of Medicine* 368:1575-1584. doi:10.1056/NEJMoa1109400.

Tang, WHW, Li, DY, Hazen, SL. 2019. Dietary metabolism, the gut microbiome, and heart failure. *Nature Reviews Cardiology* 16:137-153. doi:10.1038/s41569-018-0108-7.

Tashiro, T, Ishida, A, Hori, M, et al. 2017. Early trace of life from 3.95 Ga sedimentary rocks on Labrador, Canada. *Nature* 549:516-518. doi:10.1038/nature24019.

Tice, MM, Lowe, DR. 2004. Photosynthetic microbial mats in the 3,416-Myr-old ocean. *Nature* 431:549-552. doi:10.1038/nature2888.

Timmis, JN, Ayliffe, MA, Huang, CY, et al. 2004. Endosymbiotic gene transfer: organelle genomes forge eukaryotic chromosomes. *Nature Reviews Genetics* 5:123-135. doi:10.1038/nrg1271.

Turnbaugh, PJ, Ley, RE, Mahowald, MA, et al. 2006. An obesity-associated gut microbiome with increased capacity for energy harvest. *Nature* 444:1027-1031. doi:10.1038/nature05414.

Vogt, NM, Kerby, RL, Dill-McFarland, KA, et al. 2017. Gut microbiome alterations in Alzheimer's disease. *Scientific Reports* 7:13537. doi:10.1038/s41598-017-13601-y.

Vrieze, A, Van Nood, E, Holleman, F, et al. 2012. Transfer of intestinal microbiota from lean donors increases insulin sensitivity in individuals with metabolic syndrome. *Gastroenterology* 143:913-916. doi:10.1053/j.gastro.2012.06.031.

Zhu, W, Gregory, JC, Org, E, *et al*. 2016. Gut microbial metabolite TMAO enhances platelet hyperreactivity and thrombosis risk. *Cell* 165:111-124. doi:10.1016/j.cell.2016.02.011.

Zierer, J, Jackson, MA, Kastenmuller, G, *et al*. 2018. The fecal metabolome as a functional readout of the gut microbiome. *Nature Genetics* 50:790-795. doi:10.1038/s41588-018-0135-7.

Zmora, N, Zilberman-Schapira, G, Suez, J, *et al*. 2018. Personalized gut mucosal colonization resistance to empiric probiotics is associated with unique host and microbiome features. *Cell* 174:1388-1405. doi:10.1016/j.cell.2018.08.041.

Zuo, T, Wong, SH, Lam, K, *et al*. 2018. Bacteriophage transfer during faecal microbiota transplantation in *Clostridium difficile* infection is associated with treatment outcome. *Gut* 67:634-643. doi:10.1136/gutjnl-2017-313952.

Chapter 8
If We All Lived to a Healthy 100

Where Would We All Park?

The informed Reader, having diligently read this book, may have come to the conclusion that healthy ageing means living to 100 years in good health.

And, if you are female, then the odds of living to 100 years in good health is much greater than if you are male, given that the ratio of female/male centenarians is very skewed towards the female (e.g. in Japan the ratio is 7:1 in favour of female centenarians).

There are currently (as of mid-2019) estimated to be 450,000 individuals claiming to be 100 years-old with a projected 3.7 million by 2050 (Pew Research) and 25 million by 2100 (Robine and Cubaynes, 2017). The 2019 figure may be somewhat inflated given that many individuals claiming to be centenarians do not have adequate documentation or exaggerate their age.

Nevertheless, the figures do indicate that we may have a future parking problem if one considers the projected age (30 to 70 years) of the Readers of this book, that is, a person aged 30 or 70, having diligently read this book, may live to 100 by 2090 or 2050 respectively.

To put these figures in perspective, globally, as of 2017, there are an estimated > 950 million individuals aged 60 or over with a projection to more than double to 2.1 billion by 2050 (United Nations). Now, we really will have a parking problem by 2050 if we all adopt a healthy ageing lifestyle as outlined in this book.

However, the author of this book takes no responsibility for any future increase in the number of individuals who successfully age (healthy ageing), thus adding to the problem of *Where Would We All Park?*'

The informed Reader may have noted that there is absolutely nothing new or radical proposed in this book with respect to healthy ageing. This book is thus uniquely different from most books on nutrition, health, lifestyle and ageing. Moreover, the *Take Home Message* can be immediately put into practice.

But before we get to the *Take Home Message*, there is one final *Pub Test* question to be answered.

Pub Test: 8.1

Question:

Do women live longer than men?

Answer:

Yes

With rare exceptions, in every country, women live longer than men. Importantly, this also applies to healthy lifespan and thus healthy ageing. In general, life expectancy at birth for women is around three to five years longer than men, with healthy life expectancy two to three years longer (see Table 1 p. 154). Healthy life expectancy is defined by the World Health Organization as 'average number of years a person can expect to live in full health by taking into account years lived in less than full health due to disease or injury'.

These are facts, not opinions, and are based on extensive data as documented on authoritative internet sites (Human Mortality Database, World Health Organization, United Nations Organization, Centers for Disease Control and Prevention).

There is much debate on the reasons for these differences, with behavioural, evolutionary and genetic factors being the main issues.

Men, on average, engage in risk-taking behaviour such as excess smoking, drinking and dangerous fast-driving leading to death and injury. There is also a higher incidence of drug use and criminal activity in men compared with women and suicide is a major cause of death for young and adult men.

Women, on the other hand, are less likely to engage in risk-taking behaviour and are more health conscious. It is also well-documented that women are more willing than men to seek medical attention when unwell.

Importantly, the life/healthy life expectancy data also apply to countries which have traditional male-dominated cultures with low participation of women in positions of authority e.g. politics, business, judiciary. An interesting example is Japan, a male-dominated society, which consistently has the highest life/healthy life expectancy for both sexes (highest or in the top three countries). In a recent book entitled *Beyond the Gender Gap in Japan*, the authors concluded that, despite high inequality, Japanese women have a high sense of well-being and many are supportive of traditional gender norms (Steel, 2019).

Although behavioural and social factors account for some of the gender differences, studies of groups with similar lifestyles (e.g. male and female non-smokers) and specific religious groups (e.g. Mormons, monks/nuns) have also concluded that females outlive males (Zarulli et al., 2017, references therein), thus indicative of a biological or evolutionary role. Furthermore, even under extreme survival conditions such as famine and epidemics, females survive better than males, with infant girls in particular surviving better than infant boys (Zarulli et al., 2017).

Proposals supporting a biological role for gender differences in lifespan include distinctions related to hormonal and immune systems, with females having a stronger immune response (references in Austad and Fisher, 2016; Zarulli et al., 2017).

Females also have two copies of the sex-linked chromosome X, thus, a fault or mutation in a gene on one of the X chromosomes may be compensated by a normal copy (or allele) on the other X chromosome. Males, on the other hand, have only one copy of the X and one copy of the Y chromosome in their sex-linked chromosomes. Thus, for example, haemophilia (X-chromosome-linked genetic disorder) is much more common in males than females.

And don't even bring up the controversial topic of the disappearing male Y chromosome; perhaps in another five to ten million years from now, when only human females are around and thus conclusively proving that females live longer than males.

Another intriguing issue is that mitochondrial DNA is almost exclusively inherited from the mother (mitochondria produce > 90% of all the energy requirements of aerobic cells, including human cells, in the form of ATP). It may not have escaped the diligent Reader's attention that there is evidence that mitochondria evolved as an endosymbiotic association between prokaryotic bacteria (proteobacteria) and primitive eukaryotic cells (Timmis *et al.*, 2004; Gray, 2012; see Chapter 7: The Gut Microbiota).

There continues to be considerable scientific debate about the role of mitochondria in the ageing process, however, this topic is beyond the scope of the present discussion. The following references may be consulted for recent updates on this topic (Srivastava, 2017; Theurey and Pizzo, 2018) [warning: discussions in these references require significant background knowledge in the biological sciences].

It should be noted that the female lifespan is significantly longer (three to five years, see Table 1) than the male, but there are smaller differences in the healthy lifespan (two to three years, see Table 1). This is sometimes termed the 'male-female survival paradox' in that females outlive males despite the universal observation that females have a higher frailty index than males. Frailty refers to poorer health and includes a wide range of clinical health parameters as well as physical and cognitive function (Kim *et al.*, 2017). Nevertheless, females are simply better survivors than males.

Although these differences are particularly pronounced at > 70 years (e.g. arthritis and musculoskeletal disorders are higher in older women than men), it is now known that differences in frailty apply from birth (Ostan *et al.*, 2016; Gordon *et al.*, 2017; Zarulli *et al.*, 2017 and references therein).

Interestingly, differences in male-female lifespan are far from obvious in animals and other living organisms (Austad and Fischer, 2016). Difficulties include conflicting data from captive and wild populations with substantial variations in social structure and behaviour. Most relevant is that data on Old World monkeys and apes show that females live longer than males (Bronikowski *et al.*, 2011; Austad and Fischer, 2016).

The bottom line is that if you are female, you have a head start (several years) with respect to healthy ageing.

Healthy Mind in a Healthy Body

I am acutely aware that there will be issues not covered in this book that the informed Reader may consider important for healthy ageing.

One issue is that of sleep. The widely recommended six to eight hr/night for optimum health in adults is very much dependent on the individual and their lifestyle. There is no doubt that a routine sleep schedule, such as going to sleep and waking up at about the same time, is important for healthy ageing. A bedroom temperature of around 18-20^{0}C is often recommended as optimum given the natural tendency for the body to cool at night.

There is a plethora of information, including excellent books, on the topic and the interested Reader is encouraged to research this issue. Keep in mind that your mobile phone is not essential for life and that, for healthy ageing (and a good night's sleep), switch-off all electronic devices well before switching off the lights. Read a book (e.g. this book), instead.

Healthy Ageing means a healthy body in a healthy mind. The former topic is addressed in this book, but it should be acknowledged that psychological health is an important issue with respect to healthy ageing. The concept of meditation (attainment of self-calm, as long practised by traditional Buddhists) and mindfulness (similar to meditation but focusing on the present) as ways of decreasing stress and depression and increasing self-awareness is way beyond the present discussion.

Psychological health is clearly related to having a purpose in life, happiness, optimism and being conscientious. All of these characteristics are important for healthy ageing.

Having a purpose in life gives you a reason for getting out of bed in the morning. This is the concept of *Ikigai* in Japanese culture (Mogi, 2017): taking pleasure in small things, the importance of living in harmony with oneself and others, and attention to detail, order and punctuality. The Marie Kondo phenomenon, decluttering and organizing your home, is quintessentially *Ikigai* and Japanese (Kondo, 2014). *Ikigai* may well be one reason why the Japanese (female and male) have long and healthy lifespans.

If you are happy and have a positive outlook on life, then you are likely to outlive the individual who has a negative outlook. Simply examine the United Nations World Happiness Index (yes, there is such an index, established since 2012, https://worldhappiness.report), and note that the top countries (Finland, Denmark, Norway, Iceland, Netherlands, Switzerland) are also highly-ranked for healthy ageing. The Danes and Norwegians have the term *Hygge* which roughly translates into 'comfort', 'cosy' or 'well-being', such as having a coffee with a friend. The terms *Ikigai* and *Hygge* are clearly indicative of 'living in harmony' or 'happiness' or 'optimism' or 'purpose in life' (having a coffee with a friend gets you out of bed in the morning) and are all measures of neurological health.

If we now look at optimism in relation to healthy ageing, there is evidence that individuals with a positive outlook on life have more favourable social and health outcomes.

In an early study of middle-aged men (n = 1,306, mean age of 60.8, 10 years of follow-up) there was a relative decreased risk (56%) of coronary heart disease death in individuals reporting high levels of optimism as compared with high levels of pessimism (Kubzansky *et al.*, 2001).

In a smaller study of healthy elderly individuals (n = 128, 56% female, mean age of 70.5), objectively measured physical health status (including physical function as well as mental and emotional health) was associated with self-rated optimism (Steptoe *et al.*, 2006). In this study, it was most significant to note that individuals with high (as compared with low) self-rated optimism also smoked less (8% versus 32.5%), walked briskly more (38% versus 23%) and had higher moderate alcohol consumption (46% versus 21.6%).

These early observations were consistent with a very recent report (n = 229,391, mean follow-up of 13.8 years) that concluded that optimism in patients was associated with lower risk of cardiovascular events (35% decreased risk) and all-cause mortality (14% decreased risk) (Rozanski *et al.*, 2019).

Optimism had also been associated with healthy ageing in two recent studies. In a study of healthy individuals at baseline (n = 5,698, 60% female, mean age of 66, 6 to 8 years of follow-up) components of healthy ageing were assessed every two years (Kim et al., 2019). Healthy ageing in the participants were assessed as free from major chronic disease, no cognitive impairment and physically active. Comparing the most to the least optimistic individuals, there was a 24% increased likelihood of maintenance of healthy ageing in the former cohort. Data were adjusted for several confounders, including smoking, socio-economic status and, significantly, depression.

In a very large study of two cohorts, one of women (n = 69,744, mean age of 69.9, 10 years of follow-up) and one of men (n = 1,429, mean age of 61.6, 30 years of follow-up) the authors concluded that optimism was related to 14.9% and 8.3% longer lifespan in women and men respectively (Lee et al., 2019). Furthermore, the odds of surviving to 85 years or older was 1.5 times greater for women and 1.7 times greater for men in comparing highest versus lowest optimism levels.

In all of these studies, the authors noted that participants with the highest optimism levels also had healthier behaviour in respect of smoking less, having a better diet and higher physical activity. Although the data were adjusted for some of these confounders, it was most notable that adjustments for healthy behaviour attenuated the influence of optimism. After adjustment for healthier behaviour, optimism was related to 8.7% (14.9% before adjustment) and 6.5% (8.3% before adjustment) longer lifespan for women and men respectively (Lee et al., 2019). Thus, it was proposed that optimism leads to healthier behaviour, a most significant association.

Conscientiousness, that is, paying attention to detail, being diligent and doing the right thing, is another term closely related to psychological health. In a landmark study on human longevity, commenced in 1921 by Dr Terman (a psychologist), n = 1,528 individuals were followed from childhood for over eight decades, that is, over a lifetime. A summary of the findings was the subject of a book, *The Longevity Project*, in which the authors concluded that individuals who were conscientious, were persistent and had strong social networks stayed healthier and lived longer (Friedman and Martin, 2011). The authors also made the point that a little bit of stress would be good for you, in that some participants who progressed to responsible and stressful career positions or had survived a traumatic event(s) lived long healthy lives.

It should be noted that the study involved children selected largely on the basis of high academic achievement and were predominantly from middle-class parents. Although the characteristics of conscientiousness and healthy ageing were clearly not restricted to individuals who were well educated and at a certain socio-economic level, it was established that high education and socio-economic levels were advantageous to healthy ageing.

The authors of *The Longevity Project* also noted that conscientious individuals tended to be, well, conscientious in respect of their health and adopted healthier behaviour, thus resulting in longer and healthier lifespans.

As outlined above, studies have also shown an association between optimism in individuals and improved health behaviour (Steptoe *et al.*, 2006; Kim *et al.*, 2019; Lee *et al.*, 2019).

Notwithstanding the differences, it will not be a quantum leap to propose that individuals characterized as optimistic or conscientious may have a common health outlook such as healthier behaviour (e.g. adopting a better diet, maintaining physical activity, smoking less, drinking in moderation) thus leading to healthy ageing.

The concept of psychological health or a healthy mind thus encompasses conscientiousness, optimism and purpose in life. One should not be too pedantic and argue the finer points about the differences amongst these traits. You may make some valid academic arguments, but you will simply miss the point. And the point is? Individuals with the above characteristics adopt lifestyles which are conducive for healthy ageing. Put simply, a healthy mind leads to healthy ageing.

Take Home Message

Healthy Ageing involves

No super genes, no super foods, no super diet, no super supplements, no super exercise, no super bugs and no super lifestyle.

Simply apply common knowledge and common sense to your lifestyle.

There is no secret ingredient for healthy ageing, that is the secret. This reminds me of the secret ingredient in the noodle soup in the movie *King Fu Panda*; there was no secret ingredient. It's just that the public believed that there had to be a secret ingredient in the delicious noodle soup. It is the same for *Healthy Ageing*.

There are no extensive lists of do's and don'ts for healthy ageing, so here then is my (biased) summary of the scientific data on healthy ageing.

No super genes

There is a genetic basis for longevity, thought to be 20-30%, but this may be on the high side given that related individuals are very likely to share many lifestyle and environmental factors including diet, education, socio-economic status and neighbourhood. The latter has become an important factor with respect to inequality and there are now numerous studies, particularly in large cities, equating neighbourhood with quality of life and healthy lifespan.

Despite rapid advances in DNA technology, one can state that, to date, there are no definitive human longevity genes. Some scientists may dispute this statement, in which case send them a sample of your DNA, a valid credit card number and request an accurate estimate of your healthy lifespan. I would not hold your breath whilst waiting for that result. Alternatively, simply apply **Pub Tests 2.1, 2.2, 2.3 and 2.4.**

No super foods

Who said that broccoli or blueberries are super foods? It's called marketing. Common knowledge says that fruit and vegetables which are high in vitamins, minerals and fibre, are good for you. Humans have been eating fruit and vegetables for thousands of years. Some may be more nutritious than others; highly coloured ones are rich in antioxidants.

There is absolutely no need to keep a daily track on the amount of fruit and vegetables you consume; some days have lots, others none at all. There is no real evidence that you have to consume two or four servings a day for health. Just make sure you eat them as part of a healthy diet, which also includes fibre

(Pub Test 4.3). And don't forget some fish and dairy; humans have been consuming them since forever.

No super diet

Most diets work (translation: you lose weight) in the short-term but long-term? **(Pub Test 4.2)**. Just think, there will be no diet and nutrition industry if diets actually worked in the long-term. The marketing is superb. The Mediterranean diet is a healthy diet but is no healthier than any other healthy diet, also taking into consideration overall lifestyle (**Pub Test 4.1**). What about calorie restriction or intermittent fasting? Possible short-term benefits but absolutely nothing but stress in the long-term **(Pub Test 4.5)**. Try the simple common sense alternative of eating a bit less and there is no need to meticulously keep a track of the calories **(Pub Test 3.1)**.

It is simply common sense to avoid consuming regularly, I repeat, regularly, sugar-sweetened beverages (including energy and sports drinks), highly processed foods and foods containing *trans*-fats (**Pub Tests 3.2 and 3.6**). On the other hand, there is little evidence that consumption of dairy and saturated fats (and fats in general) is detrimental to healthy ageing (**Pub Tests 3.3, 3.4 and 3.5**). There is no evidence that a vegetarian diet is healthier than a non-vegetarian diet, in comparing individuals with comparable healthy lifestyles (**Pub Test 4.4**).

No super supplements

Here again, the marketing is superb. For the healthy and wealthy, supplements are the answer to even better health but poorer wealth. There is simply no scientific evidence that taking supplements such as multivitamins, antioxidants and fish oil is advantageous to healthy ageing (**Pub Tests 4.6, 4.7 and 4.8**).

A healthy diet will provide all the above plus much more. The placebo effect is decisive, and for individuals who claim benefit from taking supplements, then psychological health may well be the important factor. There is nothing wrong with that.

No super exercise

Once again, the marketing is superb. Think of the number of gyms, fitness centres and personal trainers out there. But in this scenario, there is a definitive truth out there. The scientific evidence is excellent that physical activity is a key element of healthy ageing (**Pub Test 6.1**). Individuals who are physically active are healthier, both self-rated and, importantly, objectively as measured by established clinical parameters.

Physical activity is very much a personal trait, some individuals enjoy going to the gym, others a simple walk in the park or walking the dog (**Pub Test 6.3**). There is no such thing as the right exercise or the best exercise or the right amount of exercise; it's an individual thing dependent on age, sex, BMI, lifestyle, time availability, location etc. It is never too late to take up physical activity; just incorporate it into your lifestyle. If you really need a guide, then at least thirty to sixty minutes every day of mild to moderate exercise for less active individuals or moderate to high exercise for those more active (**Pub Test 6.2**). There is nothing wrong with more than sixty min/day of physical activity. The bottom line is *Keep Moving*; your life is dependent on it.

No super bugs

Microorganisms are the most important organisms on Earth and are absolutely essential for all life, including humans (**Pub Tests 7.1 and 7.2**). It is not coincidental, therefore, to note that the human gut health (the microbiota in the gut) is a really hot topic not only on social media but also in the scientific literature. The most notable success of gut microbiota research has been for faecal microbiota transplants in the effective treatment of recurring antibiotic-resistant *Clostridium difficile* infections (**Pub Test 7.6**).

Gut health has been reported to be associated with everything from obesity, inflammatory bowel disorders, cardiovascular disease, autistic spectrum disorder, Alzheimer's, Parkinson's to depression, to name just a few, a most impressive list. Individuals diagnosed with these disorders are reported to have gut microbiota compositions which are different or less diverse (fewer different types of microbes in the gut) as compared with those without symptoms. The market for probiotics and prebiotics, claimed to be effective in the restoration of a healthy gut microbiota, is massive and, and I know this is repetitive, the marketing is superlative (**Pub Test 7.7**). There is low-moderate evidence that probiotics assist colitis in infants and reduces antibiotic-associated diarrhoea (not to be confused with restoring normal gut microbiota after a course of antibiotics for which there is little scientific evidence).

Here is the spoiler. Notwithstanding the remarkable advances in DNA and related technologies as applied to gut microbiota research, there is no definition or quantification of what constitutes a normal healthy gut microbiota (**Pub Tests 7.3, 7.4 and 7.5**). In fact, we are unable to identify a high proportion of the gut microbiota, including the all-important viruses. Furthermore, what are the functions of the hundreds or thousands of different species/strains of microbes in the gut and how do they interact? When one states that individuals with clinical symptoms of a certain disorder have a different or less diverse gut microbiota as compared with one without that disorder, we really need to know what the composition and function of the normal healthy gut microbiota is. This is no easy task, given that it is known that gut microbiota is very much an individual trait. And another thing, analysis of microbiota in the faeces (essentially a waste product of metabolism, easily accessible, generally free and most frequently analyzed in scientific studies) does not fully reflect the gut microbiota, particularly with respect to function.

The bottom line is there are no super bugs identified as yet. However, scientific research on human gut microbiota and health in the next few years will not only be highly informative but will also provide more than a few surprises. I have a gut feeling about that.

No super lifestyle

Adopt a balanced, prudent, conscientious lifestyle with a touch of optimism. Do not be too concerned regarding your DNA inheritance, it really is your lifestyle and psychological health that counts. As for diet, forget all those diets, calories and supplements, simply minimize sugar-sweetened beverages and highly processed foods. There is nothing wrong with pizza, cakes, doughnuts, pies, fast foods etc. Simply don't consume them regularly; that means no more than once or twice a week (not to be misinterpreted as pizza one day, cakes next day, pies next day etc). Fruit and vegetables, certainly. No need to keep a diary, but consume them as part of a healthy diet. And if you enjoy coffee or a drink (moderation), no worries (**Pub Tests 5.1 and 5.2**).

The Most Important Take Home Message for Healthy Ageing:

Keep Moving (and Keep Breathing)

The *Pub Test* Questions and Answers form the basis of this book and these are collated at the end of this Chapter.

Chapter 2 Genes and Healthy Ageing
A Beginner's Guide to DNA

Pub Test 2.1:

Question:
In deep and meaningful discussions, and after having a few drinks, in a pub or bar with friends, can analysis of your DNA at age 25, 50 or 70, accurately provide information that you will live to be a centenarian in relatively good health?

Answer:
No
Although it is common knowledge that a family history of longevity (and good health) suggests the likelihood of long-lived offspring, other lifestyle factors are significantly more important than the genetics. On the other hand, analysis of your DNA can be informative in respect of specific genetically inherited disorders and diseases.

Pub Test 2.2

Question:
Will the determination of your DNA telomere length in your leucocytes provide a good measure of your projected longevity?

Answer:
No
A single determination of telomere length in an individual at, say, age 50 is not that useful. On the other hand, if one also had the telomere lengths at birth, early teens and early adulthood, then perhaps an indication of how the individual was ageing could be provided. Nobody currently aged 50 or more will have had their

telomeres measured at birth, early teens and early adulthood (the latter certainly not accurately). Furthermore, for any meaningful measure one would also have to have a control cohort of individuals (ideally hundreds) matched for a myriad of lifestyle and environmental factors, only possible in large observational studies.

Pub Test 2.3:

Question:
Will analysis of your DNA methylation age or epigenetic age accurately state that you, say at age 25, 50 or 70, will have a healthy lifespan to your eighties and beyond?

Answer:
No
DNA methylation age or epigenetic age may provide an estimate for rate of ageing, but any meaningful interpretation will also require comparative data from many other individuals (hundreds) of similar sex, age, ethnicity and lifestyle. Furthermore, do you have your DNA methylation age at birth and at appropriate chronological points and what about the data for the control cohort as a comparison?

Pub Test 2.4:

Question:
Do established clinical markers of health provide a good indication of your healthy ageing?

Answer:
Yes
Clinical markers may well indicate potential issues such as in high blood pressure, high BMI, high cholesterol, heart, liver and kidney problems, anaemia and type 2 diabetes. Next time, also check out your score on physical activity.

Chapter 8: If We All Lived to a Healthy 100: Where Would We All Park?

Chapter 3 Nutrition 101

What Are the Facts on Fats and Sugars?

Pub Test 3.1

Question:
Is a calorie the same as a food calorie?

Answer:
No
A calorie is most definitely not a food calorie.
The calorie unit is the energy released from pure fat, pure carbohydrate or pure protein as measured under strictly defined laboratory conditions. However, food is rarely consumed as pure protein, fat or carbohydrate. The nature of the food matrix (e.g. the chemical structure of the food including the digestible and non-digestible components such as the fibre content), the chemical composition of the food (e.g. vitamins, minerals) and the digestion process (including method of food preparation) are all key issues with respect to estimation of calorie intake. The concept that 'a calorie in = a calorie out' is totally misleading.

Pub Test 3.2:

Question:
Are *trans*-fats from chemical modification of vegetable oils bad for health?

Answer:
Yes
There is good scientific evidence that *trans*-fats increase the 'bad' cholesterol (LDL-cholesterol) and decrease the 'good'

cholesterol (HDL-cholesterol). One should always read the label on packaged foods to check the content of *trans*-fats. The advice is to minimize intake as it is difficult to totally eliminate *trans*-fats from the modern diet given that many foods, particularly baked and fried foods, still contain significant amounts.

Pub Test 3.3:

Question:
Are saturated fats bad for health?

Answer:
No
However, if your diet also includes high amounts of saturated fats and refined carbohydrates from highly processed foods (e.g. pastries, pies, cakes, cookies, packaged foods) and sugar (particularly soft drinks or soda), you will have a problem.

Pub Test 3.4:

Question:
Is regular dairy bad for you?

Answer:
No
There is no scientific evidence which shows that regular dairy fat is a health hazard (unless you have an allergy to dairy), in fact the evidence is neutral or in most studies positive for health.

Pub Test 3.5:

Question:
Are fats bad for health?

Answer:
No

In fact, fats are essential for health. For example, fats are an integral part of the brain and a proper balance of saturated and unsaturated fats is essential to maintain our cell membranes (e.g. in the nucleus, mitochondria) at equilibrium for optimum functioning at 37°C.

Pub Test 3.6:

Question:
Is sugar a health hazard?

Answer:
Yes

The added (hidden) sugar in highly processed foods and the liquid calories in sugar-sweetened beverages provide sugar calories in easily digestible forms which the body readily absorbs, leading to a rapid spike in blood glucose and insulin. There is consensus that sugar in foods such as fruit, vegetables and dairy is much less harmful in that the food matrix acts as a buffer and results in the slow, controlled release of sugar into the bloodstream and organs. Moreover, the nutrients (fibre, carbohydrates, fats, proteins, minerals, vitamins, antioxidants) in the food matrix are an added bonus.

Chapter 4 Diets and Dietary Supplements

The Truth, the Whole Truth and Nothing but the Science

Pub Test 4.1:

Question:
Is the Mediterranean diet the key to health and, importantly, healthy ageing?

Answer:
No
The Mediterranean diet is certainly a healthy diet for individuals currently on an unhealthy diet (and unhealthy lifestyle). However, people living in comparable developed countries with diets radically different from the Mediterranean diet have just as long life expectancies and, importantly, healthy life expectancies.

Pub Test 4.2:

Question:
Do weight-loss diets work

(a) in the short-term?
(b) in the long-term?

Answer:

(a) In the short-term, Yes
   Most diets result in some weight loss in the short-term
(b) In the long-term, No
   Long-term (beyond one year) weight-loss diets do not work for the majority of individuals due to lack of compliance to the diet and the natural equilibrium of the body to return to a weight close to the pre-diet weight.

Pub Test 4.3:

Question:
Is dietary fibre important for healthy ageing?

Answer:
Yes

There is scientific consensus that dietary fibre from fruit, vegetables and whole grains is a key factor in healthy ageing. The quality of the dietary fibre is an important parameter, with fibre from low-quality processed foods a negative factor. The latter foods are also likely to be high in sugar and salt.

Pub Test 4.4:

Question:
Is a vegetarian or vegan diet better for healthy ageing than a healthy non-vegetarian diet?

Answer:
No

There is no published scientific evidence that a vegetarian or vegan diet is any better for healthy ageing than a *healthy* non-vegetarian diet that includes fruit, vegetables, dairy, fish and moderate intake of red meat (< two servings/week). Lifestyles (e.g. physical activity, social interactions, economic status) and not just a healthy diet play key roles in healthy ageing.

Pub Test 4.5:

Question:
Does a calorie restriction diet (20 to 25% decrease in daily calorie intake) add years to a healthy lifespan?

Answer:
No

The evidence is simply not there. Maintaining, for example, a 20% calorie restriction (CR) diet for more than six months is extremely difficult for even the most dedicated individual. There are so many issues related to calorie restriction that to recommend it to maintain health and as a means for healthy ageing in free-living humans is non-sensible.

For example, at what age should one commence the CR diet? How long does it take to maintain the CR diet? What level of CR, 10%, 20% is deemed beneficial? What can or can't you eat, and what about nutrient deficiency? What about physical activity and can one really fully participate in social and competitive sport? What are the social consequences of daily interactions with family, friends or work colleagues, especially in relation to eating and drinking?

Pub Test 4.6:

Question:
Does taking multivitamin and mineral supplements have benefits for healthy ageing?

Answer:
No

There is simply no good evidence that multivitamin and mineral supplements will extend healthy ageing lifespan. A healthy diet will provide all the necessary vitamins and minerals for good health.

Pub Test 4.7:

Question:
Does taking antioxidant supplements provide positive health outcomes?

Answer:
No

Several decades of scientific studies clearly show that antioxidant supplements provide little health benefit and, indeed, may even have a negative health outcome. By comparison, intake of antioxidants via a healthy diet such as real, minimally processed food has substantial health benefits.

Pub Test 4.8:

Question:
Does taking fish oil supplements (omega-3 fatty acids) have clear health benefits related to cardiovascular health and brain development or slow/prevent the onset of dementia/Alzheimer's?

Answer:
No
There is little evidence for health benefits of fish oil supplements despite many decades of scientific research. On the other hand, there is reasonable evidence that dietary intake of fish has positive health benefits.

Chapter 5 Alcohol and Coffee

Drinking to Your Healthy Ageing

Pub Test 5.1:

Question:
Does light to moderate drinking (1 to 2 standard drinks/day) have positive health effects?

Answer:
Yes
Light to moderate drinking is the key word, with females drinking less than males. However, your overall lifestyle and socio-economic status are key factors for health. Drinking in moderation

has to be accompanied by a healthy diet, not smoking, being physically active, maintaining a social network and having regular health checks. Cheers!

Pub Test 5.2:

Question:
Does drinking coffee or tea have any health benefits?

Answer:
Yes
The important concepts are the same as in the case of light-moderate alcohol consumption. It is where you drink, with whom you drink and why you drink. *It is the overall lifestyle of individuals who drink coffee, tea and alcohol (light-moderate) that influences their health.*

Chapter 6 Physical Activity

Keep Calm and Walk the Dog

Pub Test 6.1:

Question:
Is maintaining physical activity important for healthy ageing?

Answer:
Yes, most definitely Yes.
Physical activity or 'Keep Moving' is one of the most, if not the most, important criterion of successful healthy ageing. Individuals who are physically active also have healthy lifestyles, such as not smoking, maintaining social contact, adopting a healthy diet and having a positive attitude.

Chapter 8: If We All Lived to a Healthy 100: Where Would We All Park?

Pub Test 6.2:

Question:
Do elite athletes live longer than the general population?

Answer:
Yes and No.
This is the only Yes/No answer to a Pub Test Question.
All studies, to date, have not fully addressed the issue of lifestyle (both pre- and post-competitive) of elite athletes. More importantly, the reference cohort, i.e. the general population, should include both healthy and unhealthy individuals from the same country of origin as the elite athlete. In other words, a truly comparable reference cohort will be individuals who are not elite athletes but with a healthy lifestyle akin to that of many (but not all) of the elite athletes (particularly post-competitive), including not smoking, being physically active, consuming a nutritious diet and being socially engaged. The differences in all-cause mortality and life expectancy between healthy and unhealthy lifestyles more than accounts for the reported differences between elite athletes and the general population.

Pub Test 6.3:

Question:
Do dog owners have longer life expectancies (healthy life expectancies) than non-dog owners?

Answer:
Yes
(One has to declare a conflict of interest [bias] here as an owner of a Labrador that requires attention and long walks).

Large and long-term studies on dog ownership have provided conflicting results due to the complexities of confounders. Physical activity such as in walking the dog (how long the walk; slow, moderate or brisk walking), breed of dog, how long the individual has owned the dog and providing companionship as in single-person households are all key confounders. On the other hand, on a positive note, there is no large long-term study that concludes that dog owners have shorter life expectancies than non-dog owners. And just one more thing, do not even attempt to research potential health benefits of ownership of other types of pets (did someone say cats?).

Chapter 7 Gut Microbiota

It's a Small World After All

Pub Test 7.1:

Question:
If all human life on Earth were eliminated, would other forms of life such as animals, plants, insects and microbes, still exist?

Answer:
Yes

In fact, non-human life will most likely thrive in the absence of humans. This experiment has already been conducted on planet Earth. Anatomically modern human-like individuals have been present on Earth for only a few million years (< 2 million years). By contrast, microorganisms have been around for a few billion years (< 4 billion years), plants < 600 million years ago, followed much later by marine organisms, insects and animals. And what about the dinosaurs?

Pub Test 7.2:

Question:
If all microbes on Earth were eliminated, would humans still be around?

Answer:
No
In fact, there will be no life of any kind: no humans, animals, plants or insects. All these life forms are dependent on oxygen (mitochondria) and photosynthesis (chloroplasts). Both mitochondria and chloroplasts have their origins in ancestral microbes. Microbes are the essence of life.

Pub Test 7.3:

Question:
Are bacteria the only microorganisms on or in the human body that have an influence on human health and disease?

Answer:
No
Although bacteria are the most abundant of the microbes associated with humans (with the possible exception of the viruses), other microbes include the archaea (a type of bacteria), the fungi (substantially lower numbers than bacteria) and the viruses. The latter, in particular, may be the key regulators of the number and types of bacteria present in the human gut. These two properties (number and type) greatly influence the function of the gut microbiota and thus the overall health of the human host.

Pub Test 7.4:

Question:
Do we fully know what microbes are present in the human gut and, therefore, what constitutes a 'standard' or healthy human gut microbiota?

Answer:
No
What constitutes a 'standard' or healthy human gut microbiota composition is currently unknown. Although there are reference data bases on microbes (thousands of microbes) which have been identified in the human gut, there are many unidentified microbes. Moreover, there is incomplete knowledge about the function of these microbes, how they interact among themselves and, most importantly, how they interact with the human host.

Pub Test 7.5:

Question:
Is the composition of the adult gut microbiota largely dependent on the genetics of the human host?

Answer:
No
The composition of the adult gut microbiota is largely dependent on diet, lifestyle and the environment. Although at birth there is initially a significant (especially in the future development of the immune system) contribution from the mother, the infant gut microbiota composition rapidly changes until, at around ages 6 to 18 months, it reflects the microbiota of the

diet, lifestyle and the environment of the individual. The adult gut microbiota is relatively stable given a stable diet, lifestyle and environment.

Pub Test 7.6:

Question:
Are faecal microbiota transplants effective for treatment of health issues associated with obesity, cardiovascular disease and inflammatory bowel disorders?

Answer:
No
Faecal microbiota transplants have been relatively successful only in the treatment of the specific case of recurring diarrhoea associated with antibiotic resistance due to *Clostridium difficile*. There are insufficient high quality studies to conclude that faecal microbiota transplant is effective for other inflammatory gut disorders.

Pub Test 7.7:

Question:
Are probiotics effective for restoration of normal gut microbiota after a course of antibiotics?

Answer:
No
There is no definitive evidence that probiotics restore normal gut microbiota after a course of antibiotics. Some studies have indicated that taking probiotics may actually inhibit or delay the restoration of normal gut microbiota. Furthermore, we currently do not know the microbiota composition and function of a typical or 'standard' healthy human gut.

Chapter 8 If We All Lived to a Healthy 100

Where Would We All Park?

Pub Test: 8.1

Question:
Do women live longer than men?

Answer:
Yes
With rare exceptions, in every country, women live longer than men. Importantly, this also applies to healthy lifespan and thus healthy ageing. In general, life expectancy at birth for women is around three to five years longer than men, with healthy life expectancy two to three years longer (see Table 1). Healthy life expectancy is defined by the World Health Organization as 'average number of years a person can expect to live in full health by taking into account years lived in less than full health due to disease or injury'.
These are facts, not opinions, and are based on extensive data as documented on authoritative internet sites (Human Mortality Database, World Health Organization, United Nations Organization, Centers for Disease Control and Prevention).

Austad, SN, Fischer, KE. Sex differences in lifespan. 2016. *Cell Metabolism* 23:1022-1033. doi:10.1016/j.cmet.2016.05.019.

Bronikowski, AM, Altmann, J, Brockman, DK, *et al*. 2011. Aging in the natural world: comparative data reveal similar mortality patterns across primates. *Science* 331:1325-1328. doi:10.1126/science.1201571.

Friedman, HS, Martin, LR. 2011. The Longevity Project. Scribe Publications: Melbourne.

Gordon, EH, Peel, NM, Samanta, M, et al. 2017. Sex differences in frailty: a systematic review and meta-analysis. *Experimental Gerontology* 89:30-40. doi:10.1016/j.exger.2016.12.021.

Gray, MW. 2012. Mitochondrial evolution. *Cold Spring Harbor Perspectives in Biology* 4:a011403. doi:10.1101/cshperspect.a011403.

Kim, ES, Hagan, KA, Grodstein, F, et al. 2017. Optimism and cause-specific mortality: a prospective cohort study. *American Journal of Epidemiology* 185:21-29. doi:10.1093/aje/kww182.

Kim, ES, James, P, Zevon, ES, et al. 2019. Optimism and healthy aging in women and men. *American Journal of Epidemiology* 188:1084-1001. doi:10.1093/aje/kwz056.

Kondo, M. 2014. The life-changing magic of tidying up: the Japanese art of decluttering and organizing. Ten Speed Press: New York.

Kubzansky, LD, Sparrow, D, Vokonas, P, et al. 2001. Is the glass half empty or half full? A prospective study of optimism and coronary heart disease in the Normative Aging Study. *Psychosomatic Medicine* 63:910-916. doi:10.1097/00006842-200111000-00009.

Lee, LO, James, P, Zevon, ES, et al. 2019. Optimism is associated with exceptional longevity in 2 epidemiologic cohorts of men and women. *Proceedings of the National Academy of Sciences* 116:18357-18362. doi:10.1073/pnas.1900712116.

Mogi, K. 2017. The Little Book of Ikigai: The Essential Japanese Way to Finding Your Purpose in Life. Quercus Editions Ltd: London.

Ostan, R, Monti, D, Gueresi, P, *et al.* 2016. Gender, aging and longevity in humans: an update of an intriguing/neglected scenario paving the way to a gender-specific medicine. *Clinical Science* 130:1711-1725. doi:10.1042/CS20160004.

Robine, J-M, Cubaynes, S. 2017. Worldwide demography of centenarians. *Mechanisms of Ageing and Development* 165:59-67. doi:10.1016/j.mad.2017.03.004.

Rozanski, A, Bavishi, C, Kubansky, LD, *et al.* 2019. Association of optimism with cardiovascular events and all-cause mortality: a systematic review and meta-analysis. *JAMA Network Open* 2:e1912200. doi:10.1001/jamanetworkopen.2019.12200.

Srivastava, S. 2017. The mitochondrial basis of aging and age-related disorders. *Genes* 8:398-421. doi:10.3390/genes8120398.

Steel, G. 2019. Editor, Beyond the Gender Gap in Japan. Michigan Monograph Japanese Studies. University of Michigan Press: Ann Arbor.

Steptoe, A, Wright, C, Kunz-Ebrecht, SR, *et al.* 2006. Dispositional optimism and health behaviour in community-dwelling older people: associations with healthy ageing. *British Journal of Health Psychology* 11:71-84. doi:10.1348/135910705X42850.

Theurey, P, Pizzo, P. 2018. The aging mitochondria. *Genes* 9:22-35. doi:10.3390/genes9010022.

Timmis, JN, Ayliffe, MA, Huang, CY, *et al.* 2004. Endosymbiotic gene transfer: organelle genomes forge eukaryotic chromosomes. *Nature Reviews Genetics* 5:123-135. doi:10.1038/nrg1271.

Zarulli, V, Jones, JAB, Oksuzyan, A, *et al.* 2017. Women live longer than men even during severe famines and epidemics. *Proceedings of the National Academy of Sciences* 115:E832-E840. doi:10.1073/pnas.1701535115.

About the Author

Ken Watson is Emeritus Professor of Microbiology at the University of New England, Armidale, Australia. He has published widely in scientific journals in articles on heat shock stress proteins, mitochondrial structure and function and unique microorganisms isolated from Antarctica. He lives on the Gold Coast, Queensland and maintains physical activity by jogging and walking the dog, Penny, the Labrador.

www.ingramcontent.com/pod-product-compliance
Lightning Source LLC
Chambersburg PA
CBHW070528090426
42735CB00013B/2898